M000034675

06/28
1. Drive thru Hood River - best milkshake ever
2. Dinner in North Bend - met Violet Sparkle ☺
06/29
1. Play in the pool, relax c̄ DeeAnn, AMAZING TRIP!!

OREGON COAST CAMPING & HIKING

TOM STIENSTRA & SEAN PATRICK HILL

How to Use This Book

ABOUT THE CAMPGROUND PROFILES

The campgrounds are listed in a consistent, easy-to-read format to help you choose the ideal camping spot. If you already know the name of the specific campground you want to visit, or the name of the surrounding geological area or nearby feature (town, national or state park, forest, mountain, lake, river, etc.), look it up in the index and turn to the corresponding page. Here is a sample profile:

Campground name and number →

1 SOMEWHERE USA CAMPGROUND

Icons noting activities and facilities at or nearby the campground

General location of the campground in relation to the nearest major town or landmark →

Scenic rating: 10

south of Somewhere USA Lake

Rating of scenic beauty on a scale of 1–10 with 10 the highest rating

BEST (

Symbol indicating that the campground is listed among the author's top picks

Each campground in this book begins with a brief overview of its setting. The description typically covers ambience, information about the attractions, and activities popular at the campground.

Campsites, facilities: This section notes the number of campsites for tents and RVs and indicates whether hookups are available. Facilities such as restrooms, picnic areas, recreation areas, laundry, and dump stations will be addressed, as well as the availability of piped water, showers, playgrounds, stores, and other amenities. The campground's pet policy and wheelchair accessibility is also mentioned here.

Reservations, fees: This section notes whether reservations are accepted, and provides rates for tent sites and RV sites. If there are additional fees for parking or pets, or discounted weekly or seasonal rates, they will also be noted here.

Directions: This section provides mile-by-mile driving directions to the campground from the nearest major town or highway.

Contact: This section provides an address, phone number, and website, if available, for the campground.

ABOUT THE ICONS

The icons in this book are designed to provide at-a-glance information on activities, facilities, and services available on-site or within walking distance of each campground.

- Hiking trails
- Biking trails
- Swimming
- Fishing
- Boating
- Canoeing and/or kayaking
- Winter sports

- Hot springs
- Pets permitted
- Playground
- Wheelchair accessible
- RV sites
- Tent sites

ABOUT THE SCENIC RATING

Each campground profile employs a scenic rating on a scale of 1 to 10, with 1 being the least scenic and 10 being the most scenic. A scenic rating measures only the overall beauty of the campground and environs; it does not take into account noise level, facilities, maintenance, recreation options, or campground management. The setting of a campground with a lower scenic rating may simply not be as picturesque that of as a higher rated campground, however other factors that can influence a trip, such as noise or recreation access, can still affect or enhance your camping trip. Consider both the scenic rating and the profile description before deciding which campground is perfect for you.

MAP SYMBOLS

Expressway	(80)	Interstate Freeway	✗	Airfield
Primary Road	(101)	U.S. Highway	✈	Airport
Secondary Road	(21)	State Highway	○	City/Town
Unpaved Road	(66)	County Highway	▲	Mountain
Ferry		Lake	⬧	Park
National Border		Dry Lake	⸝⸝	Pass
State Border		Seasonal Lake	◉	State Capital

ABOUT THE TRAIL PROFILES

Each hike in this book is listed in a consistent, easy-to-read format to help you choose the ideal hike. From a general overview of the setting to detailed driving directions, the profile will provide all the information you need. Here is a sample profile:

Map number and hike number →

1 SOMEWHERE USA HIKE

Round-trip mileage → 9.0 mi/5.0 hrs

(unless otherwise noted) and the approximate amount of time needed to complete the hike (actual times can vary widely, especially on longer hikes)

Difficulty and quality ratings

at the mouth of the Somewhere River ←

BEST (

General location of the trail, named by its proximity to the nearest major town or landmark

Symbol indicating that the hike is listed among the author's top picks

Each hike in this book begins with a brief overview of its setting. The description typically covers what kind of terrain to expect, what might be seen, and any conditions that may make the hike difficult to navigate. Side trips, such as to waterfalls or panoramic vistas, in addition to ways to combine the trail with others nearby for a longer outing, are also noted here. In many cases, mile-by-mile trail directions are included.

User Groups: This section notes the types of users that are permitted on the trail, including hikers, mountain bikers, horseback riders, and dogs. Wheelchair access is also noted here.

Permits: This section notes whether a permit is required for hiking, or, if the hike spans more than one day, whether one is required for camping. Any fees, such as for parking, day use, or entrance, are also noted here.

Maps: This section provides information on how to obtain detailed trail maps of the hike and its environs. Whenever applicable, names of U.S. Geologic Survey (USGS) topographic maps and national forest maps are also included; contact information for these and other map sources are noted in the Resources section at the back of this book.

Directions: This section provides mile-by-mile driving directions to the trailhead from the nearest major town.

Contact: This section provides an address and phone number for each hike. The contact is usually the agency maintaining the trail but may also be a trail club or other organization.

ABOUT THE ICONS

The icons in this book are designed to provide at-a-glance information on the difficulty and quality of each hike.

The **difficulty rating** (rated **1-5** with **1** being the lowest and **5** the highest) is based on the steepness of the trail and how difficult it is to traverse

The **quality rating** (rated **1-10** with **1** being the lowest and **10** the highest) is based largely on scenic beauty, but also takes into account how crowded the trail is and whether noise of nearby civilization is audible

ABOUT THE DIFFICULTY RATINGS

Trails rated 1 are very easy and suitable for hikers of all abilities, including young children.

Trails rated 2 are easy-to-moderate and suitable for most hikers, including families with active children 6 and older.

Trails rated 3 are moderately challenging and suitable for reasonably fit adults and older children who are very active.

Trails rated 4 are very challenging and suitable for physically fit hikers who are seeking a workout.

Trails rated 5 are extremely challenging and suitable only for experienced hikers who are in top physical condition.

MAP SYMBOLS

Expressway	80	Interstate Freeway	✈	Airfield
Primary Road	101	U.S. Highway	✈	Airport
Secondary Road	21	State Highway	○	City/Town
Unpaved Road	66	County Highway	▲	Mountain
Ferry		Lake	▲	Park
National Border		Dry Lake	⁄	Pass
State Border		Seasonal Lake	◉	State Capital

ABOUT THE MAPS

This book is divided into chapters based on major regions in the state; an overview map of these regions precedes the table of contents. Each chapter begins with a map of the region, which is further broken down into detail maps. Sites are noted on the detail maps by number.

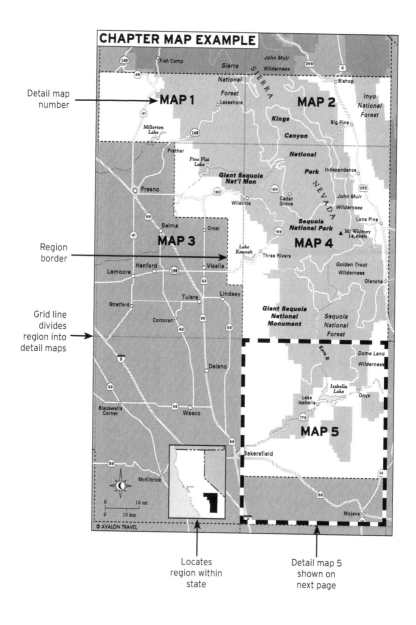

Detail map number

Region border

Grid line divides region into detail maps

Locates region within state

Detail map 5 shown on next page

Locates detail
map within
region

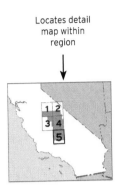

Map
number → **Map 5**

Sites shown
on detail map → **Sites 106-119**

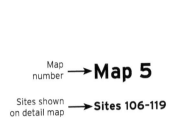

Site number ⟶

Region
border ⟶

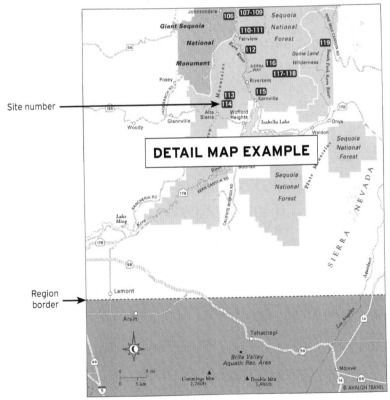

DETAIL MAP EXAMPLE

Camping and Hiking Tips

HIKING ESSENTIALS

In Oregon, there are those days when you get off work and want to head out for a couple hours of hiking. A day hike is a day hike, and you certainly don't need to lug 30 pounds of tents, stoves, and sleeping bags on your back. But this is absolutely no excuse not to be prepared. The forests resound with stories of people who got lost wandering off the trail, getting hurt or worse. The number one Boy Scout rule for the mountains, shorelines, and deserts of Oregon is *be prepared*. Here's a standard list any good outdoors person should adhere to.

Food and Water

Be sure to carry enough food on even the shortest hike, the reason being you never know if you'll get caught in the woods longer than anticipated. Outdoor stores, even grocery stores, carry a great abundance of high-energy trail food that is lightweight and easy to pack. As far as food goes, suit your tastes but also consider what your body needs. Salty foods replenish much needed sodium lost in sweat. Sugary foods maintain, well, your sugar levels, and they also give good bursts of energy (there are all sorts of great sugar-syrups in little packets for the big burst you need to make it up that final hill). Carbohydrates and proteins are a necessity, as your body will need them for energy and a little muscle repair. In general, bring more food than you think you'll need.

Though food is important, not to mention a great thing to have while you're sitting beside that mountain lake you've been walking for hours to get to, it is water that is far and away the real necessity. What will get you in the woods, even kill you, is not starvation but dehydration. Heat sickness, which can quickly degenerate into hyperthermia, can be damaging if not deadly. On a shorter, easier hike, play it safe and bring at least two quarts of water in your pack. An easy and novel solution is the CamelBak and other such products—small backpacks perfect for day hiking, with plenty of room for food, water, and the rest of the essentials. I swear by it, as does everyone I know who uses one. When I'm properly equipped, I'm carrying upwards of six quarts of water.

If you plan on backpacking and need to carry less weight, be sure to invest in a water filter or some other method of purifying. Never drink straight from the creek! Backcountry water has, unfortunately, largely been infected with *Giardia lamblia* and *Cryptosporidium,* two microscopic organisms that cause a plethora of terrible gastrointestinal problems, the likes of which hardly need to be discussed here. Iodine is still a staple for many backpackers, and there are all sorts of newfangled ways to purify water, including ultraviolet light.

Trail Map and Compass

You'd be surprised how empowering a map can be, especially when you can read it well. Never go on a hike without a map. Despite trail signs, getting confused in the backcountry is more common an occurrence than you'd think. Signs can disappear or get blown down. Trails, too, have a way of sometimes getting lost in certain areas, especially in places with many so-called "user trails" (made by people walking off the designated trail). The best maps are topographic, which can be used in conjunction with a compass to easily pinpoint your position. Plus, they give a good sense of the lay of the land—the more detailed the better. You can find nearby trails and even start adventuring cross-country into areas without trails. But it is imperative to know what you're doing first; one wrong adjustment of the compass can land you miles off track.

You can easily obtain maps from outdoors stores and from the management agencies of the area you are visiting. See the *Resources* chapter for names and contact information for those agencies and for USGS topographical maps, National Forest maps, and maps from commercial services.

A compass is an essential tool for keeping you on track. Take a class from an outdoor group, or a store like REI, and learn to use it correctly and effectively. Many people use GPS devices, but they may not work in some areas. A dense forest canopy may run you the risk of losing a signal, so why depend on it? Knowledge is power, and the compass and map make use of that knowledge.

> ## SOCKS
>
> You cannot underestimate the value of good socks, your cushion against blisters, moisture, and soreness. Hiking socks should be thick enough to fit snugly and cushion your feet all around. Buy plenty, especially for extended backpacking trips, or plan to wash the ones you do have. Dirty, damp, and worn-out socks will not do what they are meant to do. Never wear cotton socks!
>
> Wool blend socks help to wick away moisture from your skin. They run around $15 a pair. Believe me, they're worth it. They are also, I have found, wonderfully warm for when you finally get your boots off at camp.

Extra Clothing

Oregon has a classic saying: Don't like the weather? Wait five minutes, it'll change. Those who say this aren't lying. Conditions fluctuate rapidly, so the right clothing is essential. Being wet and cold is not only uncomfortable, but also downright dangerous. Cotton is the worst clothing to wear: When it gets wet, it stays wet. Wool, the old standby, gets wet and heavy. Today's hiking clothes are manufactured to be waterproof and quick-drying, and even to wick moisture away from the skin. Many clothes are also UV resistant. And they're lightweight, to boot.

You should always carry a lightweight jacket that is both waterproof and wind-resistant. Breathable jackets control your heat, as well. Think ahead if your hike will change in altitude: the higher you go, the colder it may get, so bring a hat and gloves, too. And an extra pair of socks can't hurt, either, particularly ones that keep your feet warm and dry.

Flashlight

You know how sometimes in winter you find yourself saying, "Wow, how'd it get so dark so early?" Well, the *last* place you want to say that is on the trail. It happens.

There is some great and lightweight gear you can use. Headlamps are all the rage, and can cast quite a powerful beam; plus, they keep your hands free. No matter what kind of light source you use, make sure you have extra batteries and an extra bulb. You'll find them very handy around the campsite, as well.

Sunglasses and Sunscreen

One of the trickiest things about hiking near or on a mountain peak is that the air is thinner and therefore—don't ask me how it works—the sun gets stronger. Thus, the mountains are a great place to get sunburned, even on a cold day. Bring both sunscreen with a high SPF and sunglasses with good UV resistance. Put on that sunscreen liberally, and at least 30 minutes before you hike. Later, put on more. Other good accessories to have on hand: a wide-brimmed hat and SPF lip balm.

Insect Repellent

Oregon is famous for its mosquitoes. I mean it. Some of the best destinations, like the mountain wildflower meadows or the lakes and rivers, are overrun with mosquitoes in late spring and early summer. There are many ways to avoid this. One, of course, is to just stay home and wait for fall. The other is to equip yourself with one of the many brands of "bug dope" available in any decent store. The most powerful ones contain a toxic chemical called DEET, which some people prefer to avoid. DEET should not be used on children, and adults should use safe levels. There are also handy mosquito nets that can be pulled over the face, and these are available in outdoors stores.

Long sleeves and long pants will help protect you from the other pest: ticks. Ticks are known to carry nasty diseases like Rocky Mountain Spotted Fever, so it's best to tuck those long pants into your socks and check yourself often. The high desert of Oregon, especially along rivers, is one place ticks frequent.

First-Aid Kit

You really only need a few things here, so frugality is okay when you're dealing with minor cuts, blisters, and sore muscles. A little antibiotic ointment, some bandages, and an anti-inflammatory medication like ibuprofen or acetaminophen can be invaluable. Also be aware of who in your party may be allergic to bee stings, as Oregon has a local ground wasp that can be nasty. Be sure to bring an epinephrine pen or other medication for those with allergies.

It never hurts to learn a little CPR, or even have some Wilderness First-Aid training. When you've gained experience hiking among the rocks, cliffs, and swift rivers, you will quickly see how many potential disasters lurk a little too close for comfort. Be prepared!

Swiss Army-Style Pocket Knife

In Oregon, say "Leatherman" and everyone will know what you're talking about. The Leatherman is a modern equivalent of the famous Swiss Army knife, and a good one has the essentials: a few blades, a can opener, scissors, and tweezers. Whether removing splinters or ticks, or cutting moleskin for that blister, this is a must-have tool.

Firestarter

At night, cold can come on quick in the Oregon mountains, and especially the desert. Starting a fire may be the ultimate necessity in an emergency, for warmth as well as a distress signal, and no hiker should be without either a butane lighter or waterproof matches—and in a state as rainy as Oregon, they should be carried in a waterproof container.

HIKING GEAR

Having the right clothing makes for a comfortable hike. Long gone are the days of climbing mountains in wool pants and hiking to the lake in a pair of cut-off jeans. Today's hiking clothes are made from largely synthetic materials designed to do breathe, meaning to release heat away from the body, and stay dry: that is, they both wick moisture away from the body and dry quickly.

Then, too, there are the feet, which are of course the most heavily used body part while hiking. Caring for your feet is the single most important thing you can do, since nothing makes for a more miserable walk than wet, cold feet or blisters. Take care when choosing footwear and don't worry about frugality: A good pair of hiking shoes or boots is one of the best investments you'll make.

Clothing

Synthetic material, as mentioned above, is what it's all about. So what to bring? With a visit to a good outdoors store, you should walk away with ten articles: synthetic T-shirts, both long sleeve and short sleeve; synthetic hiking shorts and pants (and many companies, like Columbia Sportswear, make those wonderful pants with removable leggings—instant shorts!); a fleece pullover, lightweight and medium-weight; lightweight thermal underwear; synthetic-blend socks that wick away moisture and stay dry; rain jacket and pants; lightweight fleece gloves; waterproof gloves; wide-brimmed sun hat; a warm pullover hat. Snug clothes are better than loose, so make sure they fit properly.

Footwear

In general, you should consider three things when looking for good hiking footwear. For one, there is **support**: a good shoe or boot needs to offer both the foot and ankle ideal support, so as to make those rocky crossings safer and less strenuous. The **weight** of footwear is as important; heavy footwear means tiresome walking, especially if you are considering a long-distance jaunt. Talk about dragging your feet! **Flexibility** will save you from that painful culprit: the blister. Flexibility must balance itself with overall boot fit, since slippage is what generally exacerbates the formation of blisters.

You should fit boots in relation to socks: the combination of the two, once mastered, will save you from sitting around the campfire at night, cutting moleskin for those welts.

There are many options for footwear, from trail running shoes and lightweight hiking boots to sturdier backpacking boots. Consider the tread on the boot, the ankle support, and whether the material is waterproof or water-resistant. Once you purchase new footwear, be sure to take a few test runs and break them in before that big backpacking trip. Your feet will applaud you.

CLIMATE AND WEATHER PROTECTION

Weather in Oregon is diverse and unpredictable. Wind, pouring rain, snow and ice, blazing sun, high and low humidity, all of these are part of the Oregon experience. It is essential to be prepared. Weather reports, especially those from the National Weather Service, help greatly, but be ready for sudden changes—especially along the coast, in the high desert, and in the mountains.

THE PACIFIC CREST TRAIL

The most famous long-distance trail through Oregon is the Pacific Crest Trail (PCT), part of the 2,650-mile trail that passes through three states between Canada and Mexico. The Beaver State has its fair share of this historic and well-used National Scenic Trail, and its 430-mile stretch is usually snow-free between July and September. There's a lot to see: the Siskiyou Mountains, Crater Lake National Park, the Oregon Cascades with its long line of volcanic peaks, and the Columbia Gorge National Scenic Area.

The PCT accounts for a number of popular day hikes, especially in Oregon's famed wilderness areas: Mount Hood, Three Sisters, and Sky Lakes to name a few. Along the way, the trail passes everything from errant graves to lava fields to the incredible Timberline Lodge.

Seasons

Oregon has roughly four seasons, and each region reflects those seasons differently. Everywhere in the state, summer, the peak season, tends to have higher temperatures (though the people of Bend, Oregon, still talk about the time it snowed on the Fourth of July). As late summer approaches, so does the occasional rain and sleet.

Autumn, too, makes for beautiful days, and is my favorite time to hike. The color displays are at a height, and days can be significantly cooler, thus making for a sweat-free ramble.

As winter approaches, so does the wind, rain, and snow. For the most part, a significant number of Oregon's mountains are snowed-in and inaccessible all winter long: check with local agencies before trying a hike in an unfamiliar place. Roads, too, tend to be snowed in, and access to trailheads can be nonexistent. Winter in Oregon, at least in the mountains (including the Cascades, the Blues, the Wallowas, and the high elevations of the Siskiyous), can stretch from November to July.

Spring brings mud and more rain, but also increasing wildflower shows.

Rain Gear

What more needs to be said? Oregonians aren't said to have webbed feet for nothing. Rain gear is crucial, and this is largely why Oregonians tend to not care if it's raining. It's not like hikers are the little kids in front of the window, glumly watching the rain, wishing they could go out. On the contrary, nothing stops hikers in Oregon.

Durable, breathable rain gear (along with waterproof or water-resistant footwear) is an investment that will allow access to many places in Oregon year-round. For the most part, the Oregon coast, the foothills of the Cascades, most of the Columbia River Gorge, and low-elevation valleys are open year-round. Take advantage of it! Much of Oregon's beauty is due to the rains. What else keeps Oregon so green?

SAFETY

Like many Western U.S. states, it is possible to run into rattlesnakes, mountain lions, and bears—not to mention poison oak and biting bugs. Here's a little information about the locals.

NON-TECHNICAL SUMMIT HIKES

Oregon is a mountain climber's dream. With numerous peaks exceeding the 10,000-foot elevation range, there are plenty of opportunities to get on top of the world and enjoy the stunning views that come with them. That being said, it is important to differentiate the kind of mountain climbs featured in this book as available to the common hiker.

A "technical" summit climb requires not just skill but equipment such as ropes, harnesses, protection gear, and other specialized tools like ice axes and crampons. Mount Hood is the most popular of all technical climbs in Oregon, and a summit climb of this kind should never be done without experienced partners and a great deal of training and conditioning. It is a sport unto itself.

Hikes recommended in this book are "non-technical" summits, meaning climbing gear is not required. The mountain hikes covered in this book are those that can be summited on trails recognized by management agencies and detailed on maps. They are generally a long, steep climb, but far safer than climbing extremely steep slopes and crossing glaciers. Think of a non-technical climb, also known as "scrambling," as a really tough hike, where the path may get arduous and you may have to cross some snow now and again.

No matter the climb – whether it be South Sister, Mount McLoughlin, or Eagle Cap – always be prepared as you would for any other hike, if not more so. Be sure to carry more than enough food, water, and clothing, and remember that any change in weather can prove disastrous. Also, pace yourself; any non-technical climb can be especially taxing if you are out-of-shape or tired. Practice on smaller climbs before attempting to bag the big peaks.

Wildlife
RATTLESNAKES
Of the 15 species of snakes in Oregon, only *Crotalus viridis,* the Western Pacific Rattlesnake, is poisonous. They are most active in the spring, summer, and early fall and can be found in parts of the Willamette Valley, the Cascade Mountain foothills, the Siskiyou Mountains, and parts of Eastern Oregon. Their most easily identifiable characteristic, of course, is that heart-stopping rattle. And it's good to stop, because once it has warned you, a rattlesnake is going to try to retreat from you. Stand still; rattlers rarely attack a nonmoving object.

Although rattlesnake bites are certainly painful, they are rarely lethal. Not all rattlesnake bites contain venom, either. If you are bitten, the best thing you can do is call 911 and drive to a hospital. Remove any restrictive clothing and don't attempt to apply a tight tourniquet. Remain calm and avoid running, which can speed venom through the body.

MOUNTAIN LIONS
Cougars, also known as mountain lions, are the largest of the big cats in Oregon. They range pretty much anywhere, and have even passed through towns and cities in the state, especially when following migrating prey such as elk. However, in all likelihood, you will never see one. Cougars will usually avoid humans at all cost. In fact, many people have been near one and never realized it.

In mountain lion country, keep children and pets close. Should you encounter a cougar, don't turn away and don't run. Instead, make yourself appear as large as possible by raising your arms, waving a stick, and opening your coat. Back away slowly, maintaining your pose and speaking loudly.

BLACK BEARS

Like cougars, black bears range widely and try to steer clear of humans. Be alert and make a little noise in bear country to let them know you're coming. If you do see one—which is unlikely, but not impossible—you'll know what it is, since black bears are the only species of bear in Oregon.

If you do encounter a bear, don't run and don't look it in the eye: bears interpret this as a sign of aggression. Instead, back away slowly. If a bear does happen to charge you, stay calm and be prepared to fight back. You can make yourself look bigger by waving your arms and opening your coat. If you have a dog, keep it leashed; an over-protective dog can put a bear on the defensive. One of the worst-case scenarios is to come between a mother bear and her cubs.

A more common way to run into a bear is at camp. Bears are attracted by not only food, and sweet food at that, but by fragrances like toothpaste and perfume. Really. If bears know, or think, that there's something tasty in your tent or your bag, like that honey-almond granola you brought, they'll have at it. Though Oregon doesn't have the same issues with bears as, say, Yosemite National Park in California, it's still wise to hide your food. Backpackers should use a bear-proof canister for overnight trips. You can also make use of a food-hang, where you hang your food by rope from a tree limb, a minimum of 20 feet off the ground and 10 feet from the tree trunk. Tie your rope to a rock and throw it over a branch at least one inch in diameter and four inches at the trunk to accomplish this.

Insects and Plants

Aside from the large mammals and reptiles, it's the little things that get you: mosquitoes, ticks, poison oak, and stinging nettles. Here's how to avoid them.

MOSQUITOES

Mosquitoes in Oregon are by far the peskiest pest of all. Come spring and summer, the valleys and mountains—even the deserts—bloom with the obnoxious buzzing and incessant biting. All this can make for a thoroughly annoying outdoor experience spent swatting and slapping.

Mosquitoes are not merely annoying; they may even be dangerous. As with other states, Oregon has had its first few experiences with West Nile Virus, though it has mostly been confined to a few infections in people, birds, and horses. Better safe than sorry. Know before you go: As snows melt in the mountains, mosquitoes are born, and this typically happens from June to August. Visiting a marshy wildlife refuge in spring? Expect skeeters. Even in deserts, you can expect hordes of them along rivers.

The worst of the worst is the Asian tiger mosquito, a non-native species thought to have been brought to America in automobile tires that contained stagnant water. You'll know them when you see them by their stripes. It's best to carry repellent and netting, or even to avoid certain areas in the peak hatching season.

TICKS

You'll want to corral a friend into a good old "tick check." Ticks find their way into the weirdest of places in an effort to lock in and draw from your blood. The frontline defense is long pants and long sleeves, and to check both your skin and your clothing after hiking. If you find a tick burrowed in, pull it straight out carefully with tweezers, grasping it firmly from the surface of the skin. It's important to get the body and head out, or you can risk infection.

Ticks are most active in spring and summer, in areas of tall grasses and shrubs. Of the four varieties of ticks in Oregon, only the Western black-legged tick is a carrier of Lyme disease. This little tick is mostly black; the larger brown ones are harmless. It's generally said that if you can save a removed tick and take it to a doctor for testing, that's a safe bet. If within a few days or a few weeks you begin to experience flu-like symptoms, see a doctor post-haste.

Dogs, too, are susceptible to ticks, so make sure to check them carefully when you've been hiking in susceptible areas.

POISON OAK

It's been said many times before, but let's say it again: "Leaves of three, let them be." Once you learn to recognize *Toxicodendron diversilobum*, it will become very familiar to you, especially in areas like southern Oregon, the Willamette Valley, and the Columbia Gorge. Otherwise, the brutal rash that can itch for weeks will teach you the hard way to remember. Even as the leaves dry, they still contain the chemical that affects us. Should you come into contact with poison oak, or think you may have, wash thoroughly with warm water and soap as soon as possible. There are several products and soap available that can deal with exposure to poison oak on the trail. As I've learned from experience, dogs pick it up on their fur. Rather than petting, offer your pooch a nice, hot bath.

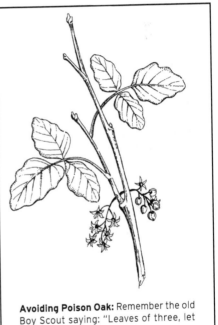

Avoiding Poison Oak: Remember the old Boy Scout saying: "Leaves of three, let them be."

STINGING NETTLES

This member of the nettle family likes to grow in clumps in the Coast Range and in the desert. Heart-shaped, coarse-toothed leaves on a stem bristling with little white hairs gives it away. If you come in contact with those hairs, the resulting sting will let you know immediately that your identification is successful. You'll have to ride out the sting for 24 hours, wondering all the while how it is possible—and delectable—to boil and eat nettles safely!

Safety on the Trail

Stories abound of unfortunate mishaps where people get lost in the wilderness for days on end, and every year seems to bring a new tale of woe. Most of these stories involve two kinds of hikers: the one who hikes alone, and the one who gets separated from a larger group. One wrong turn off a trail, or simply not paying attention in the midst of a huge mountain meadow, can have dire consequences. Weather, too, can have an impact on your safety—for example, getting caught on a ridgeline in a lightning storm (and this one comes from experience!) calls for quick thinking.

Should you find yourself lost, your first priority is to remain calm. Know that it's far better to stay put where you are than to try to keep moving; rescuers will be looking for where you were last known to be (this is why it's so important to fill out wilderness permits at trailheads). Emergency gear, especially a whistle and signaling device, will come in handy here, since rescuers will be listening and looking for signs.

What's the best way to avoid trouble? Simply this: Always tell someone where you'll be. Tell someone at home your travel plans and register with a local ranger station, especially if your plan is to hike into a remote wilderness area. Be specific and detail the area you're visiting, the times you intend to travel, and how long you think you'll be out. It's the responsible thing to do, and it saves searchers much time and effort should you become lost.

Driving Safely

If you think weather can wreak havoc on a trail, try a road. Many of the approaches to trailheads in Oregon require driving on dirt roads that can quickly turn to mud or, worse, can result in a washout. Always check road conditions before you go by calling the Oregon Department of Transportation at 511 or checking www.tripcheck.com. Detailed weather reports and forecasts are available through the National Weather Service online at www.nws.noaa.gov.

Make sure that your car is properly equipped. Fuel up often, check the oil and the brakes, and make sure you've got a spare tire. Have emergency road equipment like snow chains, flashers, and a cell phone.

Make sure your directions are accurate (even mine!). Carry a good atlas of Oregon, like the DeLorme or Benchmark, and don't rely exclusively on Internet maps or GPS devices. If all else fails, ask directions.

Check snow levels. Every year in recent memory has seen individuals or families getting trapped in the snow in the mountains. Just because it's raining in Portland doesn't mean it is at Mount Hood; most likely, it's piling up snow quick. Avoid roads closed in winter or otherwise impassable. Forest Service roads are not shortcuts; stick to main routes and get there safely.

HIKING ETHICS
Trail Etiquette

As wonderful as it is to think like Henry David Thoreau and head for the woods for a little soul-searching solitude, don't expect to find it all the time. Expect instead a lot of other intrepid hikers looking for their own Walden Pond, too. Here are some simple rules to follow to assure a good time for everyone.

WILDERNESS ETHICS

Congressionally designated Wilderness Areas are unique, and are preserved under certain criteria. It's important to maintain the wilderness experience for everyone by limiting human impact. Here are some basic guidelines:

Campfires: Gone are the days of singing around the campfire. For the most part, campfires are discouraged – if not outright prohibited – due to catastrophic forest fires rampant in the Western United States. Land management agencies have decreed that cooking is best done on a backpacking stove. Lighting can be provided by a variety of devices, from flashlights to headlamps.

Water sources: It is imperative to keep Oregon's waters clean. When camping near any lake, stream, or river, give yourself at least 100 feet distance from the waterline before pitching that tent. Like-wise, wash all your cooking gear, socks, and hands by carrying water at least 100 feet away from the water source.

Campsites: When you pitch a tent, be aware of where you are plopping down. A misplaced tent can crush sensitive flowers and damage an area for years. You should always camp on a durable surface, such as rock, or even on sand or dead and dry organic matter – never on live vegetation. This helps maintain the environment for all and prevents area closures for rehabilitation.

Garbage: No one is impressed by a trashed campsite. Who wants to see another campfire ring filled with broken glass and blackened cans, or a campsite ringed by toilet paper wads? No matter what you bring, pack out your garbage. Neither burn nor bury it. That goes for human waste, too.

Maintain the silence. You and everyone else come to the wilderness to get away from the usual hustle and bustle of civilization. Be courteous to all the other hikers by refraining from undue noise. Avoid loud conversations, shouting, and above all, cell phones. This way, too, you're more likely to encounter wildlife and hear the falling water and wind in the trees.

Yield to other users accordingly. Standard rules on yielding apply for the three main user groups—hikers, horses, and bikers. In general, bikes must yield to everyone, and hikers should yield to horses.

Stay on maintained trails. Evidence of breaking this rule is everywhere. Degraded switchbacks and the ubiquitous "user trail" show for certain that people are taking shortcuts and wandering off-trail. Don't use closed trails or enter closed areas; often, they have been closed for restoration or because of overuse. Wandering off-trail tramples vegetation and in the end may force management agencies to limit access for everyone.

Hiking with Children

Always keep children close, especially in areas with cliffs and fast-moving water. Consider the trail carefully before taking children, as many routes are too difficult for them. By choosing appropriate trails, you'll make trips memorable and enjoyable for everyone.

Hiking with Dogs

It's possible that there's no more dog-friendly state than Oregon. That being so, you're sure to run into dogs on the trail or to want to bring your own. And what could be more charming than a dog carrying its own pack with little mitts on its paws?

Regardless, dogs open a whole new can of worms in the outdoors. For one thing, chasing wildlife is a leading reason why dogs get lost in the wilderness. A dog on a leash is a dog that goes home again.

Because of conflicts between hikers and pets, dogs are no longer allowed on many trails in Oregon, or are restricted to a leash on others. Some trails, like the Deschutes River Trail in Central Oregon, no longer allow dogs off-leash, but this may not be obvious at the trailhead. It's best to call the area's managing agency for up-to-date rules. If a posted sign says that dogs must be on a leash, follow it strictly. Otherwise, you could well end up with a ticket.

If a dog is allowed off-leash, as in many forest and wilderness areas, take care that your dog responds appropriately to verbal commands, for the dog's own safety. Why worry? Carry a leash or get good dog training and just enjoy the trip for you and your dog both.

Avoiding Crowds

On the one hand, you can hike into a place like Big Indian Gorge on a summer weekend and not see a soul but for a few deer. On the other hand, you can go to Multnomah Falls, trying to get to the top to hike on up to Larch Mountain and fight your way through throngs of tourists, day-trippers, kids with ice cream cones, and parents in flip-flops pushing strollers. What to do? With a little foresight, you can find a bit of solitude after all.

Avoid the weekends. Weekends are notorious for the so-called "weekend warrior" out for a Saturday afternoon. If you get the chance, take your hike when everyone else is at work. From Tuesday through Thursday seems to be the best, and quietest, time.

Be the first one at the trailhead. If you arrive at a trailhead at around 10 or 11 A.M. like most people do, you'll have trouble finding a parking spot and staying out of the parade. But get there at 6 A.M.? Now you're talking. More than likely, you'll be the only one there.

Hike more than just summer. For most of Oregon, the on-season is summer. Memorial Day (which can be horrendous) and Labor Day (even worse) and everything in between means everyone is out for that brief respite between rains. But once the kids are in school and everyone is secure in the usual routine, *now* is the time to get out.

Avoid the popular hikes. If you have a need for peace and quiet on an August weekend afternoon, then maybe Crater Lake is not your best bet. But then nearby Mount Bailey might be. Choose off-the-beaten-path journeys and you're less likely to see the casual tourist.

Hike in the rain. Any bad weather will do, and if you have good gear you can be out looking at wildflowers in the spring rain while the rest of the world is home keeping their feet warm. Oregon is a place of many moods: gale-force winds, fog, clouds, and rain. These make life more interesting—and memorable.

Leave No Trace

As Henry David Thoreau once said, "In wilderness is the preservation of the world." So how do we preserve our wilderness? The Center for Outdoor Ethics offers these simple dictums to "Leave only footprints and take only pictures":

Plan ahead and prepare. Know the special regulations of the area you are visiting. Be prepared. Schedule your trips to avoid high-use times. Visit in small groups. Repackage your food to minimize waste.

Travel and camp on durable surfaces. Use established trails and campsites. Keep campsites small. In pristine areas, disperse use to prevent the creation of camps or trails.

Dispose of waste properly. Pack it in, pack it out. Deposit human waste in a "cathole" dug 6–8 inches at least 200 feet from water, camp, and trails; cover and disguise when finished. Pack out toilet paper and hygiene products. To wash yourself or dishes, carry water 200 feet away from streams and lakes. If you must use soap, make sure it's biodegradable. Scatter the water when done.

Leave what you find. Examine, but do not touch or remove, cultural or historic structures and artifacts. Leave rocks, plants, and natural objects as you find them. Avoid introducing non-native species. Do not build structures or furniture or dig trenches.

Minimize campfire impacts. Use a stove for cooking, a candle for lighting. Where fires are permitted, use established fire rings, pans, or mounds. Keep fires small and use only ground material to burn. Burn wood and coals to ash, douse completely, and scatter the cool ashes.

Respect wildlife. Remember that you are only a visitor in the wilderness, but it is home to animals. Observe wildlife from a distance, and do not approach or follow. Never feed animals. Store your food securely and control your pets. Avoid wildlife during times of mating, nesting, and raising young.

Be considerate of other visitors. Respect others and protect the quality of their experience. Be courteous. Camp away from other people. Let nature's sounds prevail.

This copyrighted information has been reprinted with permission from the Leave No Trace Center for Outdoor Ethics. For more information or materials, please visit www.lnt.org or call 303/442-8222 or 800/332-4100.

Permits and Land Use

There are different permits you'll need for each of Oregon's 115 state parks, 13 national forest, and five state forests. Many trails on National Forest land, but not all, require the Northwest Forest Pass to park within a quarter-mile of a posted trailhead. These cost $5 a day or $30 for a yearly pass.

Most wilderness areas on National Forest land require a free wilderness permit (available at trailheads) to enter. There are exceptions, such as the Obsidian Trail or the Pamelia Lake area, which require a free special permit beforehand, secured simply by calling the ranger station.

Oregon State Parks vary widely. Some require a day-use fee, while others are free. Many of the more popular parks require a day-use fee, but the waysides—especially along beaches—tend to be free.

The Bureau of Land Management, National Forest Service, and National Park Service manage Oregon's national monuments, national recreation areas, Crater Lake National Park, and the Columbia Gorge National Scenic Area. In addition to the information provided in this book, be sure to contact the appropriate agency for up-to-date information on fees and permits.

OREGON COAST CAMPING

© STEVE ESTVANIK/123rf.com

BEST CAMPGROUNDS

Most Scenic
Honey Bear Campground & RV Resort, **page 77.**

Families
Fort Stevens State Park, **page 30.**
Honey Bear Campground & RV Resort, **page 77.**

Fishing
Waldport/Newport KOA, **page 49.**
Port of Siuslaw RV Park and Marina, **page 55.**
Carter Lake, **page 57.**

Hiking
Nehalem Falls, **page 33.**
Cape Lookout State Park, **page 38.**
Cape Blanco State Park, **page 71.**

Waterfalls
Nehalem Falls, **page 33.**
Alsea Falls, **page 51.**

Waterfront Campgrounds
Loon Lake Recreation Area, **page 64.**
Laird Lake, **page 73.**

Wildlife-Viewing
Cape Lookout State Park, **page 38.**
Seal Rocks RV Cove, **page 47.**
Port of Siuslaw RV Park and Marina, **page 55.**
Harris Beach State Park, **page 83.**

If you want to treat yourself to vacation memories

you'll treasure forever, take a drive and then set up camp along U.S. 101 on the Oregon Coast. Here you'll see some of the most dramatic coastal frontage in North America: tidewater rock gardens, cliff-top views that seem to stretch to forever, vast sand dunes, protected bays, beautiful streams with giant salmon and steelhead (in fall and winter), and three major national forests. I prefer cruising north to south, in the right lane close to the coastline and with the wind behind me; it often seems I'm on the edge of Never Never Land.

If you're heading down from Washington, you'll cross the Columbia River on the border of Oregon and Washington. The river is so wide here that it looks like an inland sea. I find that the best way to appreciate this massive waterway is to get off the main highway and explore the many coastal streams by two-lane road. There are numerous routes, from tiny Highway 15 on the Little Nestucca River to well-known Highway 38 along the beautiful Umpqua.

The most spectacular region on the coast may be the Oregon Dunes National Recreation Area, which spans roughly from Coos Bay north past Florence to near the mouth of the Siuslaw River. Whenever I visit, I feel like I'm instantly transported to another universe. I have a photo of the dunes in my office. While I'm writing, I often look at the image of a lone raptor soaring past a pyramid of sand – it's my window to this wonderful otherworld.

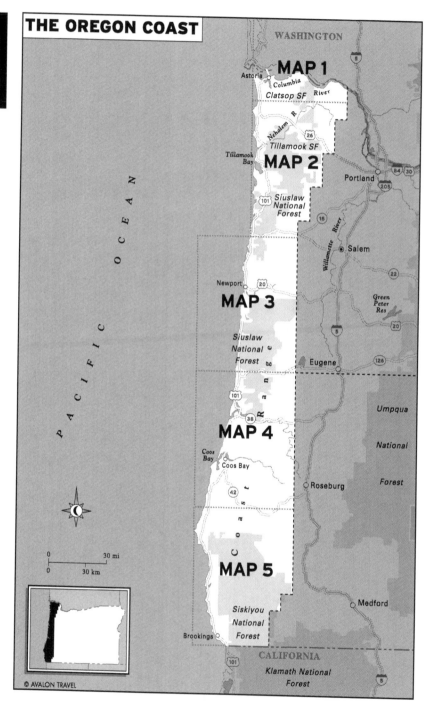

THE OREGON COAST

WASHINGTON

Astoria

Columbia River

MAP 1

Clatsop SF

Nehalem R

Tillamook SF

26

Tillamook Bay

MAP 2

Portland

84 30

205

101

Siuslaw National Forest

18

Willamette River

Salem

22

Newport

20

MAP 3

Green Peter Res

Siuslaw National Forest

Coast Range

Eugene

126

5

20

101

Umpqua

38

MAP 4

National

Coos Bay

Coos Bay

Roseburg

Forest

42

Coast Range

0   30 mi

0   30 km

MAP 5

Medford

Siskiyou National Forest

Brookings

CALIFORNIA

101

Klamath National Forest

5

PACIFIC OCEAN

© AVALON TRAVEL

Map 1

Campgrounds 1-3

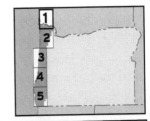

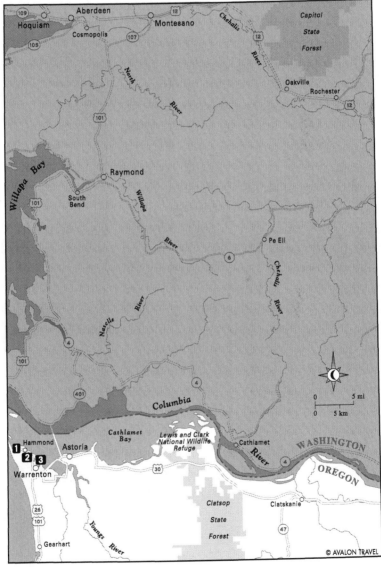

Map 2

Campgrounds 4-32

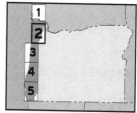

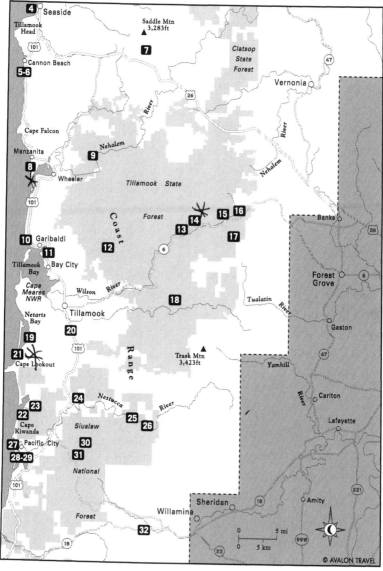

Map 3

Campgrounds 33-59

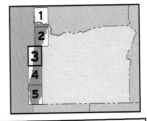

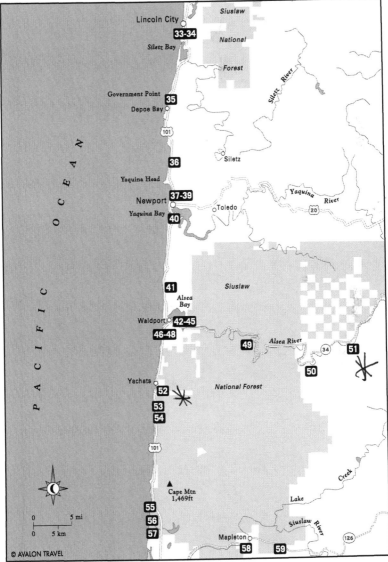

CAMPING

Map 4

Campgrounds 60-95

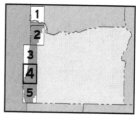

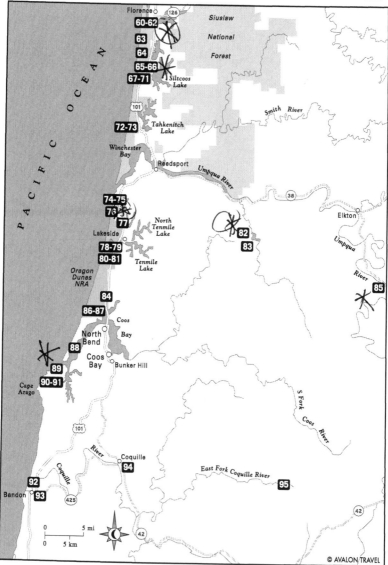

Map 5

Campgrounds 96-130

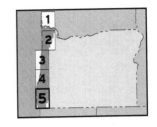

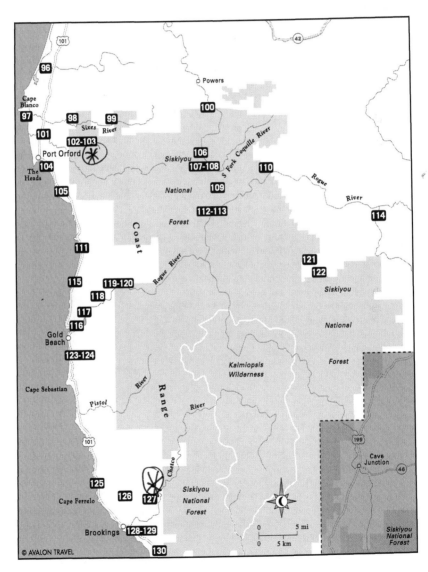

◧ FORT STEVENS STATE PARK

Scenic rating: 8

at the mouth of the Columbia River

BEST (

This classic spot is set at the northern tip of Oregon, right where the Columbia River enters the Pacific Ocean. At 3,700 acres, the park offers nine miles of biking trails, six miles of hiking trails, swimming, boating, fishing, and wildlife-viewing in a landscape of forests, wetlands, and dunes. The trailhead for the Oregon Coast Trail is here as well. History buffs will find a museum, tours of the fort and artillery batteries, and the remains of the *Peter Iredale* shipwreck.

Campsites, facilities: There are 476 sites with full or partial hookups for tents or RVs up to 60 feet long, 19 sites for tents or small RVs (no hookups), a camping area for hikers and bicyclists, and 15 yurts. Picnic tables and fire grills are provided. Drinking water, restrooms with flush toilets and showers, dump station, a transfer and recycling station, two picnic shelters, firewood, and a playground are available. Boat docks and launching facilities are nearby. Some facilities are wheelchair accessible. Leashed pets are permitted.

Reservations, fees: Reservations are accepted at 800/452-5687 or www.oregonstateparks.org ($8 reservation fee). RV sites are $18–27 per night, tent sites are $13–21 per night, $4–6 per night per person for hikers/bikers, yurts are $30–41 per night, $5 per night per additional vehicle. Some credit cards are accepted. Open year-round.

Directions: From Portland, turn west on U.S. 26 and drive 73 miles to the junction with U.S. 101. Turn right (north) on U.S. 101 and drive about 15 miles (about 0.25 mile past the Camp Rilea Army Base). Turn west on Perkins Road/Highway 104 at the sign for Fort Stevens State Park and drive about one mile to Ocean View Cemetery Road. Turn left and drive about 2.5 miles (Ocean View Cemetery Road becomes Ridge Road) to the park entrance.

Contact: Fort Stevens State Park, 503/861-1671 or 800/551-6949, www.oregonstateparks.org.

◨ ASTORIA/WARRENTON SEASIDE KOA

Scenic rating: 3

near Fort Stevens State Park

This campground is nestled in a wooded area adjacent to Fort Stevens State Park, and tours of that historical military site can be arranged. This camp provides an excellent alternative if the state park campground is full. A host of activities are available in the immediate area, including beachcombing, bicycling, deep-sea fishing, hiking, and kayaking. Horse stables are within 10 miles.

Campsites, facilities: There are 311 sites with full or partial hookups for tents or RVs of any length, 54 cabins, and two lodges. Some sites are pull-through. Picnic tables and fire pits are provided. Cable TV, 30- and 50-amp service, modem hookups, wireless Internet service, restrooms with showers, security, public phone, coin laundry, meeting room, firewood, limited groceries, ice, snack bar, RV supplies, propane gas, and a picnic area are available. Recreational facilities include a playground, game room, recreation field, bicycle rentals, miniature golf, horseshoe pits, spa, and a heated indoor swimming pool. Some facilities are wheelchair accessible. Leashed pets are permitted with some restrictions.

Reservations, fees: Reservations are accepted at 800/562-8506. Sites are $39.55–199 per night, $6.50 per person per night for more than two people, $2 per pet per night, $5 per night per additional vehicle unless towed. Some credit cards are accepted. Open year-round.

Directions: From Portland, turn west on U.S. 26 and drive 73 miles to the junction with U.S. 101. Turn right (north) on U.S. 101 and drive about 15 miles (about 0.25 mile past the Camp Rilea Army Base). Turn west on Perkins Road/Highway 104 at the sign for Fort Stevens State Park and drive about one mile to Ocean View Cemetery Road. Turn left and drive about 2.5 miles (Ocean View Cemetery Road becomes Ridge Road) to the campground directly across from the state park.

Contact: Astoria/Warrenton Seaside KOA, 503/861-2606, fax 503/861-3209, www.koa.com.

3 KAMPERS WEST RV PARK

Scenic rating: 7

near Fort Stevens State Park

Just four miles from Fort Stevens State Park, this privately run camp offers full RV services. Nearby recreation possibilities include an 18-hole golf course, hiking trails, and marked bike trails.

Campsites, facilities: There are 163 sites with full or partial hookups for RVs of any length, a small area for tents only, and three park-model cabins. Drinking water and picnic tables are provided, and some sites have fire pits. Restrooms with flush toilets and showers, propane gas, dump station, coin laundry, and ice are available. A store and a café are within one mile. Leashed pets are permitted.

Reservations, fees: Reservations are accepted. RV sites are $36 per night, and tent sites are $28 per night. Some credit cards are accepted. Open year-round.

Directions: From Portland, turn west on U.S. 30 and drive 105 miles north and west to Astoria and the junction of U.S. 101. Turn south and drive 6.5 miles to the Warrenton/Hammond Junction. Turn right (west) on

Warrenton and drive 1.5 miles to the campground on the right.

Contact: Kampers West RV Park, 503/861-1814, fax 503/861-3620, www.kamperswest.com.

4 VENICE RV PARK

Scenic rating: 3

on the Neawanna River

This park along the Neawanna River—one of two rivers running through Seaside—is less than a mile from the beach. A great bonus: Crab pot rentals are available. Seaside offers beautiful ocean beaches for fishing and surfing, moped and bike rentals, shops, and a theater. The city provides swings and volleyball nets on the beach. An 18-hole golf course is nearby.

Campsites, facilities: There are 26 sites for RVs of any length (full hookups, some pull-through) and six tent sites. Drinking water, cable TV, and picnic tables are provided. Restrooms with flush toilets and showers, picnic area and a coin laundry are available. A store and a café are within one mile. Leashed pets are permitted.

Reservations, fees: Reservations are accepted. RV sites are $27.25 per night (with camp membership), tent sites are $18 per night, $2 per person per night for more than two people, $2 per night per additional vehicle, and $2 per pet per night. Some credit cards are accepted. Open year-round.

Directions: From Portland on I-5, turn west on U.S. 26 and drive 73 miles to the junction with U.S. 101. Turn north on U.S. 101 and drive 5.25 miles to Seaside. Continue to the north end of town and bear left (west) on 24th Avenue. The campground is on the corner (do not cross the bridge) at 1032 24th Avenue.

Contact: Venice RV Park, 503/738-8851, www.shopseaside.com/vrv.

CAMPING

5 SEA RANCH RV PARK

Scenic rating: 9

in Cannon Beach

This park is set in a wooded area with nearby access to the beach. Activities at the camp include stream fishing, horseback riding, and swimming on the seashore. A golf course is six miles away, and the historic Lewis and Clark Trail is nearby. Elk hunters camp here in season. The beach and the town of Cannon Beach are within walking distance of the park.

Campsites, facilities: There are 80 sites with full or partial hookups for tents or RVs up to 40 feet long and seven cabins. Picnic tables and fire rings are provided. Restrooms with showers, horse rentals, and a dump station are available. Supplies are available within two miles. Leashed pets are permitted.

Reservations, fees: Reservations are accepted. RV sites are $30–90 per night, tent sites are $23 per night; and it costs $2 per person per night for more than two people, $3 per night per additional vehicle, and $10 per pet per night. Some credit cards are accepted. Open year-round.

Directions: From Portland on I-5, turn west on U.S. 26 and drive 73 miles to the junction with U.S. 101. Turn south on U.S. 101 and drive three miles to the Cannon Beach exit. Take that exit and drive on Fir Street for 0.3 mile to the park on the left.

Contact: Sea Ranch RV Park, 503/436-2815, www.searanchrv.com.

6 RV RESORT AT CANNON BEACH

Scenic rating: 9

near Ecola State Park

This private resort is located about seven blocks from one of the nicest beaches in the region and about two miles from Ecola State Park. From the town of Cannon Beach, you can walk for miles in either direction. Nearby recreational facilities include marked bike trails, a riding stable, and tennis courts. The city shuttle service stops here.

Campsites, facilities: There are 100 sites with full hookups for RVs of any length; some are pull-through sites. Picnic tables and fire pits are provided. Restrooms with flush toilets and showers, cable TV, propane gas, firewood, recreation hall, playground, horseshoe pits, basketball court, convenience store, spa, coin laundry, ice, gasoline, playground, and a heated swimming pool (year-round) are available. Leashed pets are permitted.

Reservations, fees: Reservations are accepted at 800/847-2231. Sites are $32–44 per night, $3 per person per night for more than two people, $3 per night per additional vehicle. Some credit cards are accepted. Open year-round.

Directions: From Portland on I-5, turn west on U.S. 26 and drive 73 miles to the junction with U.S. 101. Turn south on U.S. 101 and drive four miles to the second Cannon Beach exit at Milepost 29.5. Exit on the left (east) and drive 200 feet to the resort.

Contact: RV Resort at Cannon Beach, 503/436-2231, fax 503/436-1527, www.cbrvresort.com.

7 SADDLE MOUNTAIN STATE NATURAL AREA

Scenic rating: 7

on Saddle Mountain

This inland camp offers a good alternative to the many beachfront parks. A 2.5-mile trail climbs to the top of Saddle Mountain, a great lookout on clear days. The park is a real find for the naturalist interested in rare and unusual varieties of plants, many of which have established themselves along the slopes of this isolated mountain.

Campsites, facilities: There are 10 primitive tent sites, a grassy overflow area for tents, and a parking lot camping area for RVs. Drinking water, garbage bins, picnic tables, and fire grills are provided. Vault toilets and a picnic area are available. Leashed pets are permitted.

Reservations, fees: Reservations are not accepted. Sites are $5–10 per night, $5 per night per additional vehicle. Open March–October.

Directions: From Portland, turn west on U.S. 26 and drive about 63 miles to just before Necanicum Junction and Saddle Mountain Road. Turn right (north) on Saddle Mountain Road and drive seven miles to the park. The road dead-ends at the park.

Contact: Ecola State Park, 503/436-2844 or 800/551-6949 (this number reaches Ecola State Park, which manages Saddle Mountain), www.oregonstateparks.org.

8 NEHALEM BAY STATE PARK

Scenic rating: 7

on Nehalem Bay

This state park on a sandy point separating the Pacific Ocean from Nehalem Bay features six miles of beach frontage. There is no ocean view from the campsites, but the sites are about 150 yards from the ocean. In 2008, beachcombers discovered a pair of historic cannons at low tide, likely dating back to an 1846 shipwreck. Crabbing and fishing on the bay are popular. The Oregon Coast Trail passes through the park. A horse camp with corrals and a 7.5-mile equestrian trail are available. There is also a two-mile bike trail. The neighboring towns of Manzanita and Nehalem offer fine dining and shopping. An airport is adjacent to the park, and there are airstrip fly-in campsites.

Campsites, facilities: There are 265 sites with partial hookups for tents or RVs up to 60 feet long, a camping area for hikers and bicyclists,

and six primitive fly-in sites next to the airport. There are also 18 yurts and 17 equestrian sites with stock corrals. Drinking water, picnic tables, and fire grills are provided. Restrooms with flush toilets and showers, dump station, playgrounds, firewood, and a meeting hall are available. Boat-launching facilities are nearby on Nehalem Bay, and an airstrip is adjacent to the park. Some facilities are wheelchair accessible. Leashed pets are permitted.

Reservations, fees: Reservations are accepted at 800/452-5687 or www.oregonstateparks.org ($8 reservation fee). Sites are $16–24 per night, $5 per night per additional vehicle, and $4–5 per person per night for hikers/bikers. Yurts are $27–36 per night; horse sites are $12–19 per night. Fly-in sites are $8–10 per night, not including tie-down. Some credit cards are accepted. Open year-round.

Directions: From Portland, drive west on U.S. 26 for 73 miles to the junction with U.S. 101. Turn south on U.S. 101 and drive 19 miles to Manzanita. Continue south on U.S. 101 for 0.75 mile to Necarney City Road. Turn right and drive 0.2 mile to a stop sign. Turn right and drive 0.75 mile to the park entrance.

Contact: Nehalem Bay State Park, 503/368-5154 or 800/551-6949, www.oregonstateparks.org.

9 NEHALEM FALLS

Scenic rating: 10

in Tillamook State Forest

BEST (

This beautiful campground, amid old-growth hemlock and spruce, is located within a two-minute walk of lovely Nehalem Falls. Note that swimming in the pool below the falls is hazardous and not advised. A half-mile loop trail follows the Nehalem River, where fishing and swimming are options.

Campsites, facilities: There are 14 sites for tents or RVs up to 40 feet long, four walk-in tent sites, and one group site for up to 20

CAMPING

people. Drinking water, picnic tables, garbage bins, recycling center, fire grills, and vault toilets are available. A camp host is on-site. Some facilities are wheelchair accessible. Leashed pets are permitted.

Reservations, fees: Reservations are accepted only for the group site at 503/842-2545. Sites are $10 per night, $2 per night per additional vehicle, walk-in sites are $5 per night, and the group site is $25 per night. Open May–October.

Directions: From Tillamook on U.S. 101 northbound, drive 22 miles to Highway 53. Turn right (east) and drive 1.3 miles to Miami Foley Road. Turn right (south) and drive one mile to Foss Road (narrow and rough). Turn left and drive seven miles to the campground on the left.

Contact: Tillamook State Forest, Tillamook District, 503/842-2545, fax 503/842-3143, www.oregon.gov.

10 BARVIEW JETTY PARK

Scenic rating: 7

near Garibaldi

This Tillamook County park covers 160 acres and is located near the beach, in a wooded area adjacent to Tillamook Bay. The sites are set on grassy hills. Nearby recreation options include an 18-hole golf course, surf and scuba fishing, and a full-service marina.

Campsites, facilities: There are 224 tent sites, 69 sites for tents or RVs of any length (full hookups), and four hiker/bicyclist sites. Some sites are pull-through. Drinking water, picnic tables, and fire pits are provided. Restrooms with flush toilets and showers, a dump station, fish-cleaning station, and day-use area are available. Groups can be accommodated. Propane gas, store, café, and ice are within one mile. Some facilities are wheelchair accessible. Leashed pets are permitted.

Reservations, fees: Reservations are accepted ($5 reservation fee) at 503/322-3522 or www.co.tillamook.or.us. Sites are $10–30 per night, $3–5 per night per each additional vehicle or tent, $5 per person per night for hikers/bikers. Some credit cards are accepted. Open year-round.

Directions: From Tillamook, drive north on U.S. 101 for 12 miles to the park on the left (two miles north of the town of Garibaldi).

Contact: Barview Jetty Park, Tillamook County, 503/322-3522, www.co.tillamook.or.us/gov/parks.

11 BIAK-BY-THE-SEA RV PARK

Scenic rating: 7

on Tillamook Bay

This park along the shore of Tillamook Bay is a prime retreat for beachcombing, clamming, crabbing, deep-sea fishing, scuba diving, and surf fishing. The nearby town of Tillamook is home to a cheese factory and a historical museum. Cape Meares State Park, where you can hike through the national wildlife preserve and see how the seabirds nest along the cliffs, makes a good side trip. There is also a golf course nearby. Note that most of the sites are monthly rentals.

Campsites, facilities: There are 45 pull-through sites with full hookups for RVs of any length and a grassy area for tents. Drinking water and cable TV are provided. Restrooms with flush toilets and coin showers and a coin laundry are available. Propane gas, a store, café, and ice are within one mile. Boat docks, launching facilities, and rentals are nearby. Leashed pets are permitted.

Reservations, fees: Reservations are accepted. Sites are $25 per night. Some credit cards are accepted. Open year-round.

Directions: From Tillamook and U.S. 101,

drive north for 10 miles to 7th Street. Turn left on 7th Street and drive to the park on the left (just over the tracks).

Contact: Biak-by-the-Sea RV Park, 503/322-2111.

12 KILCHIS RIVER PARK

Scenic rating: 8

on the Kilchis River

Riverfront campsites are the highlight at this Tillamook County campground. The campground is forested and gets moderate use. Hiking trails are available. Other recreational options include boating, fishing, and swimming.

Campsites, facilities: There are 63 sites for tents or RVs of any length (no hookups), hiker/bicyclist sites, and group sites. Picnic tables, drinking water, flush toilets, and fire pits are provided. A playground, garbage bins, boat launch, day-use area, pay phone, coin showers, dump station, basketball court, and a volleyball court are available. A camp host is on-site. Leashed pets are permitted.

Reservations, fees: Reservations are accepted ($5 reservation fee) at 503/842-6694 or www.co.tillamook.or.us. Sites are $12–15 per night, $3 per night per additional vehicle, and $5 per person per night for hikers and bicyclists. Open May–September.

Directions: From Tillamook and U.S. 101, take the Alderbrook Loop/Kilches Park exit. Turn onto Alderbrook Loop and drive northeast for approximately one mile to Kilches River Road. Turn right and drive approximately four miles to the park at the end of the road.

Contact: Kilchis River Park, Tillamook County, 503/842-6694, www.co.tillamook.or.us/gov/parks.

13 JONES CREEK

Scenic rating: 7

on the Wilson River in Tillamook State Forest

Set in a forest of alder, fir, hemlock, and spruce, campsites here are spacious and private. The adjacent Wilson River provides opportunities for steelhead and salmon fishing (artificial lures only). A scenic 3.8-mile trail runs along the riverfront. The camp fills up on weekends July–Labor Day.

Campsites, facilities: There are 29 sites for tents or RVs (27 sites are 50 feet long and one is 72 feet long and pull-through), nine walk-in tent sites, and one group site for up to 80 people. Drinking water, picnic tables, and fire grills are provided. Vault toilets, garbage bins, firewood, and a horseshoe pit are available. A camp host is on-site. Some facilities are wheelchair accessible. Leashed pets are permitted.

Reservations, fees: Reservations are accepted only for the group site at 503/842-2545. Sites are $10 per night, $2 per night per additional vehicle, walk-in sites are $5 per night, and the group site is $25 per night. Open May–October.

Directions: From Portland, turn west on U.S. 26 and drive 24 miles to Highway 6. Turn west on Highway 6 and drive 28 miles to Milepost 22.7 and North Fork Road. Turn right and drive 0.25 mile to the campground on the left.

Contact: Tillamook State Forest, Tillamook District, 503/842-2545, fax 503/842-3143, www.oregon.gov.

14 ELK CREEK WALK-IN

Scenic rating: 7

on Elk Creek in Tillamook State Forest

This small campground is set among alder, fir, and maple on Elk Creek and borders the

CAMPING

Wilson River. The Elk Mountain trailhead is here and a good swimming hole is nearby. Note that Elk Creek is closed to fishing; call ahead for fishing information on the Wilson River, as regulations often change.

Campsites, facilities: There are 15 walk-in tent sites. Drinking water, picnic tables, fire grills, and vault toilets are available. Garbage must be packed out. Some facilities are wheelchair accessible. Leashed pets are permitted.

Reservations, fees: Reservations are not accepted. Sites are $5 per night, $2 per night per additional vehicle. Open early May–October.

Directions: From Portland, turn west on U.S. 26 and drive 24 miles to Highway 6. Turn west on Highway 6 and drive 23 miles to Milepost 28 and the campground entrance road on the right. Turn right on Elk Creek Road and drive 0.5 mile to the campground on the left.

Contact: Tillamook State Forest, Forest Grove District, 503/357-2191, www.oregon.gov.

15 JORDAN CREEK OHV

Scenic rating: 6

near Jordan Creek in Tillamook State Forest

This off-highway vehicle (OHV) camp is set at the bottom of a scenic, steep canyon next to Jordan Creek. Wooded campsites are clustered around a central parking area, and the park caters to OHV campers. There are almost 40 miles of OHV trails, varying from moderate to difficult. Note that in order to ride an ATV on roads, you need an ATV sticker, a driver's license, and a spark arrestor. There's no fishing in Jordan Creek.

Campsites, facilities: There are six sites for tents or RVs of any length. Overflow RV camping is allowed in the main parking lot. There is no drinking water. Picnic tables, fire grills, garbage bins, and vault toilets are available. Leashed pets are permitted.

Reservations, fees: Reservations are not accepted. Sites are $10 per night, $2 per night per additional vehicle. Open March–November.

Directions: From Tillamook on U.S. 101, turn east on Highway 6 and drive 17.9 miles to Jordan Creek Road. Turn right and drive 2.2 miles to the campground on the right.

Contact: Tillamook State Forest, Tillamook District, 503/842-2545, fax 503/842-3143, www.oregon.gov.

16 GALES CREEK

Scenic rating: 7

on Gales Creek in Tillamook State Forest

Gales Creek runs through this heavily forested camp. The Gales Creek Trailhead is accessible from camp, providing access to hiking and mountain biking opportunities. A day-use picnic area is also available.

Campsites, facilities: There are 19 sites for tents or RVs up to 35 feet long and four walk-in tent sites. Drinking water, picnic tables, fire grills, garbage bins, and vault toilets are available. Some facilities are wheelchair accessible. Leashed pets are permitted.

Reservations, fees: Reservations are not accepted. RV sites are $10 per night, walk-in tent sites are $5 per night, and an additional vehicle is $2 per night. Open early May–October.

Directions: From Portland, turn west on U.S. 26 and drive 24 miles to Highway 6. Turn west on Highway 6 and drive 17 miles to the campground entrance road (Rogers Road) on the right at Milepost 35. Turn right on Rogers Road and drive one mile to the campground.

Contact: Tillamook State Forest, Forest Grove District, 503/357-2191, www.oregon.gov.

17 BROWNS CAMP OHV

Scenic rating: 6

in Tillamook State Forest

This camp is located next to the Devil's Lake Fork of the Wilson River and has sites with and without tree cover. Surrounded by miles of OHV trails, it caters to off-highway vehicle campers. Don't expect peace and quiet. No fishing is allowed here.

Campsites, facilities: There are 29 sites for tents or RVs up to 45 feet long. Drinking water, picnic tables, fire grills, garbage bins, and vault toilets are available. Some facilities are wheelchair accessible. Leashed pets are permitted.

Reservations, fees: Reservations are not accepted. Sites are $10 per night, $2 per night per additional vehicle. Open March–November.

Directions: From Portland, turn west on U.S. 26 and drive 24 miles to Highway 6. Turn west on Highway 6 and drive 19 miles to Beaver Dam Road. Turn left (south) and drive 2.5 miles to Scoggins Road. Turn left (southeast) and drive 0.5 mile to the campground.

Contact: Tillamook State Forest, Forest Grove District, 503/357-2191, www.oregon.gov.

18 TRASK RIVER PARK

Scenic rating: 7

on the Trask River

This is a popular campground and park that gets moderate use primarily from the locals in Tillamook County. Some campsites are shaded. Fishing for trout and steelhead is available in season; check current fishing regulations.

Campsites, facilities: There are 63 sites for tents or RVs of any length (no hookups) and a hiker/bicyclist area. Picnic tables, garbage service, and fire pits are provided. Drinking water, vault toilets, and a day-use area are available. A camp host is on-site. Some facilities are wheelchair accessible. Leashed pets are permitted.

Reservations, fees: Reservations are accepted ($5 reservation fee) at 503/842-4559 or www.co.tillamook.or.us. Sites are $10–15 per night, $3 per night for additional vehicle, and $5 per person per night for hikers/bicyclists. Some credit cards are accepted. Open year-round.

Directions: From Tillamook and U.S. 101, turn east on 3rd Street. Drive 2.5 miles to Trask River Road. Turn right and drive 1.5 miles, turning left to stay on Trask River Road. Continue 10 miles to the park.

Contact: Trask River Park, Tillamook County, 503/842-4559, www.co.tillamook.or.us/gov/parks.

19 NETARTS BAY RV PARK & MARINA

Scenic rating: 8

on Netarts Bay

This camp is one of three on the east shore of Netarts Bay. A golf course is eight miles away. Sunsets and wildlife-viewing are notable here. Some sites are filled with rentals for the summer season.

Campsites, facilities: There are 88 sites with full hookups for RVs of any length; some are pull-through sites. Drinking water and picnic tables are provided, and fire rings are available at some sites. Restrooms with flush toilets and showers, propane gas, a meeting room, coin laundry, playground, horseshoe pits, crab-cooking facilities, crab bait, and ice are available. Boat docks, launching facilities, and rentals are available on-site. A store and a café are within one mile. Leashed pets are permitted, with a two-pet maximum.

Reservations, fees: Reservations are recommended. Sites are $28–35 per night, $5 per night per additional vehicle. Some credit cards are accepted. Monthly rentals are available. Open year-round.

CAMPING

Directions: From Tillamook and Netarts Highway/Highway 131, drive west on Netarts Highway for six miles to the campground entrance.

Contact: Netarts Bay RV Park & Marina, 503/842-7774, www.netartsbay.com.

20 PLEASANT VALLEY RV PARK

Scenic rating: 8

on the Tillamook River

Pleasant Valley RV Park sits along the Tillamook River. The park is very clean and provides easy access to many recreation options in the immediate area.

Campsites, facilities: There are 10 tent sites and 76 pull-through sites with full or partial hookups for RVs of any length, plus two cabins. Drinking water and picnic tables are provided and some sites have fire rings. Restrooms with flush toilets and showers, propane gas, dump station, firewood, a meeting room, cable TV, modem access, convenience store, coin laundry, ice, and a playground are available. Boat-launching facilities are nearby. Leashed pets are permitted.

Reservations, fees: Reservations are accepted. RV sites are $28–32 per night, tent sites are $18 per night, $2 per person per night for more than two people; cabins are $29 per night. Some credit cards are accepted. Open year-round.

Directions: From Tillamook and U.S. 101, drive south on U.S. 101 for 7 miles to the campground entrance on the right (west).

Contact: Pleasant Valley RV Park, 503/842-4779, fax 503/842-2293, www.pleasantvalleyrvpark.com.

21 CAPE LOOKOUT STATE PARK

Scenic rating: 8

near Netarts Bay

BEST (

This park is set on a sand spit between Netarts Bay and the Pacific. There are more than eight miles of wooded trails, including the Cape Lookout Trail which follows the headland for more than two miles. Another walk will take you out through a variety of estuarine habitats along the five-mile sand spit that extends between the ocean and Netarts Bay. With many species to view, this area is a paradise for birdwatchers. You might also catch the local hang gliders and paragliders that frequent the park. Fishing is another option here.

Campsites, facilities: There are 173 sites for tents or RVs (no hookups), 38 sites with full hookups for RVs up to 60 feet long, a tent camping area for hikers and bicyclists, two group tent sites for up to 25 people each, three cabins, and 13 yurts. Picnic tables and fire grills are provided. Restrooms with flush toilets and showers, dump station, garbage bins, meeting hall and picnic shelter, summer interpretive programs, and firewood are available. Some facilities are wheelchair accessible. Leashed pets are permitted.

Reservations, fees: Reservations are accepted at 800/452-5687 or www.oregonstateparks.org ($8 reservation fee). RV sites are $16–24 per night, tent sites are $12–19 per night, $4–5 per person per night for hikers/bikers, $40–71 per night for group sites, $45–76 per night for cabins, and $27–36 per night for yurts, $5 per night per additional vehicle. Some credit cards are accepted. Open year-round.

Directions: From Tillamook and U.S. 101, turn east on 3rd Street (becomes Netarts Highway). Drive approximately five miles to Whiskey Creek Road. Turn left and drive approximately seven miles to the park on the right.

Contact: Cape Lookout State Park, 503/842-4981, www.oregonstateparks.org.

22 WHALEN ISLAND PARK

Scenic rating: 6

in the Sandlake Estuary

This park is located in the Sandlake Estuary and is close to the beach and Nestucca Bay. The campground is fairly open and has a few trees.
Campsites, facilities: There are 34 sites for tents or RVs of any length (no hookups) and two hiker/bicyclist sites. Picnic tables and fire pits are provided. Drinking water, flush and chemical toilets, dump station, a day-use area, and a boat launch are available. A camp host is on-site during the summer. Some facilities are wheelchair accessible. Leashed pets are permitted.
Reservations, fees: Reservations are accepted ($5 reservation fee). Sites are $10–15 per night, $3 per night per additional vehicle, and $5 per person per night for hikers and bicyclists. Open March–November; check for current status at other times of year.
Directions: From Tillamook and U.S. 101, drive south for 11 miles to Sand Lake Road. Turn right (west) and drive approximately 55 miles to a stop sign. Turn left to stay on Sand Lake Road. Continue 4.75 miles south to the park entrance road on the right.
Contact: Whalen Island Park, Tillamook County, 503/965-6085, www.co.tillamook.or.us/gov/parks.

23 SANDBEACH, EAST DUNES, AND WEST WINDS OHV

Scenic rating: 5

in Siuslaw National Forest

Sandbeach campground is set along the shore of Sand Lake, which is actually more like an estuary than a lake since the ocean is just around the bend. This area is known for its beaches with large sand dunes, which are popular with off-road-vehicle enthusiasts. It's noisy and can be windy. East Dunes and West Winds, which used to be the overflow parking area, are nearby. This is the only coastal U.S. Forest Service camping area for many miles, and it's quite popular. If you're planning a trip for midsummer, be sure to reserve far in advance. Holiday permits are required ($10 at the district office) for three-day holiday weekends.
Campsites, facilities: At Sandbeach, there are 101 sites for tents or RVs; West Winds has 51 sites for tents or RVs; and East Dunes has 51 sites for tents or RVs. There are no hookups and RV length limit is 60 feet long. Picnic tables and fire pits are provided. Drinking water, garbage bins, and flush toilets are available. A camp host is on-site at each campground. Leashed pets are permitted.
Reservations, fees: Reservations are accepted during the summer season at 877/444-6777 or www.recreation.gov ($10 reservation fee). Sites at Sandbeach are $20 per night; sites at East Dunes and West Winds are $15 per night. Additional vehicles cost $8 per night at all campgrounds. Open year-round.
Directions: From Tillamook on U.S. 101, drive south for 11 miles to County Road 8. Turn right (west) on County Road 8 and drive approximately 12 miles to the campground.
Contact: Siuslaw National Forest, Hebo Ranger District, 503/392-3161, fax 503/392-4203, www.fs.fed.us.

24 CAMPER COVE RV PARK AND CAMPGROUND

Scenic rating: 6

on Beaver Creek

This small, wooded campground along Beaver Creek is set just far enough off the highway to provide quiet. The park can be used as a base camp for anglers, with seasonal steelhead and

CAMPING

salmon fishing in the nearby Nestucca River. It gets crowded here, especially in the summer, so be sure to make a reservation if possible. Ocean beaches are four miles away.

Campsites, facilities: There are 50 sites with full hookups for RVs up to 40 feet long, five tent sites, and three cabins. Drinking water, fire pits, and picnic tables are provided. Restrooms with flush toilets and coin showers, dump station, firewood, recreation hall, coin laundry, and ice are available. Leashed pets are permitted.

Reservations, fees: Reservations are accepted. RV sites are $28 per night, tent sites are $20 per night, $3 per person per night for more than two people and $3 per night per additional vehicle. Open year-round.

Directions: From Tillamook and U.S. 101, drive south on U.S. 101 for 12 miles to the park entrance on the right (west), three miles north of Beaver.

Contact: Camper Cove RV Park and Campground, 503/398-5334, www.campercovecampground.com.

25 ROCKY BEND

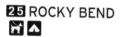

Scenic rating: 5

on the Nestucca River in
Siuslaw National Forest

This campground along the Nestucca River is a little-known, secluded spot that provides guaranteed peace and quiet. There isn't much in the way of recreational activities out here, but clamming, fishing, hiking, and swimming are available along the coast, a relatively short drive away.

Campsites, facilities: There are six tent sites. Picnic tables and fire pits are provided. Vault toilets are available. There is no drinking water and garbage must be packed out. Leashed pets are permitted.

Reservations, fees: Reservations are not accepted. There is no fee for camping. Open year-round.

Directions: On U.S. 101 southwest of Portland, drive to the tiny town of Beaver and Blaine Road. Turn east on Blaine Road (keep right; Blaine Road turns into Nestucca River Access Road) and drive 15.5 miles to the campground on the right.

Contact: Siuslaw National Forest, Hebo Ranger District, 503/392-5100, fax 503/392-5143, www.fs.fed.us.

26 DOVRE, FAN CREEK, ALDER GLEN

Scenic rating: 5

on the Nestucca River

This is a series of three BLM campgrounds set along the Nestucca River. The camps, separated by alder trees and shrubs, are near the river, and some have river views. Tourists don't know about these spots. The Nestucca is a gentle river, with the water not deep enough for swimming.

Campsites, facilities: Dovre has 10 sites, Fan Creek has 11 sites, and Alder Glen has 11 sites—all for tents or small RVs. Picnic tables and fire grills are provided. Drinking water and vault toilets are available. Garbage must be packed out. Some facilities, including a fishing pier at Alder Glen, are wheelchair accessible. Leashed pets are permitted.

Reservations, fees: Reservations are not accepted. Sites are $10 per night, $4 per night per additional vehicle with a limit of two vehicles per site. Open year-round.

Directions: On U.S. 101 southwest of Portland, drive to the tiny town of Beaver and Blaine Road. Turn east on Blaine Road (keep right; Blaine Road turns into Nestucca River Access Road) and drive 17.5 miles to Alder Glen. Continue east for seven more miles to reach Fan Creek and nine more miles to reach Dovre.

Contact: Bureau of Land Management, Salem District, 503/375-5646, fax 503/375-5622, www.blm.gov.

27 WOODS COUNTY PARK

Scenic rating: 6

on the Kilchis River

This small Tillamook County park is not well known outside the local area and gets fairly light use. The campground is grassy with few trees. Salmon fishing is a possibility; check current regulations.

Campsites, facilities: There are seven tent sites and five sites for RVs up to 40 feet long. Picnic tables and fire pits are provided. Drinking water, flush toilets, garbage containers, and a day-use area are available. A camp host is on-site. Leashed pets are permitted.

Reservations, fees: Reservations are accepted ($5 reservation fee) at 503/965-5001 or www.co.tillamook.or.us. Sites are $15–25 per night, $3 per night per additional vehicle. Open May–October, weather permitting.

Directions: From Tillamook and U.S. 101, drive approximately 25 miles south to Resort Drive. Turn right (west) and drive three miles (road changes to Brooten Drive) to the park on the right.

Contact: Woods County Park, Tillamook County, 503/965-5001, www.co.tillamook.or.us/gov/parks.

28 CAPE KIWANDA RV RESORT

Scenic rating: 8

near Cape Kiwanda State Park

This park is set a short distance from Cape Kiwanda State Park, which is open for day use only. Highlights at the park include a boat launch and hiking trails that lead out to the cape. Four miles south at Nestucca Spit, there is another day-use park, providing additional recreational options. The point extends about three miles and is a good spot for bird-watching. The campsites do not have ocean views, but the ocean is across the road and within walking distance. Surfing is an option.

Campsites, facilities: There are 150 sites with full hookups for RVs up to 65 feet long, 13 tent sites, and 14 camping cabins. Some sites are pull-through. Drinking water, fire rings, and picnic tables are provided. Restrooms with flush toilets and showers, dump station, modem access, a heated swimming pool (year-round), hot tub, an exercise room, firewood, a recreation hall, coin laundry, propane, a seafood market, deli, gift shop, automated teller machine (ATM), sandboard rentals, and a playground are available. Gasoline, a store, and a café are within one mile. Boat docks, launching facilities, and rentals are nearby. Leashed pets are permitted.

Reservations, fees: Reservations are accepted. RV sites are $40.95–43.95 per night, tent sites are $26 per night, $2–4 per person per night for more than two people, and $4 per night per additional vehicle. Some credit cards are accepted. Open year-round.

Directions: From Tillamook and U.S. 101, drive south on U.S. 101 for 25 miles to the Pacific City exit and Brooten Road. Turn right on Brooten Road and drive three miles toward Pacific City and Three Capes Drive. Turn left, cross the bridge, and bear right on Three Capes Drive. Continue one mile north to the park on the right.

Contact: Cape Kiwanda RV Resort, 503/965-6230, fax 503/965-6235, www.capekiwandarvpark.com.

29 WEBB PARK

Scenic rating: 7

near Cape Kiwanda

This public campground provides an excellent alternative to the more crowded commercial RV parks off U.S. 101. Although not as

CAMPING

developed, it offers a quiet, private setting and access to the ocean. Fishing and swimming are among your options here. The camp is adjacent to Cape Kiwanda and provides convenient access to the beach.

Campsites, facilities: There are 31 sites for tents or RVs (no hookups), seven sites with partial hookups for RVs up to 40 feet long, and a hiker/bicyclist site. Picnic tables and fire pits are provided. Drinking water, a dump station, fish-cleaning station, and restrooms with flush toilets and showers are available. Beach launching is nearby. Leashed pets are permitted.

Reservations, fees: Reservations are accepted ($5 reservation fee) at 503/965-5001 or www.co.tillamook.or.us. Sites are $15–25 per night, $3 per night per additional vehicle, and $5 per person per night for hikers/bikers. Some credit cards are accepted. Open May–September.

Directions: From Tillamook and U.S. 101, drive south on U.S. 101 for 25 miles to the Pacific City exit and Highway 30. From Pacific City, turn right (north) and drive to the four-way stop at McPhillips Drive. Turn left on McPhillips Drive and drive 0.5 mile to Cape Kiwanda and the park on the right.

Contact: Webb Park, Tillamook County Parks, 503/965-5001, www.co.tillamook.or.us/gov/parks.

30 HEBO LAKE

Scenic rating: 7

on Hebo Lake in Siuslaw National Forest

This U.S. Forest Service campground along the shore of Hebo Lake is a secluded spot with sites nestled under trees. The trailhead for the eight-mile-long Pioneer-Indian Trail is located in the campground. The trail around the lake is wheelchair accessible.

Campsites, facilities: There are 15 sites for tents or RVs up to 18 feet long. Picnic tables and fire pits are provided. Drinking water,

garbage bins, and vault toilets are available. Boats with electric motors are allowed on the lake, but gas motors are not. Some facilities are wheelchair accessible. Leashed pets are permitted.

Reservations, fees: Reservations are not accepted. Sites are $12 per night, $5 per night per additional vehicle. Open from mid-April to mid-November, weather permitting.

Directions: On U.S. 101 southwest of Portland, drive to the town of Hebo and Highway 22. Turn east on Highway 22 and drive 0.25 mile to Forest Road 14. Turn left (east) and drive five miles to the campground on the right.

Contact: Siuslaw National Forest, Hebo Ranger District, 503/392-5100, fax 503/392-5143, www.fs.fed.us.

31 CASTLE ROCK

Scenic rating: 4

on Three Rivers in Siuslaw National Forest

This tiny spot along Three Rivers provides tent campers with an inland alternative to the large beachfront RV parks popular on the Oregon coast. Fishing can be good here. Though primitive, this camp is located along the edge of the highway and can fill up quickly.

Campsites, facilities: There are four tent sites. Picnic tables, garbage bins, and a vault toilet are provided. There is no drinking water. Leashed pets are permitted.

Reservations, fees: Reservations are not accepted. There is no fee for camping. Open year-round, weather permitting.

Directions: On U.S. 101 southwest of Portland, drive to the town of Hebo and Highway 22. Turn east on Highway 22 and drive five miles to the campground on the right.

Contact: Siuslaw National Forest, Hebo Ranger District, 503/392-5100, fax 503/392-5143, www.fs.fed.us.

32 WANDERING SPIRIT RV PARK

🏊 🎣 🐎 🏕 ♿ 🚐 ⛺

Scenic rating: 6

on Rock Creek

The major draw here is the nearby casino, but there is the added benefit of shaded sites next to Rock Creek, which provides fishing and swimming options. The Yamhill River is 0.5 mile away. Fishing is good for steelhead and salmon in season. Golf courses and wineries are available within 10 miles. There is a combination of monthly rentals and overnighters at this park.

Campsites, facilities: There are 129 sites with full hookups for RVs up to 45 feet long, 10 tent sites, and four park-model cabins. Some sites are pull-through. Drinking water, cable TV, wireless Internet service, modem access, restrooms with showers, dump station, coin laundry, RV storage, RV supplies, and a convenience store are available. Propane, a clubhouse, basketball hoop, an exercise room, and a game room are also available on-site. A 24-hour free bus shuttles campers to and from the Spirit Mountain Casino, restaurants, and shops less than two miles away. Some facilities are wheelchair accessible. Leashed pets are permitted.

Reservations, fees: Reservations are accepted at 800/390-6980. RV sites are $26 per night, tent sites are $16 per night, $2 per person per night for more than two people. Monthly rates are available. Some credit cards are accepted. Open year-round.

Directions: From Salem, drive west on Highway 22 about 25 miles to Highway 18. Turn west on Highway 18 and drive seven miles to the park on the left.

Contact: Wandering Spirit RV Park, 503/879-5700, fax 503/879-5171.

33 DEVIL'S LAKE STATE PARK

🏊 🛶 🚤 🎣 🏕 ♿ 🚐 ⛺

Scenic rating: 7

on Devil's Lake

Oregon's only coastal camp in the midst of a city, Devil's Lake is the center of summertime activity. A take-your-pick deal: You can boat, canoe, fish, kayak, or water ski. A walking path extends from the campground to the boat launch 0.25 mile away. For something different, head west and explore the seven miles of beaches. Lincoln City also has a number of arts and crafts galleries and a weekend farmers market during the summer. East Devil's Lake is two miles east and offers a boat ramp and picnic facilities.

Campsites, facilities: There are 54 sites for tents or small RVs (no hookups), 33 sites for tents or RVs up to 55 feet long (full hookups), 10 yurts, and a separate area for hikers and bikers. Picnic tables and fire grills are provided. Drinking water, cable TV, garbage bins, restrooms with flush toilets and showers, an amphitheater, and firewood are available. Boat docks and launching facilities are nearby. Some facilities are wheelchair accessible. Leashed pets are permitted.

Reservations, fees: Reservations are accepted at 800/452-5687 or www.oregonstateparks.org ($8 reservation fee). RV sites are $17-23 per night, $5 per night per additional vehicle, tent sites are $13-17 per night, $4 per person per night for hikers/bikers, and yurts are $29 per night. Boat mooring is $7 per night. Some credit cards are accepted. Open year-round.

Directions: From Lincoln City and U.S. 101, take the 6th Street exit. Drive east on 6th Street for one block to the park on the right.

Contact: Devil's Lake State Park, 503/994-2002 or 800/551-6949, www.oregonstateparks.org.

CAMPING

34 KOA LINCOLN CITY

Scenic rating: 7

on Devils Lake

This area offers opportunities for beach-combing, fishing, and tidepool-viewing along a seven-mile stretch of beach. Nearby recreation options include a casino, factory outlets, a golf course, skateboard park, and tennis courts.

Campsites, facilities: There are 15 tent sites and 81 sites with full or partial hookups for RVs up to 60 feet long, including some pull-through sites, and 30- and 50-amp service is available. There are also 14 cabins. Picnic tables and fire pits are provided. Drinking water, cable TV, modem access, restrooms with flush toilets and showers, dump station, public phones, convenience store, snack bar, gift shop, propane gas, ice, RV supplies, video and DVD rentals, game room, coin laundry, meeting room, firewood, and a playground are available. Leashed pets are permitted.

Reservations, fees: Reservations are accepted at 800/562-2791. RV sites are $20–32 per night, tent sites are $20–25 per night, $3 per person per night for more than two people, $7.50 per night per additional vehicle. Some credit cards are accepted. Open year-round.

Directions: From Portland, drive south on Highway 99 West to Highway 18. Turn west on Highway 18 and drive 47 miles to U.S. 101. Turn south on U.S. 101 and drive 1.5 miles to East Devil's Lake Road. Turn east on East Devil's Lake Road and drive one mile to the park on the left.

Contact: KOA Lincoln City, 541/994-2961, fax 541/994-9454, www.koa.com.

35 SEA AND SAND RV PARK

Scenic rating: 9

near Siletz Bay

Beachcombing for fossils and agates is popular at this oceanfront park near Gleneden Beach on Siletz Bay. Some sites have ocean views and pleasant terraces. The Siletz River and numerous small creeks are in the area. The park is located 3.5 miles north of Depoe Bay.

Campsites, facilities: There are 109 sites with full hookups for RVs up to 35 feet long. Drinking water, cable TV, fire pits, and picnic tables are provided. Restrooms with flush toilets and showers, dump station, firewood, and a coin laundry are available. A store, café, and ice are within one mile. Leashed pets are permitted.

Reservations, fees: Reservations are accepted. Sites are $29–57 per night, $2 per person per night for more than two people, and $5 per night per additional vehicle unless towed. Open year-round.

Directions: From Lincoln City and U.S. 101, drive south for nine miles on U.S. 101 to the park entrance (on the beach side of the highway).

Contact: Sea and Sand RV Park, 541/764-2313.

36 BEVERLY BEACH STATE PARK

Scenic rating: 7

near Newport

This beautiful campground is set in a wooded, grassy area on the east side of U.S. 101. Treed campsites sit along Spencer Creek. A tunnel leads under the roadway to a beach that stretches from Yaguna Head to the Otter Rock headlands. A one-mile hiking trail is available. Just a mile to the north lies a small day-use state park called Devil's Punchbowl, named for an unusual bowl-shaped rock formation with caverns under it where the waves rumble about. For some great ocean views, head north one more mile to the Otter Crest Wayside. The Oregon Coast Aquarium is within a few minutes' drive.

Campsites, facilities: There are 128 sites for tents or small RVs, 128 sites with full or partial hookups for tents or RVs up to 65 feet long, a special camping area for hikers and bicyclists, and five group sites for tents or RVs (no hookups) that can accommodate up to 25 people each. There is also a village of 21 yurts. Picnic tables and fire grills are provided. Drinking water, restrooms with flush toilets and showers, cable TV, a playground, a day-use area, garbage bins, and a dump station are available. Some facilities are wheelchair accessible. Leashed pets are permitted.

Reservations, fees: Reservations are accepted at 800/452-5687 or www.oregonstateparks.org ($8 reservation fee). Sites are $13–26 per night, $5 per night per additional vehicle, $4–6 per person per night for hikers/bikers, $30–40 per night for yurts, and $44–77 for group sites. Some credit cards are accepted. Open year-round.

Directions: From Newport and U.S. 101, drive north on U.S. 101 for seven miles to the park entrance on the east side.

Contact: Beverly Beach State Park, 541/265-9278 or 800/551-6949, www.oregonstateparks.org.

37 AGATE BEACH RV PARK

Scenic rating: 6

near Newport

This park is located about half a mile from Agate Beach Wayside, a small state park with beach access. Agate hunting can be good. Sometimes, a layer of sand covers the agates, and you have to dig a bit. But other times,

wave action clears the sand, unveiling the agates at low tides. Beverly Beach State Park is 4.5 miles north. About half of the sites are filled with monthly rentals. There are no ocean views from the campsites.

Campsites, facilities: There are 32 sites with full or partial hookups for RVs up to 40 feet long. Drinking water, cable TV, and picnic tables are provided. Restroom with flush toilets and showers, dump station, and a coin laundry room are available. A store and ice are within one mile. Leashed pets are permitted, with some restrictions.

Reservations, fees: Reservations are accepted. Sites are $22.50 per night, $1 per person per night for more than two people, and $1 per night per additional vehicle. Some credit cards are accepted. Open year-round.

Directions: From Newport and U.S. 101, drive to the north end of town. The park is on the east side of the road.

Contact: Agate Beach RV Park, 541/265-7670.

38 HARBOR VILLAGE RV PARK

Scenic rating: 6

on Yaquina Bay

This wooded and landscaped park is set near the shore of Yaquina Bay. Nearby recreation options include clamming, crabbing, deep-sea fishing, an 18-hole golf course, hiking trails, and a full-service marina.

Campsites, facilities: There are 40 sites with full hookups for RVs up to 35 feet long. Note that there are also 100 sites for full-time renters and a mobile-home park for ages 55 and up. Drinking water, cable TV, wireless Internet service, modem access, and picnic tables are provided. Restrooms with flush toilets and showers and a coin laundry are available. Propane gas, a store, and a café are within one mile. Boat docks, launching

CAMPING

facilities, and rentals are nearby. Leashed pets are permitted.

Reservations, fees: Reservations are accepted at 888/818-0002. Sites are $30 per night, $5 per person per night for more than two people. Some credit cards are accepted. Open year-round.

Directions: In Newport, drive south on John Moore Road for 0.5 mile to the bay and Bay Boulevard. Bear left and drive a short distance to the park entrance on the left.

Contact: Harbor Village RV Park, 541/265-5088, fax 541/265-5895, www.harborvillag-ervpark.com.

39 PORT OF NEWPORT MARINA AND RV PARK

Scenic rating: 7

on Yaquina Bay

This public park is set along the shore of Yaquina Bay near Newport, a resort town that offers a variety of attractions. Among them are ocean fishing, a museum and aquarium at the nearby Hatfield Marine Science Center, the Undersea Garden, the Waxworks, Ripley's Believe It or Not, and the Lincoln County Historical Society Museum. Nearby recreation options include an 18-hole golf course, hiking trails, and a full-service marina.

Campsites, facilities: There are 143 sites with full hookups for RVs up to 45 feet long. Restrooms with flush toilets and showers, cable TV, Wi-Fi, modem access, dump station, convenience store, coin laundry, fish-cleaning station, and ice are available. A marina with boat docks and launching facilities is available on-site. Some facilities are wheelchair accessible. Leashed pets are permitted.

Reservations, fees: Reservations are accepted at 541/867-3321. Sites with hookups are $29.73–40.78 per night, sites without hookups are $17.68 per night, $1 per person per night for more than two people. Weekly rates

are available. Some credit cards are accepted. Open year-round.

Directions: From Newport and U.S. 101, drive south for 0.5 mile (over the bridge) to Marine Science Drive. Turn right (east) and drive 0.5 mile to the park entrance on the left.

Contact: Port of Newport Marina and RV Park, 541/867-3321, fax 541/867-3352, www.portofnewport.com.

40 SOUTH BEACH STATE PARK

Scenic rating: 7

near Newport

This park along the beach offers opportunities for beachcombing, boating, crabbing, fishing, hiking, and windsurfing. The Oregon Coast Trail passes right through the park. A nature trail circles the campground, and there are hiking and bicycling trails to the beach. A primitive hike-in campground is also available. A naturalist provides campground talks during the summer season. Kayak trips are an option during the summer. The park is within walking distance of Oregon Aquarium. Newport attractions include the Hatfield Marine Science Center, the Undersea Garden, the Waxworks, Ripley's Believe It or Not, and the Lincoln County Historical Society Museum.

Campsites, facilities: There are 228 sites with partial hookups for tents or RVs up to 45 feet long, six primitive tent sites, a dispersed camping area (without designated sites) for hikers and bicyclists, and an overflow area for RVs. There are also three group sites for up to 25 people each and 27 yurts. Picnic tables and fire grills are provided. Drinking water, restrooms with flush toilets and showers, garbage bins, recycling, a dump station, Wi-Fi, horseshoe pits, playground, a day-use area, meeting hall, and firewood are available. A camp host is on-site. Some facilities are wheelchair accessible. Leashed pets are permitted.

Reservations, fees: Reservations are accepted at 800/452-5687 or www.oregonstateparks. org ($8 reservation fee). Sites are $18–27 per night, $5 per night per additional vehicle, $4–6 per person per night for hikers/bicyclists (three-night limit), $10 for primitive tent sites, $44–77 per night for group sites, and $30–40 per night for yurts. Some credit cards are accepted. Open year-round.

Directions: From Newport and U.S. 101, drive south for three miles to the park entrance on the right.

Contact: South Beach State Park, 541/867-4715 or 800/551-6949, www.oregonstateparks. org.

41 SEAL ROCKS RV COVE

Scenic rating: 8

near Seal Rock State Park

BEST (

This RV park is situated on the rugged coastline near Seal Rock State Park (open for day use only), where you may find seals, sea lions, and a variety of birds. The ocean views are stunning, and some sites have views.

Campsites, facilities: There are 28 sites with full hookups for RVs of any length and 16 tent sites with electricity. Drinking water, picnic tables, and fire rings are provided. Firewood and restrooms with flush toilets and showers are available. A store, a café, and ice are within one mile. Leashed pets are permitted.

Reservations, fees: Reservations are accepted. RV sites are $29–36 per night, tent sites are $20–24 per night, $1–3 per person per night for more than two people, and there's a $3 one-time fee for an additional vehicle unless towed. Winter rates are available. Open year-round.

Directions: From Newport and U.S. 101, drive south for 10 miles to the town of Seal Rock. Continue south on U.S. 101 for 0.25 mile to the park entrance on the left.

Contact: Seal Rocks RV Cove, 541/563-3955, www.sealrocksrv.com.

42 DRIFT CREEK LANDING

Scenic rating: 6

on the Alsea River

Drift Creek Landing is set along the shore of the Alsea River in a heavily treed and mountainous area. The Oregon Coast Aquarium is 15 miles away, and an 18-hole golf course is nearby. There are 10 mobile homes with long-term renters on this property, and more than one-third of the RV sites are taken by monthly renters.

Campsites, facilities: There are 49 sites with full hookups for RVs of any length, five sites for tents, and three cabins. Drinking water and picnic tables are provided. Restroom with flush toilets and showers, cable TV, propane gas, recreation hall, convenience store, snack bar, coin laundry, boat docks, boat rentals, and launching facilities are available. Leashed pets are permitted.

Reservations, fees: Reservations are accepted. RV sites are $22 per night, and tent sites are $15 per night; it's $2 per person per night for more than two people and $5 per night per additional vehicle. Some credit cards are accepted. Open year-round.

Directions: From Newport and U.S. 101, drive south for 14 miles to Waldport and Highway 34. Turn east on Highway 34 and drive 3.8 miles to the campground.

Contact: Drift Creek Landing, 541/563-3610, fax 541/563-5234.

43 FISHIN' HOLE RV PARK & MARINA

Scenic rating: 6

on the Alsea River

This campground is one of several along the shore of the Alsea River. Kayaking and canoeing are popular. Some of the sites here are filled with monthly rentals.

CAMPING

Campsites, facilities: There are 24 sites with full or partial hookups for RVs of any length, six sites for tents, one rental home, and one cabin. Drinking water and picnic tables are provided, and fire pits are available on request. Restrooms with flush toilets and showers, coin laundry, recreation room, bait and tackle, boat docks, boat rentals, and launching facilities are available. Leashed pets are permitted.

Reservations, fees: Reservations are accepted at 877/770-6137. Tent sites are $17 per night, RV sites are $21–23 per night, and it's $5 per person per night for more than two people and $5 per night per additional vehicle. Some credit cards are accepted. Open year-round.

Directions: From Newport and U.S. 101, drive south for 14 miles to Waldport and Highway 34. Turn east on Highway 34 and drive four miles to the entrance on the left.

Contact: Fishin' Hole RV Park & Marina, 541/563-3401.

44 CHINOOK RV PARK

Scenic rating: 7

on the Alsea River

This park is set along the shore of the Alsea River, about 3.5 miles from the ocean. The park is filled primarily with monthly rentals, although several RV sites are reserved for short-term campers. Campsites are rented on a space-available basis.

Campsites, facilities: There are six sites for tents and 34 sites with full or partial hookups for RVs up to 40 feet long. Picnic tables are provided. Drinking water, cable TV, wireless Internet service, restrooms with flush toilets and showers, a picnic area, ice, and a coin laundry are available. A store is within 1.5 miles. Boat docks are nearby. Propane gas and boat launching facilities are available 3.5 miles away. Leashed pets are permitted.

Reservations, fees: Reservations are accepted. RV sites are $22–27 per night, tent sites are $15.75–17.50 per night, $3 per person per night for more than two people. Open year-round.

Directions: From Newport and U.S. 101, drive south for 14 miles to Waldport and Highway 34. Turn east on Highway 34 and drive 3.3 miles to the park entrance on the left.

Contact: Chinook RV Park, 541/563-3485, www.chinookrvpark.com.

45 TAYLOR'S LANDING RV PARK

Scenic rating: 9

on the Alsea River

This wooded campground is set along the scenic Alsea River. Fall, when the salmon fishing is best, is the prime time here, and the park often fills up. Recreation options include hiking trails, marked bike trails, the Oregon Coast Aquarium, the Sea Lion Caves, and a marina.

Campsites, facilities: There are 81 sites for tents or RVs of any length (full hookups). Drinking water, cable TV, and picnic tables are provided. Restrooms with flush toilets and showers, propane gas, a café, coin laundry, community fire ring, and boat docks and rentals are available. Boat launching facilities are nearby. Leashed pets are permitted.

Reservations, fees: Reservations are accepted. Sites are $27 per night, $1 per person per night for more than two people. Monthly rates are available. Open year-round.

Directions: From Newport and U.S. 101, drive south for 14 miles to Waldport and Highway 34. Turn east on Highway 34 and drive seven miles to the entrance on the right.

Contact: Taylor's Landing RV Park, phone/fax 541/528-3388, www.taylorslandingrvpark-marina.com.

46 WALDPORT/NEWPORT KOA

🚶 🚴 🛶 🚐 🐕 🛝 🚌 ⛺

Scenic rating: 8

on Alsea Bay

BEST (

This pretty park, set amid some of the oldest pine trees in Oregon, is located within walking distance of the beach, the bay, and downtown Waldport—and to top it off, some of the campsites have beautiful ocean views. Alsea Bay's sandy and rocky shoreline makes this area a favorite with anglers. The crabbing and clamming can also be quite good. Kite flying is popular. South Beach State Park, about five miles north on U.S. 101, offers more fishing and a boat ramp along Beaver Creek. It's open for day use only. Other nearby recreation options include hiking trails, marked bike trails, the Oregon Coast Aquarium, the Sea Lion Caves, and a marina.

Campsites, facilities: There are 10 tent sites and 66 sites for RVs up to 45 feet long (full hookups), and 15 cabins. Picnic tables and fire pits are provided; drinking water and cable TV are also available. Restrooms with flush toilets and showers, wireless Internet service, modem access, recreation room, propane gas, dump station, store, café, coin laundry, playground, and ice are available. Boat docks, launching facilities, and boat rentals are nearby. A café is within one mile. Leashed pets are permitted, with certain restrictions.

Reservations, fees: Reservations are accepted at 800/562-3443. RV sites are $46.50–59.50 per night, tent sites are $25–26 per night, $2–5 per person per night for more than two people. Some credit cards are accepted. Open year-round.

Directions: From Newport and U.S. 101, drive south for approximately 14 miles to Milepost 155 at the north end of the Alsea Bay Bridge. The park is on the west side of the bridge.

Contact: Waldport/Newport KOA, 541/563-2250, fax 541/563-4098, www.koa.com.

47 BEACHSIDE STATE RECREATION SITE

🚶 🚴 🏊 🛶 🐕 ♿ 🚐 ⛺

Scenic rating: 7

near Alsea Bay

This state park offers about nine miles of beach and is not far from Alsea Bay and the Alsea River. Sites are close to the beach. Nearby attractions include clamming, crabbing, and fishing, as well as hiking and driving tours, tidepools, an aquarium, three lighthouses, science centers, and visitors centers. South Beach State Park, about five miles north on U.S. 101, offers more fishing and a boat ramp along Beaver Creek (day use only).

Campsites, facilities: There are 42 sites for tents, 32 sites with partial hookups for RVs up to 30 feet long, two yurts, and a special camping area for hikers and bicyclists. Picnic tables and fire grills are provided. Drinking water, garbage bins, restrooms with flush toilets and showers, recycling, and firewood are available. A horseshoe pit is available nearby. Some facilities are wheelchair accessible. Leashed pets are permitted.

Reservations, fees: Reservations are accepted at 800/452-5687 or www.oregonstateparks. org ($8 reservation fee). RV sites are $18–21 per night, $5 per night per additional vehicle, tent sites are $13–17 per night, $4 per person per night for hikers/bicyclists, and yurts are $30 per night. Some credit cards are accepted. Open mid-March–October, weather permitting.

Directions: From Newport and U.S. 101, drive south for 16 miles to Waldport. Continue south on U.S. 101 for four miles to the park entrance on the west side of the road.

Contact: Beachside State Recreation Site, 541/563-3220, fax 541/563-3657, www.oregonstateparks.org.

CAMPING

48 TILLICUM BEACH
🚶 🏊 🏕 🚐 ⛺

Scenic rating: 8

in Siuslaw National Forest

Oceanview campsites are a big draw at this campground just south of Beachside State Park. Since it's just off the highway and along the water, this camp fills up very quickly in the summer, so expect crowds. Nearby forest roads provide access to streams in the mountains east of the beach area.

Campsites, facilities: There are 61 sites for tents or RVs up to 60 feet long; some sites have partial hookups. Picnic tables and fire grills are provided. Flush toilets, garbage bins, firewood, and drinking water are available. Leashed pets are permitted.

Reservations, fees: Reservations are accepted at 877/444-6777 or www.recreation.gov ($10 reservation fee). Sites are $22 per night, $6 per night per additional vehicle. Open year-round, with reduced capacity in winter.

Directions: From Newport and U.S. 101, drive south for 14 miles to Waldport. Continue south on U.S. 101 for 4.5 miles to the campground entrance on the right.

Contact: Siuslaw National Forest, Waldport Ranger District, 541/563-3211 or 541/547-3679 (concessionaire), fax 541/563-8449, www.fs.fed.us.

49 CANAL CREEK
🚶 🏕 👫 🚐 ⛺

Scenic rating: 5

on Canal Creek in Siuslaw National Forest

There's one key thing you must know: Vehicles must be able to cross a small creek to access this site. That accomplished, this pleasant little campground is just off the beaten path in a large, wooded, open area along Canal Creek. It feels remote because of the creek that runs through the campground and the historic

homesites nearby, with old fruit trees on the grounds. Yet it has easy access and is close to the coast and all the amenities. The climate here is relatively mild, but, on the other hand, there is the rain in winter—lots of it.

Campsites, facilities: There are 11 sites for tents or RVs up to 22 feet long, plus a group area for up to 100 people. Picnic tables and fire grills are provided. Vault toilets are available. There is no drinking water and garbage must be packed out. The group site has a picnic shelter and a play area. Leashed pets are permitted.

Reservations, fees: Reservations are not accepted for family sites but are required for group sites at 877/444-6777 or www.recreation.gov ($10 reservation fee). Sites are $17 per night, $6 per night per additional vehicle; group sites are $115–165 per night. Open year-round for individual camping. The group sites are open mid-May–mid-September.

Directions: From Albany, drive west on U.S. 20 for 15 miles to Philomath and Highway 34. Turn south on Highway 34 and drive 52 miles to Forest Road 3462. Turn left (south) and drive four miles to the camp.

Contact: Siuslaw National Forest, Waldport Ranger District, 541/563-3211 or 541/547-3679, fax 541/563-3124, www.fs.fed.us.

50 BLACKBERRY
🚶 🏊 🏕 🐕 🚐 ⛺

Scenic rating: 7

on the Alsea River in Siuslaw National Forest

Blackberry makes a good base camp for a fishing trip on the Alsea River. The U.S. Forest Service provides boat launches and picnic areas at several spots along this stretch of river. Often, there is a camp host who can give you inside information on nearby recreational opportunities. Large fir trees and lawns separate the sites.

Campsites, facilities: There are 32 sites for tents or RVs of any length. Picnic tables and fire grills are provided. Drinking water, garbage bins, and flush toilets are available. There is no firewood. A boat ramp is on-site. Leashed pets are permitted.

Reservations, fees: Reservations are not accepted. Sites are $20 per night, $6 per night per additional vehicle. Open year-round.

Directions: From Albany, drive west on U.S. 20 for 15 miles to Philomath and Highway 34. Turn south on Highway 34 and drive 41 miles to the campground entrance on the left.

Contact: Siuslaw National Forest, Waldport Ranger District, 541/563-3211, fax 541/563-3124, www.fs.fed.us.

51 ALSEA FALLS

Scenic rating: 8

adjacent to the south fork of the Alsea River

BEST

Enjoy the beautiful surroundings of Alsea Falls by exploring the trails that wander through this park and lead to a picnic area by the falls. Trails to McBee Park and Green Peak Falls are accessible from the campground along the south fork of the river. The campsites are situated in a 40-year-old forest of Douglas fir and vine maple. On a warm day, Alsea Falls offers cool relief along the river. The area was named after its original inhabitants, the Alsea people.

Campsites, facilities: There are 16 sites for tents or RVs up to 30 feet long. Picnic tables and fire pits are provided. Drinking water, vault toilets, and garbage bins are available. Leashed pets are permitted.

Reservations, fees: Reservations are not accepted. Sites are $10 per night, $5 per night per additional vehicle. Open late May-early September.

Directions: From Albany, drive west on U.S. 20 for nine miles to Corvallis. Turn left (south) onto Highway 99 and drive 15 miles to County Road 45120. Turn right (west) and drive five miles to Alpine Junction. Continue

along the South Fork Alsea Access Road for nine miles to the campground on the right.

Contact: Bureau of Land Management, Salem District Office, 503/375-5646, fax 503/375-5622, www.blm.gov.

52 CAPE PERPETUA

Scenic rating: 8

on Cape Creek in Siuslaw National Forest

This U.S. Forest Service campground is set along Cape Creek in the Cape Perpetua Scenic Area. The visitor information center provides hiking and driving maps to guide you through this remarkable region; maps highlight the tidepools and picnic spots. The coastal cliffs are perfect for whale-watching December–March. Neptune State Park is just south and offers additional rugged coastline vistas.

Campsites, facilities: There are 38 sites for tents or RVs up to 45 feet long, plus one group site that can accommodate up to 50 people and 12 vehicles. Picnic tables and fire grills are provided. Flush toilets, drinking water, dump station, firewood, and garbage bins are available. A camp host is on-site. Some facilities are wheelchair accessible. Leashed pets are permitted.

Reservations, fees: Reservations are accepted at 877/444-6777 or www.recreation.gov ($10 reservation fee). Sites are $22 per night, $6 per night per additional vehicle; group sites are $115 per night. Open May–September.

Directions: From Newport and U.S. 101, drive south for 23 miles to Yachats. Continue three miles south on U.S. 101 to the entrance on the left.

Contact: Siuslaw National Forest, Waldport Ranger District, 541/563-3211 or 541/547-3676 (concessionaire), fax 541/563-3124, www.fs.fed.us; Cape Perpetua Visitors Center, 541/547-3289.

53 SEA PERCH RV PARK

Scenic rating: 8

near Cape Perpetua

Sea Perch sits right in the middle of one of the most scenic areas on the Oregon coast. This private park just south of Cape Perpetua has sites 75 feet from the beach and lawn areas, plus its own shell museum and gift shop. Surf fishing and windsurfing are options here, or head to Cape Perpetua for whale-watching and tidepooling. Big rigs are welcome here.

Campsites, facilities: There are 29 sites with full or partial hookups for RVs of any length. Some sites are pull-through. Drinking water and picnic tables are provided. Restrooms with flush toilets and coin showers, dump station, firewood, recreation hall, coin laundry, ice, convenience store, wireless Internet access, modem hookups, picnic area, and a beach are available. Leashed pets are permitted.

Reservations, fees: Reservations are accepted. Sites are $45–60 per night, $5 per person per night for more than four, $15 per night for an additional vehicle if it cannot be parked on your site. Some credit cards are accepted. Open year-round.

Directions: From Newport and U.S. 101, drive south for 23 miles to Yachats. Continue south on U.S. 101 for 6.5 miles to the campground at Milepost 171 on the right.

Contact: Sea Perch RV Park, 541/547-3505, fax 541/547-3368, www.seaperchrvpark.com.

54 ROCK CREEK

Scenic rating: 7

on Rock Creek in Siuslaw National Forest

This little campground is set along Rock Creek just 0.25 mile from the ocean. It's a premium spot for coastal-highway travelers, although it

can get packed very quickly. An excellent side trip is to Cape Perpetua, a designated scenic area a few miles up the coast. The cape offers beautiful ocean views and a visitors center that will supply you with information on nature trails, picnic spots, tidepools, and where to find the best viewpoints in the area.

Campsites, facilities: There are 15 sites for tents or RVs up to 22 feet long. Fire grills and picnic tables are provided. Flush toilets, garbage bins, and drinking water are available. Leashed pets are permitted.

Reservations, fees: Reservations are not accepted. Sites are $22 per night, $6 per night per additional vehicle. Open mid-May–September.

Directions: From Newport and U.S. 101, drive south for 23 miles to Yachats. Continue south on U.S. 101 for 10 miles to the campground entrance on the left.

Contact: Siuslaw National Forest, Waldport Ranger District, 541/563-3211 or 541/547-3679 (concessionaire), fax 541/563-3124, www.fs.fed.us.

55 CARL G. WASHBURNE STATE PARK

Scenic rating: 7

near Florence

Even though busy Highway 101 lies right next to Washburne State Park, a bank of native plants shields campers from most road noise, so you hear the roar of the ocean instead of traffic. Sites are spacious, with some abutting China Creek, and elk are frequent visitors. Short hikes lead from the campground to a two-mile-long beach, extensive tidepools along the base of the cliffs, and a three-mile trail to Heceta Head Lighthouse. Just three miles south of the park are the Sea Lion Caves, where an elevator takes visitors down into a cavern for an insider's view of the life of a sea lion.

Campsites, facilities: There are 56 sites for

tents or RVs up to 45 feet long (full hookups), seven primitive walk-in sites, two yurts, and a hiker/biker camping area. Picnic tables, fire pits, drinking water, garbage bins, and a dump station are provided. Firewood and restrooms with flush toilets and showers are available. Leashed pets are permitted.

Reservations, fees: Reservations are not accepted, except for yurts. RV sites are $17–26 per night, tent sites are $13–21 per night, $4–5 per person per night for hikers/bicyclists, and yurts are $29–39 per night; $5 per night per additional vehicle. Some credit cards are accepted. Open year-round.

Directions: From Florence and U.S. 101, drive north for 12.5 miles to the park entrance road (it is well signed, 10 miles south of the town of Yachats). Turn east and drive a short distance to the park.

Contact: Carl G. Washburne State Park, 541/547-3416 or 800/551-6949, www.oregonstateparks.org.

56 ALDER DUNE

Scenic rating: 7

near Alder Lake in Siuslaw National Forest

This wooded campground is situated near four lakes—Alder Lake, Dune Lake, Mercer Lake (the largest), and Sutton Lake. A boat launch is available at Sutton Lake. An excellent recreation option is to explore the expansive sand dunes in the area by foot (there is no off-road-vehicle access here). Side trips include the Sea Lion Caves, Darlington State Park, Jessie M. Honeyman Memorial State Park, and the Indian Forest, just four miles north.

Campsites, facilities: There are 39 sites for tents or self-contained RVs (no hookups) up to 62 feet long. Picnic tables and fire grills are provided. Flush toilets, garbage bins, and drinking water are available. Leashed pets are permitted.

Reservations, fees: Reservations are accepted

at 877/444-6777 or www.recreation.gov ($10 reservation fee). Sites are $20 per night. Open year-round, weather permitting.

Directions: From Florence and U.S. 101, drive north for eight miles to the campground on the left.

Contact: Siuslaw National Forest, Reedsport Ranger District, 541/271-6000, fax 541/271-1563, www.fs.fed.us.

57 SUTTON

Scenic rating: 7

near Sutton Lake in Siuslaw National Forest

This campground is located adjacent to Sutton Creek, not far from Sutton Lake. Vegetation provides some privacy between sites. Holman Vista on Sutton Beach Road offers a beautiful view of the dunes and ocean. Wading and fishing are both popular. A hiking trail system leads from the camp out to the dunes. There is no off-road-vehicle access here. An alternative camp is Alder Dune to the north.

Campsites, facilities: There are 80 sites, 20 with partial hookups, for tents or RVs up to 30 feet long and two group sites for up to 50 and 100 people, respectively. Picnic tables and fire grills are provided. Flush toilets, garbage bins, and drinking water are available. A boat ramp is nearby. Leashed pets are permitted.

Reservations, fees: Reservations are accepted at 877/444-6777 or www.recreation.gov ($10 reservation fee). Sites are $20–22 per night and $50–75 per night for group sites. Open May–December.

Directions: From Eugene, drive west on Highway 126 for 61 miles to Florence and U.S. 101. Turn north on U.S. 101 and drive six miles to Sutton Beach Road (Forest Road 794). Turn left (northwest) and drive 1.5 miles to the campground entrance.

Contact: Siuslaw National Forest, Reedsport Ranger District, 541/271-6000, fax 541/271-1563, www.fs.fed.us.

58 MAPLE LANE RV PARK AND MARINA

Scenic rating: 5

on the Siuslaw River

This park along the shore of the Siuslaw River in Mapleton is close to hiking trails. The general area is surrounded by Siuslaw National Forest land. A U.S. Forest Service map details nearby backcountry side-trip options. Fall is the most popular time of the year here, as it's prime time for salmon fishing on the Siuslaw. Most sites are taken by monthly renters.

Campsites, facilities: There are five tent sites and 39 sites with full hookups for RVs up to 35 feet long. Some sites are pull-through. Drinking water, restrooms with flush toilets and showers, and propane gas are available. A bait and tackle shop is open during the fishing season. Boat docks and launching facilities are on-site. A store, café, and ice are nearby. Small pets (under 15 pounds) are permitted.

Reservations, fees: Reservations are accepted. RV sites are $25–30 per night, tent sites are $18 per night, $1.50 per night for more than two people, and $2 per night per additional vehicle. Monthly rates are available. Open year-round.

Directions: From Eugene, drive west on Highway 126 for 47 miles to Mapleton. Continue on Highway 126 for 0.25 mile past the business district to the park entrance on the left.

Contact: Maple Lane RV Park and Marina, 541/268-4822.

59 ARCHIE KNOWLES

Scenic rating: 6

on Knowles Creek in Siuslaw National Forest

This little campground along Knowles Creek about three miles east of Mapleton is rustic, with a mix of forested and lawn areas, yet it offers easy proximity to the highway.

Campsites, facilities: There are nine sites for tents or RVs up to 16 feet long. Picnic tables and fire grills are provided. Flush toilets, garbage bins, and drinking water are available. Leashed pets are permitted.

Reservations, fees: Reservations are not accepted. Sites are $15 per night. Open May–early September, weather permitting.

Directions: From Eugene, drive west on Highway 126 for 44 miles to the campground entrance (three miles east of Mapleton).

Contact: Siuslaw National Forest, Reedsport Ranger District, 541/271-6000, fax 541/271-1563, www.fs.fed.us.

60 HARBOR VISTA COUNTY PARK

Scenic rating: 6

near Florence

This county park out among the dunes near the entrance to the harbor offers a great lookout point from its observation deck. The park is perched above the North Jetty of the Siuslaw River and encompasses 15 acres. Beach access is one mile away. A number of side trips are available, including to the Sea Lion Caves, Darlington State Park, Jessie M. Honeyman Memorial State Park, and the Indian Forest, just four miles north. Florence also has displays of Native American dwellings and crafts.

Campsites, facilities: There are 38 sites with partial hookups for tents or RVs up to 60 feet long. Picnic tables, fire rings, and garbage bins are provided. Restrooms with flush toilets and coin showers, dump station, drinking water, pay phone, and a playground are available. A camp host is on-site. Some facilities are wheelchair accessible. Leashed pets are permitted.

Reservations, fees: Reservations are accepted at 541/682-2000 ($10 reservation fee). Sites are $20 per night, $6.50 per night per additional vehicle. Some credit cards are accepted. Open year-round.

Directions: From Florence and U.S. 101, drive north for four miles to 35th Street. Turn left and drive to where it dead-ends into Rhododendron Drive. Turn right and drive 1.4 miles to North Jetty Road. Turn left and drive half a block to Harbor Vista Road. Turn left and continue to the campground at 87658 Harbor Vista Road.

Note: Follow these exact directions. Previous visitors to this park taking a different route will discover that part of Harbor Vista Road is now gated.

Contact: Harbor Vista County Park, 541/997-5987, www.co.lane.or.us/.

61 B AND E WAYSIDE MOBILE HOME AND RV PARK

Scenic rating: 5

near Florence

Adjacent to this landscaped RV park is a 28-unit mobile home park for ages 55 and up. Some sites at the RV park are taken by monthly rentals. Nearby recreation options include two golf courses and a riding stable, two miles away.

Campsites, facilities: There are 24 sites with full hookups for RVs of any length. Picnic tables are provided. Restrooms with flush toilets and showers, dump station, recreation room, modem access, and a coin laundry are available. Propane gas, a store, ice, a café, and a restaurant are within two miles. Boat-launching facilities are nearby. Small, leashed pets are permitted.

Reservations, fees: Reservations are accepted. Sites are $24 per night, $2 per person per night for more than two people. Weekly and monthly rates are available. Open year-round.

Directions: From Florence and U.S. 101, drive north for 1.8 miles to the park on the right.

Contact: B and E Wayside Mobile Home and RV Park, 541/997-6451.

62 PORT OF SIUSLAW RV PARK AND MARINA

Scenic rating: 8

on the Siuslaw River

BEST (

This public resort can be found along the Siuslaw River in a grassy, urban setting. Anglers with boats will find that the U.S. 101 bridge support pilings make good spots for crabbing, as well as fishing for perch and flounder. A new set of docks with drinking water, electricity, gasoline, security, and a fish-cleaning station are available. The Sea Lion Caves and estuary are a bonus for wildlife lovers, and nearby lakes make swimming and waterskiing a possibility. Golf is within driving distance, and horses can be rented about nine miles away.

Campsites, facilities: There are 10 tent sites and 92 sites with full or partial hookups for tents or RVs of any length. Drinking water, cable TV, and picnic tables are provided. Restrooms with flush toilets and showers, dump station, coin laundry, wireless Internet service, and boat docks are available. A café, grocery store, and ice are within one mile. Some facilities are wheelchair accessible. Leashed pets are permitted.

Reservations, fees: Reservations are accepted at 541/997-3040 or www.portofsiuslaw.com ($10 reservation fee). Sites are $22–30 per night, $2 per night per additional vehicle. Weekly rates available. Some credit cards are accepted. Open year-round.

Directions: From Florence and U.S. 101, drive south to Nopal Street. Turn left (east) and drive two blocks to 1st Street. Turn left and drive 0.25 mile to the park at the end of the road.

Contact: Port of Siuslaw RV Park and Marina, 541/997-3040, www.portofsiuslaw.com.

CAMPING

63 JESSIE M. HONEYMAN MEMORIAL STATE PARK

Scenic rating: 7

near Cleowax Lake

This popular state park is within walking distance of the shore of Cleowax Lake and adjacent to the dunes of the Oregon Dunes National Recreation Area. Dunes stretch for two miles between the park and the ocean. The dunes here are quite impressive, with some reaching to 500 feet. In the winter, the area is open to OHV use. For thrill-seekers, sand-board rentals (for sand-boarding on the dunes) are available in nearby Florence. The two lakes in the park offer facilities for boating, fishing, and swimming. A one-mile hiking trail with access to the dunes is available in the park, and off-road-vehicle trails are nearby in the sand dunes.

Campsites, facilities: There are 187 sites for tents or RVs (no hookups) up to 60 feet long, 168 sites with full or partial hookups for RVs, a camping area for hikers and bicyclists, six group tent areas for up to 25 people and 10 vehicles each, and 10 yurts. Picnic tables, garbage bins, and fire grills are provided. Drinking water, restrooms with flush toilets and showers, a dump station, seasonal interpretive programs, a playground, an amphitheater, and firewood are available. A meeting hall and picnic shelters can be reserved. Boat docks and launching facilities are nearby. Some facilities are wheelchair accessible. Leashed pets are permitted.

Reservations, fees: Reservations are accepted at 800/452-5687 or www.oregonstateparks.org ($8 reservation fee). RV sites are $17–26 per night, tent sites are $13–21 per night, $5 per night per additional vehicle, $4–5 per person per night for hikers/bicyclists, $29–39 per night for yurts, and $43–76 per night for group sites. Some credit cards are accepted. Open year-round.

Directions: From Florence and U.S. 101, drive south for three miles to the park entrance on the west side of the road.

Contact: Jessie M. Honeyman Memorial State Park, 541/997-3641 or 800/551-6949, www.oregonstateparks.org.

64 LAKESHORE RV PARK

Scenic rating: 5

on Woahink Lake

Here's a prime area for vacationers. This park is set along the shore of Woahink Lake, a popular spot to fish for bass, bluegill, catfish, crappie, perch, and trout. It's adjacent to Jessie M. Honeyman Memorial State Park and the Oregon Dunes National Recreation Area. Off-road-vehicle access to the dunes is four miles northeast and three miles south of the park. Hiking trails through the dunes can be found at Honeyman Memorial State Park. Some sites are filled with monthly rentals.

Campsites, facilities: There are 20 sites with full hookups for RVs of any length; some are pull-through sites. Picnic tables and cable TV are provided. Drinking water, restrooms with flush toilets and showers, modem access, wireless Internet service, and a coin laundry are available. A café is within three miles. Boat docks are nearby. Leashed pets are permitted.

Reservations, fees: Reservations are accepted at 866/240-4269. Sites are $29 per night, $2 per person per night for more than two people. Monthly rentals are available. Open year-round.

Directions: From Florence and U.S. 101, drive south for four miles to Milepost 195. The park is on the left (east side of road).

Contact: Lakeshore RV Park, 541/997-2741, www.lakeshorerv.com.

65 MERCER LAKE RESORT

Scenic rating: 7

on Mercer Lake

This resort is in a forested setting situated above the shore of Mercer Lake, one of a number of lakes that have formed among the ancient dunes in this area. The 375-acre lake has 11 miles of shoreline and numerous coves. Fishing for rainbow trout and largemouth bass in the stocked lake is the most popular activity. A sandy swimming beach is also available, and the ocean is four miles away.

Campsites, facilities: There are 10 sites with full or partial hookups for RVs up to 40 feet long and 10 cabins. Some sites are pull-through. No open fires are allowed. Drinking water, cable TV, and picnic tables are provided. Restrooms with flush toilets and showers, dump station, convenience store, coin laundry, and ice are available. Boat docks, launching facilities, and fishing boat rentals are on-site. Leashed pets are permitted.

Reservations, fees: Reservations are accepted at 800/355-3633. Sites are $22–35 per night, $2 per night per additional vehicle, $5 per night per pet. Some credit cards are accepted. Open year-round.

Directions: From Florence and U.S. 101, drive north for five miles to Mercer Lake Road. Turn east and drive just under one mile to Bay Berry Lane. Turn left and drive to the resort.

Contact: Mercer Lake Resort, 541/997-3633, www.mlroregon.com.

66 CARTER LAKE

Scenic rating: 9

on Carter Lake in
Oregon Dunes National Recreation Area

BEST (

This campground sits on the north shore of Carter Lake, and you can fish almost right from your campsite. Boating and fishing are permitted on this long, narrow lake, which is set among dunes overgrown with vegetation. The nearby Taylor Dunes Trail is a half-mile, wheelchair-accessible trail to the dunes past Taylor Lake. Hiking is allowed in the dunes, but there is no off-road-vehicle access here. If you want off-road access, head north one mile to Siltcoos Road, turn west, and drive 1.3 miles to Driftwood II.

Campsites, facilities: There are 22 sites for tents or RVs up to 30 feet long. Picnic tables, garbage service, and fire grills are provided. Drinking water, flush toilets, and firewood are available. A camp host is on-site. Leashed pets are permitted.

Reservations, fees: Reservations are accepted at 877/444-6777 or www.recreation.gov ($10 reservation fee). Sites are $17–20 per night, $5 per night per additional vehicle. Open May–September.

Directions: From Florence and U.S. 101, drive south for 8.5 miles to Forest Road 1084. Turn right on Forest Road 1084 and drive west 200 yards to the camp.

Contact: Oregon Dunes National Recreation Area, Visitors Center, 541/271-3611, fax 541/750-7244.

67 DRIFTWOOD II

Scenic rating: 6

near Siltcoos Lake in
Oregon Dunes National Recreation Area

Primarily a campground for off-road vehicles, Driftwood II is set near the ocean, but without an ocean view, in the Oregon Dunes National Recreation Area. It has off-road-vehicle access. Several small lakes, the Siltcoos River, and Siltcoos Lake are nearby. Note that ATV use is prohibited between 10 P.M. and 6 A.M.

Campsites, facilities: There are 68 sites for tents or RVs up to 59 feet long, including 10 pull-through sites. Picnic tables, garbage service, and fire grills are provided at back-in sites but not at the 10 pull-through sites. Drinking water and restrooms with flush toilets and showers are available. A dump station is within five miles. Boat docks, launching facilities, and rentals can be found about four miles away on Siltcoos Lake. Some facilities are wheelchair accessible. Leashed pets are permitted.

Reservations, fees: Reservations are accepted at 877/444-6777 or www.recreation.gov ($10 reservation fee). Sites are $20 per night. Open year-round.

Directions: From Florence and U.S. 101, drive south for seven miles to Siltcoos Beach Road. Turn right and drive 1.5 miles west to the campground.

Contact: Oregon Dunes National Recreation Area, Visitors Center 541/271-6000 or 541/271-3611, fax 541/750-7244.

68 LAGOON

Scenic rating: 9

near Siltcoos Lake in
Oregon Dunes National Recreation Area

One of several campgrounds in the area, this camp is located along the lagoon, about one mile from Siltcoos Lake and set 0.5 mile inland. The Lagoon Trail offers prime wildlife-viewing for marine birds and other aquatic species.

Campsites, facilities: There are 41 sites for tents or RVs of any length. Picnic tables, garbage service, and fire grills are provided. Drinking water and flush and vault toilets are available. A camp host is on-site. Boat docks, launching facilities, and rentals are nearby on Siltcoos Lake. A telephone and a dump station are within five miles. Some facilities are wheelchair accessible. Leashed pets are permitted.

Reservations, fees: Reservations are accepted

at 877/444-6777 or www.recreation.gov ($10 reservation fee). Sites are $20 per night. Open year-round.

Directions: From Florence and U.S. 101, drive south for seven miles to Siltcoos Beach Road. Turn right on Siltcoos Beach Road and drive west for 1.2 miles to the campground.

Contact: Oregon Dunes National Recreation Area, Visitors Center 541/271-6000 or 541/271-3611, fax 541/750-7244.

69 DARLINGS RESORT AND MARINA

Scenic rating: 7

on Siltcoos Lake

This park, in a rural area along the north shore of Siltcoos Lake, is adjacent to the extensive Oregon Dunes National Recreation Area. Sites are right on the lake; fish from your picnic table. An access point to the dunes for hikers and off-road vehicles is just across the highway. The lake has a full-service marina. About half the sites are taken by monthly rentals.

Campsites, facilities: There are 14 sites with partial hookups for RVs up to 38 feet long. Cable TV, drinking water, fire pits, and picnic tables are provided. Restrooms with flush toilets and coin showers, firewood, convenience store, tavern, deli, boat docks, boat rentals, launching facilities, and a coin laundry are available. Leashed pets are permitted.

Reservations, fees: Reservations are accepted. Sites are $29.96 per night, $5 per night per additional vehicle. Some credit cards are accepted. Open year-round.

Directions: From Florence and U.S. 101, drive south for five miles to North Beach Road. Turn left (east) and drive 0.25 mile to Darlings Loop Road. Turn right and drive 0.25 mile to the resort.

Contact: Darlings Resort and Marina, 541/997-2841, www.darlingsresortrv.com.

70 TYEE

Scenic rating: 6

on the Siltcoos River in
Oregon Dunes National Recreation Area

This wooded campground along the shore of the Siltcoos River provides an alternative to Driftwood II and Lagoon. Fishing is permitted at the nearby lake, where there is a canoe portage trail and a boat ramp. Off-road-vehicle access to the dunes is available from Driftwood II, and there are hiking trails in the area.

Campsites, facilities: There are 16 sites for tents or RVs up to 30 feet long. Picnic tables, garbage service, and fire grills are provided. Drinking water, vault toilets, firewood, and a day-use area with horseshoe pits are available. A camp host is on-site. A store, boat docks, launching facilities, and rentals are nearby. Some facilities are wheelchair accessible. Leashed pets are permitted.

Reservations, fees: Reservations are accepted at 877/444-6777 or www.recreation.gov ($10 reservation fee). Sites are $17–18.35 per night, $5 per night per each additional vehicle. Open May–September.

Directions: From Florence and U.S. 101, drive south for six miles to the Westlake turnoff. Take that exit and continue a short distance to the campground.

Contact: Oregon Dunes National Recreation Area, Visitors Center 541/271-6000 or 541/271-3611, fax 541/750-7244; campground management 541/997-4479.

71 WAXMYRTLE

Scenic rating: 7

near Siltcoos Lake in
Oregon Dunes National Recreation Area

One of three camps in the immediate vicinity, Waxmyrtle is adjacent to Lagoon and less than a mile from Driftwood II. The camp is near the Siltcoos River and a couple of miles from Siltcoos Lake, a good-sized lake with boating facilities where you can fish. A pleasant hiking trail here meanders through the dunes and along the estuary.

Campsites, facilities: There are 57 sites for tents or RVs of any length. Picnic tables, garbage service, and fire grills are provided. Drinking water and flush toilets are available. A camp host is on-site. Boat docks, launching facilities, and rentals are nearby on Siltcoos Lake. Leashed pets are permitted.

Reservations, fees: Reservations are accepted at 877/444-6777 or www.recreation.gov ($10 reservation fee). Sites are $20 per night. Open year-round.

Directions: From Florence and U.S. 101, drive south for seven miles to Siltcoos Beach Road. Turn right and drive 1.3 miles west to the campground.

Contact: Oregon Dunes National Recreation Area, Visitors Center 541/271-6000 or 541/271-3611, fax 541/750-7244.

72 TAHKENITCH LANDING

Scenic rating: 6

near Tahkenitch Lake in
Oregon Dunes National Recreation Area

This camp overlooking Tahkenitch Lake (Lake of Many Fingers) has easy access to excellent fishing.

Campsites, facilities: There are 29 sites for tents or RVs up to 40 feet long. Picnic tables and garbage service are provided. Vault toilets, boat-launching facilities, and a floating dock are available, but there is no drinking water. A camp host is on-site. Leashed pets are permitted.

Reservations, fees: Reservations are accepted at 877/444-6777 or www.recreation.gov ($10 reservation fee). Sites are $17–19 per night, $5 per night per additional vehicle. Open year-round.

CAMPING

Directions: From Florence and U.S. 101, drive south for 14 miles to the campground on the east side of the road.

Contact: Oregon Dunes National Recreation Area, Visitors Center 541/271-6000 or 541/271-3611, fax 541/750-7244; campground management 541/997-4479.

73 TAHKENITCH

Scenic rating: 7

near Tahkenitch Lake in
Oregon Dunes National Recreation Area

This very pretty campground with dense vegetation is set in a wooded area across the highway from Tahkenitch Lake, which has numerous coves and backwater areas for fishing. A hiking trail close to the camp goes through the dunes out to the beach, as well as to Threemile Lake. If this camp is full, Tahkenitch Landing provides space nearby.

Campsites, facilities: There are 26 sites for tents or RVs up to 30 feet long. Picnic tables, garbage service, and fire grills are provided. Drinking water, firewood, and flush toilets are available. A camp host is on-site. Boat docks and launching facilities are on the lake across the highway. Some facilities are wheelchair accessible. Leashed pets are permitted.

Reservations, fees: Reservations are accepted at 877/444-6777 or www.recreation.gov ($10 reservation fee). Sites are $16.83–19.80 per night, $5 per night per additional vehicle. Open mid-May–September.

Directions: From Florence and U.S. 101, drive south for 14 miles. The campground entrance is on the right.

Contact: Oregon Dunes National Recreation Area, Visitors Center 541/271-6000 or 541/271-3611, fax 541/750-7244; campground management 541/997-4479.

74 DISCOVERY POINT RESORT & RV PARK

Scenic rating: 7

on Winchester Bay

This resort sits on the shore of Winchester Bay, adjacent to sandy dunes, in a fishing village near the mouth of the Umpqua River. The park was designed around motor sports, and ATVs are available for rent. It is somewhat noisy, but that's what most people come for.

Campsites, facilities: There are five tent sites, 60 sites with full hookups for RVs of any length, 13 cabins, and two condos. Some sites are pull-through. Picnic tables and fire pits are provided at most sites. Restrooms with flush toilets and showers, drinking water, cable TV, convenience store, coin laundry, a weekend snack bar, and ice are available. A dump station and propane gas are within one mile. Boat docks and launching facilities are nearby. Leashed pets are permitted.

Reservations, fees: Reservations are accepted. RV sites are $28–33 per night, tent sites are $14–16 per night, condos are $260–275 per night, $7 per night per each additional vehicle. Call for cabin rates. Some credit cards are accepted. Open year-round.

Directions: From Reedsport and U.S. 101, drive south for two miles to Winchester Bay and Salmon Harbor Drive. Turn right at Salmon Harbor Drive and proceed west for one mile to the resort on the left.

Contact: Discovery Point Resort & RV Park, 541/271-3443, www.discoverypointresort.com; ATV rentals, 541/271-9357.

75 WINDY COVE COUNTY PARK

🏃 ⛵ 🏊 ⛺ 🐕 ♿ 🚐 ⛺

Scenic rating: 7

adjacent to Salmon Harbor at Winchester Bay

This Douglas County park actually comprises two campgrounds, Windy Cove A and B. Set near ocean beaches and sand dunes, both offer a variety of additional recreational opportunities, including an 18-hole golf course, hiking trails, and a lighthouse.

Campsites, facilities: There are 33 tent sites and 64 sites with full or partial hookups for RVs up to 60 feet long. Drinking water and picnic tables are provided. Fire pits are provided at some Windy A sites, but not at Windy B sites. Restrooms with flush toilets and showers and cable TV are available. Propane gas, dump station, a store, café, coin laundry, and ice are within one mile. Boat docks, launching facilities, boat charters, and rentals are nearby. Some facilities are wheelchair accessible. Leashed pets are permitted.

Reservations, fees: Reservations are accepted for selected Windy B sites only at 541/957-7001. Sites are $15–20 per night, $3 per night per additional vehicle. Some credit cards are accepted. Open year-round.

Directions: From Reedsport and U.S. 101, drive south for three miles to the Windy Cove exit near Winchester Bay. Take that exit and drive west to the park on the left.

Contact: Windy Cove County Park, Windy B, 541/271-5634; Windy A, 541/271-4138, www.co.douglas.or.us/parks.

76 UMPQUA LIGHTHOUSE STATE PARK

🏃 ⛵ 🏊 ⛺ 🐕 🚐 ⛺

Scenic rating: 7

on the Umpqua River

This park is located near Lake Marie and less than a mile from Salmon Harbor on Winchester Bay. A one-mile trail circles Lake Marie, and swimming and non-motorized boating are allowed. Near the mouth of the Umpqua River, this unusual area features dunes as high as 500 feet. Hiking trails lead out of the park and into the Oregon Dunes National Recreation Area. The park offers more than two miles of beach access on the ocean and 0.5 mile along the Umpqua River. The adjacent lighthouse is still in operation, and tours are available during the summer season.

Campsites, facilities: There are 24 sites for tents or RVs up to 45 feet long (no hookups), 20 sites with full hookups for RVs up to 45 feet long, a hiker/bicyclist camp, two cabins, two rustic yurts, and six deluxe yurts. Picnic tables and fire pits are provided. Drinking water, garbage bins, restrooms with flush toilets and showers, and firewood are available. Boat docks and launching facilities are on the Umpqua River. Leashed pets are permitted.

Reservations, fees: Reservations are accepted at 800/452-5687 or www.oregonstateparks.org ($8 reservation fee). RV sites are $16–24 per night, tent sites are $12–19 per night, $5 per night for an additional vehicle, $4–5 per person per night for hikers/bikers, $35–39 per night for cabins, $27–36 per night for rustic yurts, and $45–76 for deluxe yurts. Some credit cards are accepted. Open year-round.

Directions: From Reedsport and U.S. 101, drive south for six miles to Umpqua Lighthouse Road. Turn right (west) and drive one mile to the park.

Contact: Umpqua Lighthouse State Park, 541/271-4118 or 800/551-6949, www.oregon stateparks.org.

CAMPING

77 WILLIAM M. TUGMAN STATE PARK

🏞️🚴🏕️🏊🛶🐕♿🚗⛺

Scenic rating: 7

on Eel Lake

This campground is set along the shore of Eel Lake, which offers almost five miles of shoreline for boating, fishing, sailing, and swimming. It's perfect for bass fishing. A boat ramp is available, but there is a 10-mph speed limit for boats. Oregon Dunes National Recreation Area is across the highway. Hiking is available just a few miles north at Umpqua Lighthouse State Park. A developed, 2.5-mile trail along the south end of the lake allows hikers to get away from the developed areas of the park and explore the lake's many outlets.

Campsites, facilities: There are 94 sites with partial hookups for tents or RVs up to 50 feet long, a camping area for hikers and bicyclists, and 16 yurts. Drinking water, fire rings, and picnic tables are provided. Restrooms with flush toilets and showers, dump station, firewood, and a picnic shelter are available. Boat docks and launching facilities are nearby. Some facilities are wheelchair accessible. Leashed pets are permitted.

Reservations, fees: Reservations are accepted at 800/452-5687 or www.oregonstateparks.org ($8 reservation fee). Sites are $12–20 per night, $5 per night per additional vehicle, $4–5 per person per night for hikers/bicyclists, and $27–39 per night for yurts. Some credit cards are accepted. Open year-round.

Directions: From Reedsport and U.S. 101, drive south for eight miles to the park entrance on the left (east side of the road).

Contact: Sunset Bay State Park, 541/759-3604 or 800/551-6949, www.oregonstateparks.org.

78 NORTH LAKE RESORT AND MARINA

🏕️🛶🚗🏠♿⛺

Scenic rating: 8

on Tenmile Lake

This 40-acre resort along the shore of Tenmile Lake is wooded and secluded, has a private beach, and makes the perfect layover spot for U.S. 101 travelers. The lake has a full-service marina, and bass fishing can be good here. About 25 percent of the sites are taken by summer season rentals.

Campsites, facilities: There are 20 tent sites and 75 sites with full or partial hookups for RVs of any length. Picnic tables are provided and there are fire pits at most sites. Restrooms with flush toilets and coin showers, dump station, firewood, convenience store, ice, phone/modem hookups, cable TV, drinking water, coin laundry, horseshoe pits, and a volleyball court are available. Boat docks, launching facilities, and a marina are also available. A café and boat rentals are nearby. Leashed pets are permitted.

Reservations, fees: Reservations are accepted. Tent sites are $20 per night; RV sites are $25 per night. Some credit cards are accepted. Open April–October.

Directions: From Reedsport and U.S. 101, drive south on U.S. 101 for 11 miles to the Lakeside exit. Take that exit east into town for 0.75 mile (across the railroad tracks) to North Lake Road. Turn left (north) and drive 0.5 mile to the resort on the left.

Contact: North Lake Resort and Marina, 541/759-3515, fax 541/759-3326, www.northlakeresort.com.

79 OSPREY POINT RV RESORT

🧍🏊🚤�— 🐴🚐⛺

Scenic rating: 7

on Tenmile Lake

Tenmile is one of Oregon's premier bass fishing lakes and yet is located only three miles from the ocean. The resort is situated in a large, open area adjacent to Tenmile Lake and 0.5 mile from North Lake. A navigable canal connects the lakes. The Oregon Dunes National Recreation Area provides nearby hiking trails, and Elliot State Forest offers wooded trails. With weekend barbecues and occasional live entertainment, Osprey Point is more a destination resort than an overnight stop.

Campsites, facilities: There are 132 sites for tents or RVs of any size (full hookups), a grassy area for tents, and five park-model cabins. Drinking water, picnic tables, and fire pits are provided. Cable TV, modem access, restrooms with flush toilets and showers, dump station, coin laundry, restaurant, cocktail lounge, convenience store, full-service marina with boat docks, launch, fishing pier, fish-cleaning station, horseshoe pits, volleyball, tetherball, recreation hall, video arcade, and a pizza parlor are available. Leashed pets are permitted.

Reservations, fees: Reservations are accepted. RV sites are $25–36 per night, tent sites are $18 per night, $3.50 per person per night for more than two people. Monthly rates are available. Some credit cards are accepted. Open year-round.

Directions: From Reedport, drive north on U.S. 101 for 11 miles to the Lakeside exit. Take that exit east into town for 0.75 mile (across the railroad tracks) to North Lake Road. Turn left (north) on North Lake Road and drive 0.5 mile to the resort on the right.

Contact: Osprey Point RV Resort, 541/759-2801, fax 541/759-3198, www.ospreypoint.net.

80 EEL CREEK

🧍🏊🚤🚤🐴🚐⛺

Scenic rating: 8

near Eel Lake in Oregon Dunes National Recreation Area

This campground along Eel Creek is located near both Eel and Tenmile Lakes. Although Tenmile Lake allows waterskiing, Eel Lake does not. Nearby trails offer access to the Umpqua Dunes Scenic Area, where you'll find spectacular scenery in an area closed to off-road vehicles. Off-road access is available at Spinreel.

Campsites, facilities: There are 38 sites for tents or RVs up to 50 feet long. Picnic tables, garbage service, and fire grills are provided. Drinking water, flush toilets, and firewood are available. A camp host is on-site. Boat docks, launching facilities, and rentals are nearby. Leashed pets are permitted.

Reservations, fees: Reservations are accepted at 877/444-6777 or www.recreation.gov ($10 reservation fee). Sites are $20 per night, $5 per night per additional vehicle. Open mid-May–September.

Directions: From Reedsport and U.S. 101, drive south for 10.5 miles to the park entrance.

Contact: Oregon Dunes National Recreation Area, Visitors Center 541/271-6000 or 541/271-3611, fax 541/750-7244.

81 SPINREEL

🧍🚤🚤🐴♿🚐⛺

Scenic rating: 6

on Tenmile Creek in Oregon Dunes National Recreation Area

Spinreel campground is set several miles inland at the outlet of Tenmile Lake in the Oregon Dunes National Recreation Area. A boat launch (for drift boats and canoes) is near the camp. Primarily for off-road-vehicle

CAMPING

enthusiasts, Spinreel's other recreational opportunities include hiking trails and off-road-vehicle access to the dunes. Off-road-vehicle rentals are available adjacent to the camp. **Campsites, facilities:** There are 37 sites for tents or RVs up to 61 feet long. Drinking water, garbage service, and flush toilets are available. Picnic tables and fire grills are provided. Firewood, store, and a coin laundry are nearby. Boat docks, launching facilities, and rentals are on Tenmile Lake. Some facilities are wheelchair accessible. Leashed pets are permitted.

Reservations, fees: Reservations are accepted at 877/444-6777 or www.recreation.gov ($10 reservation fee). Sites are $20 per night. Open year-round.

Directions: From Coos Bay, drive north on U.S. 101 for 10 miles to the campground entrance road (well signed). Turn northwest and drive one mile to the campground.

Contact: Oregon Dunes National Recreation Area, Visitors Center 541/271-6000 or 541/271-3611, fax 541/750-7244.

82 LOON LAKE RECREATION AREA

Scenic rating: 8

on Loon Lake

BEST (

Loon Lake was created 1,400 years ago when a nearby mountain crumbled and slid downhill, damming a creek with house-sized boulders. Today, the lake is half a mile wide and nearly two miles long, covers 260 acres, and is more than 100 feet deep in places. Its ideal location provides a warm, wind-sheltered summer climate for various water activities. A nature trail leads to a waterfall about half a mile away. Evening interpretive programs are held during summer weekends.

Campsites, facilities: There are 57 sites for tents or RVs of any length; some sites can be combined into a group site for up to 12

people. Picnic tables and fire pits are provided. Drinking water, restrooms with flush toilets and showers, garbage bins, dump station, basketball court, firewood, playground, horseshoe pits, volleyball, fish-cleaning station, a sand beach, and a boat ramp and moorings are available. Some facilities are wheelchair accessible, including the fishing pier. Leashed pets are permitted in the campground, but not on the beach or in the day-use area.

Reservations, fees: Reservations are accepted at 877/444-6777 or www.recreation.gov ($10 reservation fee). Sites are $18 per night, $7 per night per additional vehicle, and $36 per night for group sites. Open late May–November, weather permitting.

Directions: From Eugene, drive south on I-5 to Exit 162 and Highway 38. Turn west on Highway 38 and drive 43 miles to Milepost 13.5 and the County Road 3 exit. Turn left (south) and drive 7.5 miles to the campground on the right.

Contact: Bureau of Land Management, Coos Bay District Office, 541/756-0100, fax 541/751-4303, www.blm.gov.

83 LOON LAKE LODGE AND RV

Scenic rating: 8

on Loon Lake

This resort boasts one mile of lake frontage and nestles among the tall trees on pretty Loon Lake. It's not a long drive from either U.S. 101 or I-5, making it an ideal layover spot for travelers eager to get off the highway. The lake offers good bass fishing, boating, swimming, and waterskiing.

Campsites, facilities: There are 25 tent sites, 40 sites with full or partial hookups for tents or RVs up to 40 feet long, four group sites for up to 20–30 people each, eight cabins, and a six-unit motel. Some RV sites are pull-through. Picnic tables and fire rings are provided. Pit toilets and drinking water are available. A restaurant, general store, wireless Internet service, ice, gas, a beach, boat ramp, dock, marina, and boat rentals are also available. Leashed pets are permitted, with certain restrictions.

Reservations, fees: Reservations are accepted. Tent sites are $19 per night, RV sites are $35 per night, $7 per person per night for more than five, $5 per night per additional vehicle. Some credit cards are accepted. Open year-round.

Directions: From Eugene, drive south on I-5 to Exit 162 and Highway 38. Turn west on Highway 38 and drive 20 miles through the town of Elkton. Continue on Highway 38 for another 22 miles until you cross a large bridge and reach Loon Lake Road. Turn left at Loon Lake Road and drive nine miles to the resort.

Contact: Loon Lake Lodge and RV Resort, 541/599-2244, fax 541/599-2274, www.loonlakerv.com.

84 OREGON DUNES KOA

Scenic rating: 5

north of North Bend, next to the
Oregon Dunes National Recreation Area

This ATV-friendly park has direct access to Oregon Dunes National Recreation Area, which offers miles of ATV trails. The fairly open campground features a landscape of grass, young trees, and a small lake. The ocean is a 15-minute drive away. Mill Casino is about six miles south on U.S. 101. Freshwater and ocean fishing are nearby. A golf course is about five miles away.

Campsites, facilities: There are 51 sites for tents or RVs of any size (full hookups), six tent sites, and nine cabins. Most sites are pull-through, and 30- and 50-amp service is available. RV sites have drinking water, picnic tables, fire pits, and cable TV provided. Drinking water, restrooms with flush toilets

and showers, wireless Internet service, modem access, coin laundry, convenience store, game room, playground, seasonal organized activities, a snack bar, firewood, propane gas, horseshoe pits, volleyball, and a picnic shelter are available. ATV rentals are nearby. Some facilities are wheelchair accessible. Leashed pets are permitted, except in cabins.

Reservations, fees: Reservations are accepted at 800/562-4236. Tent sites are $18–32 per night, RV sites are $25–55 per night, and it costs $3.25–5 per person per night for more than two people and $4.50 per night per additional vehicle. Some credit cards are accepted. Open year-round.

Directions: From Coos Bay, drive north on U.S. 101 past North Bend for nine miles to Milepost 229. The campground entrance road is on the left.

Contact: Oregon Dunes KOA, 541/756-4851, fax 541/756-8838, www.koa.com.

85 TYEE

Scenic rating: 7

on the Umpqua River

Here's a classic spot along the Umpqua River with great salmon, smallmouth bass, and steelhead fishing in season. Boat launches are available a few miles upstream and downstream of the campground. Eagleview Group camp, a BLM campground, is one mile away.

Campsites, facilities: There are 15 sites for tents or RVs up to 70 feet long. Drinking water, garbage service, fire grills, and picnic tables are provided. Vault toilets, a day-use area with horseshoe pits, and a pavilion are available. A camp host is on-site. A store is within one mile. Some facilities are wheelchair accessible. Leashed pets are permitted.

Reservations, fees: Reservations are not accepted. Sites are $10 per night, $4 per night for each additional vehicle. Open mid-March–November.

Directions: From Roseburg, drive north on I-5 to Exit 136 and Highway 138. Take that exit and drive west on Highway 138 for 12 miles. Cross Bullock Bridge and continue to County Road 57. Turn right and drive 0.5 mile to the campground entrance.

Contact: Bureau of Land Management, Roseburg District, 541/440-4930, fax 541/440-4948, www.blm.gov.

86 WILD MARE HORSE CAMP

Scenic rating: 7

in Oregon Dunes National Recreation Area

This horse camp has paved parking, with single and double corrals. No off-road vehicles are allowed within the campground. Horses can be ridden straight out into the dunes and to the ocean; they cannot be ridden on developed trails, such as Bluebill Lake Trail. The heavily treed shoreline gives rise to treed sites with some bushes.

Campsites, facilities: There are 11 horse campsites for tents or RVs up to 61 feet long. There is a maximum of two vehicles per site. Picnic tables and fire pits are provided. Drinking water, vault toilets, and garbage bins are available. Leashed pets are permitted.

Reservations, fees: Reservations are accepted at 877/444-6777 or www.recreation.gov ($10 reservation fee). Sites are $20 per night. Some credit cards are accepted. Open year-round.

Directions: From Coos Bay, drive north on U.S. 101 for 1.5 miles to Horsfall Dunes and Beach Access Road. Turn left and drive west for one mile to the campground access road. Turn right and drive 0.75 mile to the campground on the left.

Contact: Oregon Dunes National Recreation Area, Visitors Center 541/271-6000 or 541/271-3611, fax 541/750-7244.

87 BLUEBILL

Scenic rating: 6

on Bluebill Lake in Oregon Dunes National Recreation Area

This campground gets very little camping pressure, although there are some good hiking trails available. It's located next to little Bluebill Lake, which sometimes dries up during the summer. A one-mile trail goes around the lake bed. The camp is a short distance from Horsfall Lake, which is surrounded by private property. If you continue west on the forest road, you'll come to a picnicking and parking area near the beach. This spot provides off-road-vehicle access to the dunes at the Horsfall day-use area and Horsfall Beach.

Campsites, facilities: There are 19 sites for tents or RVs of any length. Picnic tables, garbage service, and fire grills are provided. Flush toilets and drinking water are available. Leashed pets are permitted.

Reservations, fees: Reservations are accepted at 877/444-6777 or www.recreation.gov ($10 reservation fee). Sites are $20 per night. Open May–September.

Directions: From Coos Bay, drive north on U.S. 101 for 1.5 miles north to Horsfall Dunes and Beach Access Road. Turn west and drive one mile to Horsfall Road. Turn northwest and drive two miles to the campground entrance.

Contact: Oregon Dunes National Recreation Area, Visitors Center 541/271-6000 or 541/271-3611, fax 541/750-7244.

88 HORSFALL

Scenic rating: 4

in Oregon Dunes National Recreation Area

Horsfall campground is actually a nice, large paved area for parking RVs; it's the staging area for off-road-vehicle access into the southern section of Oregon Dunes National Recreation Area. If Horsfall is full, try nearby Horsfall Beach, an overflow area with 34 tent and RV sites.

Campsites, facilities: There are 69 sites for RVs up to 52 feet in length. Picnic tables and fire rings are provided. Drinking water, garbage service, restrooms with flush toilets and coin showers, and a pay phone are available. Some facilities are wheelchair accessible. Leashed pets are permitted.

Reservations, fees: Reservations are accepted at 877/444-6777 or www.recreation.gov ($10 reservation fee). Sites are $20 per night. Open year-round.

Directions: From Coos Bay, drive north on U.S. 101 for 1.5 miles to Horsfall Road. Turn west on Horsfall Road and drive about one mile to the campground access road. Turn on the campground access road (well signed) and drive 0.5 mile to the campground.

Contact: Oregon Dunes National Recreation Area, Visitors Center 541/271-6000541/271-3611, fax 541/750-7244.

89 SUNSET BAY STATE PARK

Scenic rating: 8

near Sunset Bay

Scenic Sunset Bay sits on the beautiful Oregon Coast, amid coastal forest and headlands. The sandy beach is secluded, protected by cliffs and conifers, and tidepooling is a popular activity. A series of hiking trails leads to Shore Acres and Cape Arago Parks. Clamming and fishing is available in nearby Charleston. Golfing and swimming are some of the recreation options here.

Campsites, facilities: There are 66 sites for tents or self-contained RVs, 63 sites with full or partial hookups for tents or RVs up to 47 feet long, a separate area for hikers and bicyclists, eight yurts, and two group camps

for up to 25 and 250 people, respectively. Drinking water, picnic tables, garbage bins, and fire grills are provided. Restrooms with flush toilets and showers, a fish-cleaning station, boat ramp, and firewood are available. A camp host is on-site. A gazebo and meeting hall can be reserved at nearby Shore Acres. A restaurant is within three miles. Some facilities are wheelchair accessible. Leashed pets are permitted, except in yurts.

Reservations, fees: Reservations are accepted at 800/452-5687 or www.oregonstateparks.org ($8 reservation fee). RV sites are $16–24 per night, tent sites are $12–19 per night, $5 per night per additional vehicle, $4–5 per person per night for hikers/bicyclists, $27–36 per night for yurts, $40–71 per night for group camps, and $2.40 per person per night for more than 25 people. Some credit cards are accepted. Open year-round.

Directions: In Coos Bay, take the Charleston/State Parks exit to Empire Coos Bay Highway. Drive west to Newmark Avenue. Bear left and continue to Cape Arago Highway. Turn left and drive about five miles south to Charleston and cross the South Slough Bridge. Continue on Cape Arago Highway about three miles to the park entrance on the left.

Contact: Sunset Bay State Park, 541/888-4902 or 800/551-6949, www.oregonstateparks.org.

90 BASTENDORFF BEACH PARK

Scenic rating: 8

near Cape Arago State Park

This campground is surrounded by large trees and provides access to the ocean and a small lake. Nearby activities include boating, clamming, crabbing, dune buggy riding, fishing, golfing, swimming, and whale-watching. Swimmers should be aware of undertows and sneaker waves. Horses may be rented near Bandon. A nice side trip is to Shore Acres State Park and Botanical Gardens, about 2.5 miles away.

Campsites, facilities: There are 35 tent sites, 56 sites with partial hookups for tents or RVs (of any length), and two cabins. Group camping is available. Picnic tables and fire pits are provided. Drinking water, restrooms with flush toilets and coin showers, and a dump station are available. A fish-cleaning station, horseshoe pits, playground, basketball courts, and a picnic area are also available. Some facilities are wheelchair accessible. Leashed pets are permitted.

Reservations, fees: Reservations are accepted for groups, cabins, and the picnic area only at 541/396-3121, ext. 354 ($10 reservation fee). Sites are $15–20 per night, $5 per night per additional vehicle, and cabins are $30 per night. Some credit cards are accepted. Open year-round.

Directions: In Coos Bay, take the Charleston/State Parks exit to Empire Coos Bay Highway. Drive west to Newmark Avenue. Bear left and continue to Cape Arago Highway. Turn left and drive about five miles south to Charleston and cross the South Slough Bridge. Continue on Cape Arago Highway for 1.25 miles to the park entrance.

Contact: Bastendorff Beach Park, 541/888-5353, www.co.coos.co.or.us/ccpark.

91 CHARLESTON MARINA RV PARK

Scenic rating: 7

on Coos Bay

This large, developed public park and marina is located near Charleston on the Pacific Ocean. Recreational activities in and near the campground include boating, clamming, crabbing, fishing (halibut, salmon, and tuna), hiking, huckleberry and blackberry picking, and swimming.

Campsites, facilities: There are 100 sites for tents or RVs up to 50 feet long (full hookups), six tent sites, and two yurts. Picnic tables are provided. No open fires are allowed. Drinking water, satellite TV, modem access, restrooms with showers, dump station, public phone, coin laundry, playground, fish-cleaning station, crab-cooking facilities, and propane gas are available. A marina with a boarding dock and launch ramp are on-site. Some facilities are wheelchair accessible. Leashed pets are permitted.

Reservations, fees: Reservations are accepted at 541/888-9512 or rvpark@charlestonmarina.com. RV sites are $22–25 per night, tent sites are $13 per night, and yurts are $31 per night. Weekly and monthly rates are available. Some credit cards are accepted. Open year-round.

Directions: In Coos Bay, take the Charleston/State Parks exit to Empire Coos Bay Highway. Drive west to Newmark Avenue. Bear left and continue to Cape Arago Highway. Turn left and drive about five miles south to Charleston and cross the South Slough Bridge. Continue to Boat Basin Drive. Turn right and drive 0.2 mile to Kingfisher Drive. Turn right and drive 200 feet to the campground on the left.

Contact: Charleston Marina RV Park, 541/888-9512, fax 541/888-6111, www.charlestonmarina.com.

92 BULLARDS BEACH STATE PARK

Scenic rating: 7

on the Coquille River

The Coquille River, which has good fishing in season for both boaters and crabbers, is the centerpiece of this park with four miles of shore access. If fishing is not your thing, the park also has several hiking trails. The Coquille River Lighthouse is at the end of the road that wanders through the park; during the summer, there are tours to the tower. Equestrians can explore the seven-mile horse trail.

Campsites, facilities: There are 185 sites with full or partial hookups for tents or RVs up to 64 feet long, a hiker/bicyclist camping area, a primitive horse camp with eight sites and three corrals, and 13 yurts. Drinking water, garbage bins, picnic tables, and fire grills are provided. Restrooms with flush toilets and showers, dump station, playground, firewood, a yurt meeting hall, and picnic shelters are available. Boat docks and launching facilities are in the park on the Coquille River. Some facilities are wheelchair accessible. Leashed pets are permitted.

Reservations, fees: Reservations are accepted at 800/452-5687 or www.oregonstateparks.org ($8 reservation fee). Sites are $16–24 per night, $5 per vehicle per night, $4–5 per person per night for hikers/bicyclists, and yurts are $27–36 per night. Horse camping is $12–19 per night. Some credit cards are accepted. Open year-round.

Directions: In Coos Bay, drive south on U.S. 101 for about 22 miles to the park on the right (west side of road), two miles north of Bandon.

Contact: Bullards Beach State Park, 541/347-3501 or 800/551-6949, www.oregonstateparks.org.

93 BANDON RV PARK

Scenic rating: 6

near Bullards Beach State Park

This in-town RV park is a good base for many adventures. Some sites are filled with renters, primarily anglers, for the summer season. Rock hounds will enjoy combing for agates and other semiprecious stones hidden along the beaches, while kids can explore the West Coast Game Park Walk-Through Safari petting zoo seven miles south of town. Bandon State Park, four miles south of town, has a nice wading spot in the creek at the north end of the park. Nearby recreation opportunities include two

18-hole golf courses, a riding stable, and tennis courts. Bullards Beach is about 2.5 miles north. Nice folks run this place.

Campsites, facilities: There are 44 sites with full hookups for RVs of any length; some are pull-through sites. Picnic tables are provided at most sites. No open fires are allowed. Restrooms with flush toilets and showers, dump station, cable TV, modem access, and a coin laundry are available. Propane gas and a store are within two blocks. Boat docks and launching facilities are nearby. Leashed pets are permitted.

Reservations, fees: Reservations are accepted at 800/393-4122. Sites are $22–24 per night, $2 per person per night for more than two people. Some credit cards are accepted. Open year-round.

Directions: From Coos Bay, drive south on U.S. 101 for 26 miles to Bandon and the Highway 42S junction. Continue south on U.S. 101 for one block to the park (located on the right at 935 2nd Street Southeast).

Contact: Bandon RV Park, 541/347-4122.

94 LAVERNE AND WEST LAVERNE GROUP CAMP

Scenic rating: 9

in Fairview on the north fork of the Coquille River

This beautiful, 350-acre park sits on a river with a small waterfall and many trees, including a myrtle grove and old-growth Douglas fir. Mountain bikers can take an old wagon road, and golfers can enjoy any of several courses. There are a few hiking trails and a very popular swimming hole. You can fish for salmon, steelhead, and trout, and the wildlife includes bears, cougars, deer, elk, and raccoons. You can take a side trip to the museums at Myrtle Point and Coos Bay, which display local indigenous items, or an old stagecoach house in Dora.

Campsites, facilities: There are 30 tent sites

and 46 RV sites with partial hookups for RVs of any length. There is also a large group site at West Laverne B that includes 22 RV sites with partial hookups. One cabin is also available. Drinking water, picnic tables, and fire pits are provided. Restrooms with flush toilets and coin showers, garbage bins, dump station, ice, playground, a picnic area that can be reserved, swimming hole (unsupervised), horseshoe pits, and volleyball and softball areas are available. A restaurant is within 1.5 miles. Propane gas, a store, and gasoline are within five miles. Some facilities are wheelchair accessible. Leashed pets are permitted.

Reservations, fees: Reservations are not accepted for family sites but are accepted for the group site and cabin ($10 reservation fee) at 541/396-3121, ext. 354. RV sites are $12–16 per night, tent sites are $10–11 per night, $5 per night per each additional vehicle. The group site is $140 per night for the first six camping units, plus $16 per night for each additional unit. The cabin is $30 per night. Some credit cards are accepted. Open year-round.

Directions: From Coos Bay, drive south on U.S. 101 for six miles to the junction with Highway 42. Turn east and drive 11 miles to Coquille and West Central. Turn left and drive 0.5 mile to Fairview McKinley Road. Turn right and drive eight miles to the Fairview Store. Continue east another five miles (past the store) to the park on the right.

Contact: Laverne County Park, Coos County, 541/396-2344, www.co.coos.or.us/ccpark.

95 PARK CREEK

🐾 🚐 ⛺

Scenic rating: 7

near Coquille

Want to be by yourself? You came to the right place. This pretty little campground offers peaceful, shady campsites under an old-growth canopy of Douglas fir, myrtle, red cedar, and western hemlock. Relax and enjoy nearby Park Creek and Middle Creek.

Campsites, facilities: There are 15 sites for tents or small RVs. Picnic tables and fire grills are provided. Vault toilets and garbage bins are available. There is no drinking water. Leashed pets are permitted.

Reservations, fees: Reservations are not accepted. There is no fee, but the stay limit is 14 days. Open year-round.

Directions: From Coos Bay, drive south on U.S. 101 for six miles to the junction with Highway 42. Turn east and drive 11 miles to Coquille and Coquille Fairview Road. Turn left (east) on Coquille Fairview Road and drive 7.5 miles to Fairview and Coos Bay Wagon Road. Turn right and drive four miles to Middle Creek Access Road. Turn left (east) and drive nine miles to the campground on the right.

Contact: Bureau of Land Management, Coos Bay District, 541/756-0100, fax 541/751-4303, www.or.blm.gov/coosbay.

96 KOA BANDON/ PORT ORFORD

🥾 🏊 🐾 🐎 🚐 ⛺

Scenic rating: 7

near the Elk River

This spot is considered just a layover camp, but it offers large, secluded sites nestled among big trees and coastal ferns. A pool and spa are available. During the summer season, a daily pancake breakfast and ice cream social are held. The Elk and Sixes Rivers, where the fishing can be good, are minutes away, and Cape Blanco State Park is just a few miles down the road.

Campsites, facilities: There are 46 tent sites and 26 pull-through sites with full hookups (20-, 30-, and 50-amp) for RVs of any length. Six cabins are also available. Picnic tables and fire rings are provided. Restrooms with flush toilets and showers, cable TV, modem access, snack bar, propane gas, dump station, firewood, recreation hall, convenience store, coin laundry, seasonal heated swimming pool, hot tub, horseshoe pits, basketball court, ice, and a playground are available. Leashed pets are permitted.

Reservations, fees: Reservations are accepted at 800/562-3298. Sites are $24–32 per night, $3 per person per night for more than two people, and $5 per night per additional vehicle. Some credit cards are accepted. Open March–November.

Directions: From Bandon, drive south on U.S. 101 for 16 miles to the campground at Milepost 286 near Langlois, on the west side of the highway.

Contact: KOA Bandon/Port Orford, 541/348-2358, www.koa.com.

97 CAPE BLANCO STATE PARK

🚶 🚴 🛶 🚤 🐎 ♿ 🚙 ⛺

Scenic rating: 8

between the Sixes and Elk Rivers

BEST (

This large park is named for the white *(blanco)* chalk appearance of the sea cliffs here, which rise 200 feet above the ocean. Sea lions inhabit the offshore rocks, and trails and a road lead to the black sand beach below the cliffs. The park offers good fishing access to the Sixes River, which runs for more than two miles through meadows and forests. There are seven miles of trails for horseback riding available and more than eight miles of hiking trails, some with ocean views. Tours of the lighthouse and historic Hughes House are available.

Campsites, facilities: There are 53 sites with partial hookups for tents or RVs up to 65 feet long. Other options include an equestrian camp with eight sites, a hiker/bicyclist camping area, four cabins, and four primitive group sites for tents or RVs for up to 25 people. Garbage bins, picnic tables, drinking water, and fire grills are provided. Firewood and restrooms with flush toilets and showers are available. Some facilities are wheelchair accessible. Leashed pets are permitted.

Reservations, fees: Reservations are not accepted for single sites, but are accepted for cabins, the group site, and the horse camp at 800/452-5687 or www.oregonstateparks.org ($8 reservation fee). Single sites are $12–20 per night, $5 per night per additional vehicle. The horse camp is $10–17 per night; the hiker/biker sites are $4–5 per person per night. The group site is $40–71 per night for the first 25 people, then $2.40–3 per additional person per night. Some credit cards are accepted. Open year-round.

Directions: From Coos Bay, turn south on U.S. 101 and drive approximately 46 miles (south of Sixes, five miles north of Port Orford) to Cape Blanco Road. Turn right (northwest) and drive five miles to the campground on the left.

Contact: Humbug Mountain State Park, 541/332-6774 or 800/551-6949, www.oregonstateparks.org. (This park is under the same management as Humbug Mountain State Park.)

98 EDSON

🛶 🚤 🐎 ♿ 🚙 ⛺

Scenic rating: 6

on the Sixes River

This is a popular campground along the banks of the Sixes River. Edson is similar to Sixes River Campground, except it has less tree cover and Sixes River has the benefit of a boat ramp.

Campsites, facilities: There are 25 sites for tents or RVs up to 30 feet long, and four group sites for up to 50 people. Picnic tables and fire grills are provided. Drinking water, vault toilets, garbage service, a boat launch, and a camp host are available. Some facilities are wheelchair accessible. Leashed pets are permitted.

Reservations, fees: Reservations are not accepted for single sites but are required for

CAMPING

group sites at 541/332-8027. Sites are $8 per night and $4 per night for each additional vehicle, with a 14-day stay limit. Open May–November, weather permitting.

Directions: From Coos Bay, drive south on U.S. 101 for 40 miles to Sixes and Sixes River Road/County Road 184. Turn left (east) on Sixes River Road and drive four miles to the campground entrance on the left. It's located before the Edson Creek Bridge.

Contact: Bureau of Land Management, Coos Bay District, 541/756-0100 or 541/332-8027, fax 541/751-4303, www.blm.gov.

99 SIXES RIVER

Scenic rating: 6

on the Sixes River

Set along the banks of the Sixes River at an elevation of 4,303 feet, this camp is a favorite of anglers, miners, and nature lovers. There are opportunities to pan or sluice for gold year-round or through a special limited permit. Dredging is permitted from July 15 through September. The camp roads are paved.

Campsites, facilities: There are 19 sites for tents or RVs up to 30 feet long. Picnic tables, garbage service, and fire grills are provided. Drinking water and vault toilets are available. Some facilities are wheelchair accessible. Leashed pets are permitted.

Reservations, fees: Reservations are not accepted. Sites are $8 per night, $4 per night for an additional vehicle, with a 14-day stay limit. Open May–November, weather permitting.

Directions: From Coos Bay, drive south on U.S. 101 for 40 miles to Sixes and Sixes River Road/County Road 184. Turn left (east) on Sixes River Road and drive 11 miles to the campground on the right. The last 0.5 mile is an unpaved road.

Contact: Bureau of Land Management, Coos Bay District, 541/756-0100, fax 541/751-4303, www.blm.gov.

100 POWERS COUNTY PARK

Scenic rating: 9

near the south fork of the Coquille River

This private and secluded public park in a wooded, mountainous area is a great stop for travelers going between I-5 and the coast. A 30-acre lake at the park provides a spot for visitors to boat and fish for trout. The lake is stocked with bass, catfish, crappie, and trout. Only electric boat motors are allowed. Swimming is not recommended because of the algae in the lake. A bike trail is available. On display at the park are an old steam donkey and a hand-carved totem pole. The biggest cedar tree in Oregon is reputed to be about 12 miles away.

Campsites, facilities: There are 30 sites for tents or RVs up to 54 feet long and 40 sites with partial hookups (20- and 30-amp). One cabin is also available. Picnic tables, fire pits, drinking water, restrooms with flush toilets and showers, a dump station, fish-cleaning station, picnic shelters, and a public phone are provided. Recreational facilities include a boat ramp, horseshoe pits, playground, basketball and volleyball courts, tennis courts, and a softball field. Supplies are available within one mile. Some facilities are wheelchair accessible. Leashed pets are permitted.

Reservations, fees: Reservations ($10 reservation fee) are accepted for the cabin only at 541/396-3121, ext. 354. RV sites are $12–16 per night, tent sites are $10–11 per night, and cabins are $30 per night. Some credit cards are accepted. Open year-round.

Directions: From Coos Bay, drive south on U.S. 101 for six miles to the junction with Highway 42. Turn east and drive 20 miles to Myrtle Point. Continue on Highway 42 to the Powers Highway (Highway 242) exit. Turn right (southwest) and drive 19 miles to the park on the right.

Contact: Powers County Park, Coos County, 541/439-2791, www.co.coos.or.us/ccpark/.

101 ELK RIVER CAMPGROUND

Scenic rating: 7

near the Elk River

This quiet and restful camp makes an excellent base for fall and winter fishing on the Elk River, which is known for its premier salmon fishing. A one-mile private access road goes to the river, so guests get their personal fishing holes. About half of the sites are taken by monthly rentals.

Campsites, facilities: There are 50 sites with full hookups for RVs up to 40 feet long; some sites are pull-through. Picnic tables are provided. No open fires are allowed. Drinking water, restrooms with showers, dump station, public phone, modem hookups, cable TV, and a coin laundry are available. Recreational facilities include a sports field, horseshoe pits, recreation hall, and a boat ramp. Some facilities are wheelchair accessible. Leashed pets are permitted.

Reservations, fees: Reservations are recommended. Sites are $20.20 per night. Weekly and monthly rates are available. Open year-round.

Directions: From Port Orford, drive north on U.S. 101 for 1.5 miles to Elk River Road (Milepost 297). Turn right (east) on Elk River Road and drive 1.8 miles to the campground on the left.

Contact: Elk River Campground, 541/332-2255.

102 LAIRD LAKE

Scenic rating: 8

on Laird Lake in Siskiyou National Forest

BEST

This secluded campground is set at 1,600 feet elevation, along the shore of pretty Laird Lake (six feet at its deepest point). Some old-growth cedar logs are in the lake. Most campers have no idea such a place exists in the area. This very private and scenic spot can be just what you're looking for if you're tired of fighting the crowds at the more developed camps along U.S. 101.

Campsites, facilities: There are four sites for tents or RVs up to 25 feet long. There is no drinking water, and garbage must be packed out. Leashed pets are permitted.

Reservations, fees: Reservations are not accepted. There is no fee for camping. Open year-round.

Directions: From Port Orford, drive north on U.S. 101 for three miles to County Road 208. Turn right and drive 7.5 miles southeast (the road becomes Forest Road 5325). Continue for 15.5 miles (the road bears to the right when you reach the gravel) to the campground. The road is paved for 11 miles and is gravel for the last 4.5 miles to the campground.

Contact: Siskiyou National Forest, Powers Ranger District, 541/439-6200, fax 541/439-6217, www.fs.fed.us.

103 BUTLER BAR

Scenic rating: 6

on the Elk River in Siskiyou National Forest

This campground, at an elevation of 800 feet, is set back from the shore of the Elk River and surrounded by old-growth and hardwood forest, with some reforested areas nearby. Across the river is the Grassy Knob Wilderness, which has no trails and is generally too rugged to hike. Check fishing regulations before fishing.

Campsites, facilities: There are seven sites for tents. Picnic tables and fire grills are provided. Vault toilets are available. There is no drinking water, and garbage must be packed out. Leashed pets are permitted.

Reservations, fees: Reservations are not accepted. There is no fee for camping. Open year-round, weather permitting.

CAMPING

Directions: From Port Orford, drive north on U.S. 101 for three miles to County Road 208. Turn right and drive 7.5 miles southeast (the road becomes Forest Road 5325). Continue for 7.5 miles to the campground. The road is paved.

Contact: Siskiyou National Forest, Powers Ranger District, 541/439-6200, fax 541/439-6217, www.fs.fed.us.

104 PORT ORFORD RV VILLAGE

🚶 🚴 🏊 🎣 🚣 🐎 🚐 ⛺

Scenic rating: 5

near the Elk and Sixes Rivers

Each evening, an informal group campfire and happy hour enliven this campground. Other nice touches include a small gazebo where you can get free coffee each morning and a patio where you can sit. Fishing is good during the fall and winter on the nearby Elk and Sixes Rivers, and the campground has a smokehouse, freezer, and fish-cleaning station. Some sites here are taken by summer season rentals or permanent residents.

Campsites, facilities: There are 47 sites with full or partial hookups for RVs of any length. Some sites are pull-through. Picnic tables are provided, and fire pits are available on request. Restrooms with flush toilets and showers, propane gas, dump station, horseshoe pits, recreation hall, and a coin laundry are available. Boat docks and launching facilities are nearby. Lake, river, and ocean are all within 1.5 miles. Leashed pets are permitted.

Reservations, fees: Reservations are accepted. Sites are $26 per night, plus $2 per person per night for more than two people. Open year-round.

Directions: In Port Orford on U.S. 101, drive to Madrona Avenue. Turn east and drive one block to Port Orford Loop. Turn left (north) and drive 0.5 mile to the camp on the left side.

Contact: Port Orford RV Village, 541/332-1041, www.portorfordrv.com.

105 HUMBUG MOUNTAIN STATE PARK

🚶 🚴 🏊 🐎 ♿ 🚐 ⛺

Scenic rating: 7

near Port Orford

Humbug Mountain, at 1,756 feet elevation, looms over its namesake state park. Fortunately, this natural guardian affords the campground some of the warmest weather on the coast by blocking cold winds from the ocean. Windsurfing and scuba diving are popular, as is hiking the three-mile trail to Humbug Peak. Both ocean and freshwater fishing are accessible nearby.

Campsites, facilities: There are 62 sites for tents or RVs (no hookups), 32 sites with partial hookups for RVs up to 55 feet long, and a hiker/bicyclist camp. Some sites are pull-through. Fire grills, picnic tables, garbage bins, and drinking water are provided. Firewood and restrooms with flush toilets and showers are available. A camp host is on-site. Some facilities are wheelchair accessible. Leashed pets are permitted.

Reservations, fees: Reservations are not accepted. RV sites are $12–20 per night, tent sites are $10–17 per night, $5 per night per additional vehicle, and $4–5 per person per night for hikers/bicyclists. The group camp is $60 per night for up to 25 people, plus $2.40 per person per night for additional persons. Some credit cards are accepted. Open year-round.

Directions: From Port Orford, drive south on U.S. 101 for six miles to the park entrance on the left.

Contact: Humbug Mountain State Park, 541/332-6774 or 800/551-6949, www.oregonstateparks.org.

106 MYRTLE GROVE

Scenic rating: 6

on the south fork of the Coquille River in
Siskiyou National Forest

This U.S. Forest Service campground is located along the south fork of the Coquille River, a little downstream from Daphne Grove, at an elevation of 500 feet. No fishing is allowed. Campsites are set under a canopy of big leaf maple and Douglas fir in a narrow, steep canyon. The Big Tree Observation Site, home to a huge Port Orford cedar, is a few miles away. The trail that runs adjacent to Elk Creek provides a prime hike. (The road to Big Tree may be closed because of slides, so be sure to check with the ranger district in advance.)

Campsites, facilities: There are five tent sites. Picnic tables and fire grills are provided. Vault toilets and garbage bins are available. There is no drinking water. Leashed pets are permitted.

Reservations, fees: Reservations are not accepted. There is no fee for camping. Open year-round.

Directions: From Coos Bay, drive south on U.S. 101 for six miles to the junction with Highway 42. Turn east and drive 20 miles to Myrtle Point. Continue on Highway 42 to Powers Highway (Highway 242). Turn right (southwest) and drive 18 miles (the road becomes County Road 90) to Powers. Continue for 4.3 miles (the road becomes Forest Road 33). Turn south and drive to the camp. The road is paved all the way to the camp.

Contact: Siskiyou National Forest, Powers Ranger District, 541/439-6200 or 541/439-6217, www.fs.fed.us.

107 DAPHNE GROVE

Scenic rating: 7

on the south fork of the Coquille River in
Siskiyou National Forest

This prime spot is far enough out of the way to attract little attention. At 1,000 feet elevation, it sits along the south fork of the Coquille River and is surrounded by old-growth cedar, Douglas fir, and maple. No fishing is allowed. The road is paved all the way to, and in, the campground, a plus for RVs and "city cars."

Campsites, facilities: There are 15 sites for tents or RVs up to 35 feet long. Picnic tables, garbage bins, and fire grills are provided. Vault toilets are available. There is no drinking water. Some facilities are wheelchair accessible. Leashed pets are permitted.

Reservations, fees: Reservations are not accepted. Sites are $6 per night, $3 per night per additional vehicle. Open year-round.

Directions: From Coos Bay, drive south on U.S. 101 for six miles to the junction with Highway 42. Turn east and drive 20 miles to Myrtle Point. Continue on Highway 42 to Powers Highway (Highway 242). Turn right (southwest) and drive 18 miles (the road becomes County Road 90) to Powers. Continue for 4.3 miles (the road becomes Forest Road 33). Continue for 10.5 miles to the campground entrance.

Contact: Siskiyou National Forest, Powers Ranger District, 541/439-6200, fax 541/439-6217, www.fs.fed.us.

108 ISLAND

Scenic rating: 7

near Coquille River Falls

Island Camp is an excellent base camp for hikers with many trailheads nearby. It is located along the south fork of the Coquille River at 1,000-foot elevation in Siskiyou National Forest. Nearby hiking opportunities include the Azalea Lake Trail, Panther Ridge Trail, Coquille River Falls Trail, and Sucker Creek Trail. Note: Do not confuse this Island Campground with the Island Campground in Umpqua National Forest.

Campsites, facilities: There are five sites for tents or RVs to 16 feet. Picnic tables and fire rings are provided. Vault toilets and garbage bins are available, but there is no drinking water. Leashed pets are permitted.

Reservations, fees: Reservations are not accepted. Sites are $6 per night. Open year-round.

Directions: From Coos Bay, drive south on U.S. 101 for six miles to the junction with Highway 42. Turn east and drive 20 miles to Myrtle Point. Continue on Highway 42 to Powers Highway (Highway 242). Turn right (southwest) and drive 18 miles (the road becomes County Road 90) to Powers. Drive south 17 miles on Forest Service Road 3300 to the campground.

Contact: Siskiyou National Forest, Powers Ranger District, 541/439-6200, fax 541/439-6217, www.fs.fed.us.

109 SRU LAKE
🏃 🛶 🎣 🚌 ⛺

Scenic rating: 8

on Squaw Lake in Siskiyou National Forest

Sru (pronounced "Shrew") campground is set along the shore of one-acre Sru Lake at 2,200 feet elevation in rich, old-growth forest. Sru is more of a pond than a lake, but it is stocked with trout in the spring. Get there early—the fish are generally gone by midsummer. The trailheads for the Panther Ridge Trail and Coquille River Falls Trail are a 10-minute drive from the campground. It's strongly advised that you obtain a U.S. Forest Service map detailing the backcountry roads and trails.

Campsites, facilities: There are seven sites

for tents or RVs up to 21 feet long. Picnic tables and fire rings are provided. Vault toilets are available. There is no drinking water, and garbage must be packed out. Leashed pets are permitted.

Reservations, fees: Reservations are not accepted. There is no fee for camping. Open year-round.

Directions: From Coos Bay, drive south on U.S. 101 for six miles to the junction with Highway 42. Turn east and drive 20 miles to Myrtle Point. Continue on Highway 42 to Powers Highway (Highway 242). Turn right (southwest) and drive 18 miles (the road becomes County Road 90) to Powers. Continue for 4.3 miles (the road becomes Forest Road 33). Continue on Forest Road 33 for 15 miles to the South Fork Coquille River Bridge. Continue on Forest Road 33 for 0.5 mile to Forest Road 3347 (paved road). Turn right and drive one mile to the camp.

Contact: Siskiyou National Forest, Powers Ranger District, 541/439-6200, fax 541/439-6217, www.fs.fed.us.

110 TUCKER FLAT
🏃 🛶 🎣 ♿ ⛺

Scenic rating: 7

on the Rogue River

Above the clear waters of Mule Creek, this campground borders the Wild Rogue Wilderness. Tucker Flat offers a trailhead into the Wild Rogue Wilderness and lots of evidence of historic mining. Mosquitoes can be a problem, and bears occasionally wander through. The historic Rogue River Ranch is just 0.25 mile away, and the museum and other buildings are open during the summer. The Rogue River Ranch is on the National Register of Historic Places. There are also scenic bridges along Mule Creek. Tucker Flat campground can also be reached by hiking the Rogue River Trail or by floating the Rogue River and hiking up past the Rogue River Ranch. Campers and hikers are advised to stop by the Medford BLM office for maps.

Campsites, facilities: There are six primitive tent sites. Picnic tables and fire grills are provided. Vault toilets and bear-proof trash cans are available. There is no drinking water. Some facilities are wheelchair accessible. Leashed pets are permitted.

Reservations, fees: Reservations are not accepted. There is no fee for camping. Open May–October, weather permitting.

Directions: From Grants Pass, drive one mile north on I-5 to Exit 61. Take that exit and drive west on Merlin-Galice Access Road for 20 miles to the Grave Creek Bridge (the second bridge over the Rogue River). Cross the bridge and drive a short distance to BLM Road 34-8-1. Turn left and drive 16 miles to BLM Road 32-8-31. Turn left and drive seven miles to BLM Road 32-9-14.2. Turn left and drive 15 miles to the campground (around the bend from the Rogue River Ranch).

Contact: Bureau of Land Management, Medford District, 541/618-2200, fax 541/618-2400, www.blm.gov.

111 HONEY BEAR CAMPGROUND & RV RESORT

🏕️🛶🏠🐕🚐⛺

Scenic rating: 10

near Gold Beach

BEST (

This campground offers wooded sites with ocean views. The owners have built a huge, authentic chalet, which contains a German deli, recreation area, and a big dance floor. On summer nights, they hold dances with live music. A restaurant is available on-site with authentic German food. A fishing pond is stocked with trout.

Campsites, facilities: There are 20 sites for tents or RVs (no hookups) and 65 sites with full hookups for RVs of any length. Thirty are pull-through sites with full hookups and

15 have patios. Picnic tables and fire rings are provided. Restrooms with flush toilets and showers, drinking water, cable TV, modem access, dump station, firewood, recreation hall, restaurant, convenience store, coin laundry, ice, and a playground are available. Leashed pets are permitted.

Reservations, fees: Reservations are accepted at 800/822-4444. Sites are $21.95 per night, $3 per person per night for more than two people, and $1 per night per additional vehicle. Open year-round, weather permitting.

Directions: From Gold Beach, drive north on U.S. 101 for eight miles to Ophir Road near Milepost 321. Turn right and drive two miles to the campground on the right side of the road.

Contact: Honey Bear Campground & RV Resort, 541/247-2765, www.honeybearrv.com.

112 ROCK CREEK

🏕️🛶🐕🚐⛺

Scenic rating: 6

near the south fork of the Coquille River in Siskiyou National Forest

This little-known camp (elevation 1,400 feet) in a tree-shaded canyon is surrounded by old-growth forest and some reforested areas. It is set near Rock Creek, just upstream from its confluence with the south fork of the Coquille River. No fishing is allowed. For a good side trip, take the one-mile climb to Azalea Lake, a small, shallow lake where there are some hike-in campsites. In July, the azaleas are spectacular.

Campsites, facilities: There are seven sites for tents or RVs up to 16 feet long. Picnic tables and fire grills are provided. Vault toilets, garbage bins, and firewood are available. There is no drinking water. Leashed pets are permitted.

Reservations, fees: Reservations are not accepted. Sites are $6 per night, $3 per night per additional vehicle. Open year-round, with limited winter facilities.

CAMPING

Directions: From Coos Bay, drive south on U.S. 101 for six miles to the junction with Highway 42. Turn east and drive 20 miles to Myrtle Point. Continue on Highway 42 to Powers Highway (Highway 242). Turn right (southwest) and drive 18 miles (the road becomes County Road 90) to Powers. Continue for 4.3 miles (the road becomes Forest Road 33). Continue on Forest Road 33 for 15 miles to the South Fork Coquille River Bridge. Continue on Forest Road 33 for 0.5 mile to Forest Road 3347 (paved road). Turn right and drive 0.5 mile to the camp.

Contact: Siskiyou National Forest, Powers Ranger District, 541/439-6200, fax 541/439-6217, www.fs.fed.us.

113 FOSTER BAR

Scenic rating: 5

on the Rogue River in Siskiyou National Forest

This camping area is set near the banks of the Rogue River. There's a take-out point for rafters. Hiking opportunities are good nearby, and you can also fish from the river bar. Agness RV Park provides a nearby camping alternative.

Campsites, facilities: There are eight sites for tents. Drinking water, flush toilets, garbage bins, and boat-launching facilities are available. A camp host is on-site. Leashed pets are permitted.

Reservations, fees: Reservations are not accepted. Sites are $5 per night, $3 per night per additional vehicle. Open year-round.

Directions: From Gold Beach on U.S. 101, turn east on County Road 595 and drive 35 miles (it becomes Forest Road 33) to the junction for Illahe and Foster Bar. Turn right on County Road 375 and drive five miles to the campground.

Contact: Rogue River, Siskiyou National Forest, Gold Beach Ranger District, 541/247-3600, fax 541/247-3617, www.fs.fed.us.

114 ALMEDA PARK

Scenic rating: 6

on the Rogue River

This rustic park, located along the Rogue River and featuring a grassy area, is popular for rafting and swimming. One of the main put-in points for floating the lower section of the river can be found right here. Fishing is also available. The Rogue River Trail is four miles west.

Campsites, facilities: There are 34 sites for tents or RVs of any length (no hookups), two group sites for tents or RVs for up to 30 people, and one yurt. Some sites are pull-through. Picnic tables and fire pits are provided. Drinking water, vault toilets, garbage bins, and a boat ramp are available. A seasonal camp host is on-site. Leashed pets are permitted.

Reservations, fees: Reservations are accepted. Sites are $19 per night, $5 per night per additional vehicle, and the yurt is $30 per night. The group site is $32 per night for up to 12 people, and $3 per person per night for more than 12 people. Open year-round.

Directions: From Grants Pass, drive north on I-5 for 3.5 miles to Exit 61 (Merlin-Galice Road). Take that exit and drive on Merlin-Galice Road for 19 miles to the park on the right. The park is approximately 16 miles west of Merlin.

Contact: Josephine County Parks, 541/474-5285, fax 541/474-5288, www.co.josephine.or.us/parks/index.htm.

115 NESIKA BEACH RV PARK

Scenic rating: 7

near Gold Beach

This RV park next to Nesika Beach is a good layover spot for U.S. 101 cruisers. An 18-hole golf course is close by. There are many long-term rentals here.

Campsites, facilities: There are six tent sites and 32 sites with full or partial hookups for RVs of any length; some sites are pull-through. Drinking water, cable TV, and picnic tables are provided; some tent sites have fire rings. Restrooms with flush toilets and showers, a dump station, convenience store, coin laundry, and ice are available. Leashed pets are permitted.

Reservations, fees: Reservations are accepted. RV sites are $20–24 per night, tent sites are $15 per night, $1 per person per night for more than two people. Monthly rates are available. Open year-round.

Directions: From Gold Beach, drive north on U.S. 101 for six miles to Nesika Road. Turn left and drive 0.75 mile west to the park on the right.

Contact: Nesika Beach RV Park, 541/247-6077, www.nesikarv.com.

116 INDIAN CREEK RESORT

Scenic rating: 7

on the Rogue River

This campground is set along the Rogue River on the outskirts of the town of Gold Beach. A few sites have river views. Nearby recreation options include boat trips on the Rogue.

Campsites, facilities: There are 26 tent sites and 90 sites with full hookups for RVs of any length; some sites are pull-through. Five park-model cabins are also available. Drinking water, cable TV hookups, and picnic tables are provided. Fire pits are provided at some sites. Restrooms with flush toilets and showers, modem access, firewood, recreation hall, convenience store, sauna, café, coin laundry, ice, and a playground are available. Propane gas is within two miles. Boat docks, launching facilities, and rentals are nearby. Leashed pets are permitted.

Reservations, fees: Reservations are accepted at 877/537-7704. RV sites are $27 per night, tent sites are $18 per night, $2 per person per

night for more than two people. Some credit cards are accepted. Open year-round, with limited winter facilities.

Directions: On U.S. 101, drive to the northern end of Gold Beach to Jerry's Flat Road (just south of the Patterson Bridge). Turn left (east) on Jerry's Flat Road and drive 0.5 mile to the resort.

Contact: Indian Creek Resort, 541/247-7704, www.indiancreekrv.com.

117 LUCKY LODGE RV PARK

Scenic rating: 6

on the Rogue River

Lucky Lodge is a good layover spot for U.S. 101 travelers who want to get off the highway circuit. Set on the shore of the Rogue River, it offers opportunities for boating, fishing, and swimming. Most sites have a view of the river. Nearby recreation options include hiking trails. About one-third of the sites are occupied by monthly renters.

Campsites, facilities: There are 31 sites with full hookups for RVs of any length, three tent sites, and two cabins. Most sites are pull-through. Drinking water and picnic tables are provided. Restrooms with flush toilets and showers, propane gas, a recreation hall, and coin laundry are available. Boat docks and rentals are within eight miles. Leashed pets are permitted.

Reservations, fees: Reservations are accepted. RV sites are $27–30 per night, tent sites $20 per night, $4 per person per night for more than two people. Open year-round.

Directions: From Gold Beach, drive north on U.S. 101 for four miles (on the north side of the Rogue River) to Rogue River Road. Turn right (east) and drive 3.5 miles to North Bank River Road. Turn right and drive 4.5 miles to the park on the right.

Contact: Lucky Lodge RV Park, 541/247-7618.

CAMPING

118 KIMBALL CREEK BEND RV RESORT

🏃 🚤 🏕 🐴 🚙 ⛺

Scenic rating: 6

on the Rogue River

Kimball Creek campground on the scenic Rogue River is just far enough from the coast to provide quiet and its own distinct character. The resort offers guided fishing trips and sells tickets for jet boat tours. Nearby recreation options include an 18-hole golf course, hiking trails, and boating facilities. Note that about one-third of the sites are monthly rentals.

Campsites, facilities: There are 62 sites with full hookups for RVs of any length, 13 tent sites, one park-model cabin, and three motel rooms. Drinking water and picnic tables are provided, and fire rings are at some sites. Restrooms with flush toilets and showers, modem access, propane gas, dump station, recreation hall, store, coin laundry, ice, and a playground are available. Boat docks are on-site, and launching facilities are nearby. Leashed pets are permitted.

Reservations, fees: Reservations are accepted at 888/814-0633. RV sites are $27–39 per night, tent sites are $25 per night, $3 per person per night for more than two people. Some credit cards are accepted. Open year-round.

Directions: From Gold Beach, drive north on U.S. 101 for one mile (on the north side of the Rogue River) to Rogue River Road. Turn right (east) and drive about eight miles to the resort on the right.

Contact: Kimball Creek Bend RV Resort, 541/247-7580, www.kimballcreek.com.

119 QUOSATANA

🏃 🚲 🚤 🛶 🐴 ♿ 🚙 ⛺

Scenic rating: 6

on the Rogue River in Siskiyou National Forest

This campground is set along the banks of the Rogue River, upstream from the much smaller Lobster Creek Campground. The campground features a large, grassy area and a barrier-free trail around the campground. Ocean access is just a short drive away, and the quaint town of Gold Beach offers a decent side trip. Nearby Otter Point State Park (day-use only) has further recreation options. The Shrader Old-Growth Trail, Lower Rogue River Trail, and Myrtle Tree Trail provide nearby hiking opportunities. Quosatana makes a good base camp for a hiking or fishing trip.

Campsites, facilities: There are 42 sites for tents or RVs up to 32 feet long. Drinking water, fire grills, garbage bins, and picnic tables are provided. Flush toilets, dump station, fish-cleaning station, and a boat ramp are available. A camp host is on-site. Some facilities are wheelchair accessible. Leashed pets are permitted.

Reservations, fees: Reservations are not accepted. Sites are $10 per night, $3 per night per additional vehicle. Open year-round.

Directions: From Gold Beach on U.S. 101, turn east on County Road 595 and drive 14.5 miles (it becomes Forest Road 33) to the campground on the left.

Contact: Rogue River Siskiyou National Forest, Gold Beach Ranger District, 541/247-3600, fax 541/247-3617, www.fs.fed.us.

120 LOBSTER CREEK

🏃 🚤 🏕 🐴 🚙 ⛺

Scenic rating: 6

on the Rogue River in Siskiyou National Forest

This small campground on a river bar along the Rogue River is about a 15-minute drive from Gold Beach, and it makes a good base for a fishing or hiking trip. The area is heavily forested with myrtle and Douglas fir, and the Shrader Old-Growth Trail and Myrtle Tree Trail are nearby.

Campsites, facilities: There are six sites for tents or RVs up to 21 feet long. Fire rings and picnic tables are provided. Drinking water, flush toilets, and garbage bins are available, as is a boat launch. A camp host is on-site. Leashed pets are permitted.

Reservations, fees: Reservations are not accepted. Sites are $6 per night, $3 per night per additional vehicle. Camping is also permitted on a gravel bar area for $5 per night. Open year-round, weather permitting.

Directions: From Gold Beach on U.S. 101, turn east on County Road 595 and drive 10 miles (it becomes Forest Road 33) to the campground on the left.

Contact: Rogue River Siskiyou National Forest, Gold Beach Ranger District, 541/247-3600, fax 541/247-3617, www.fs.fed.us.

121 BIG PINE

Scenic rating: 4

on Myers Creek in Siskiyou National Forest

This little campground (elevation 2,400 feet) is set near the banks of Myers Creek in a valley of large pine and Douglas fir. Many sites are right on the creek, and all are shaded. One of the world's tallest ponderosa pine trees grows near the campground. A 1.1-mile barrier-free interpretive trail starts at the campground, and a day-use area is available.

Campsites, facilities: There are 14 tent sites. Picnic tables and fire grills are provided. Vault toilets, drinking water, and garbage bins are available. Some facilities are wheelchair accessible. Leashed pets are permitted.

Reservations, fees: Reservations are not accepted. Sites are $5 per night, $2 per night per additional vehicle. Open late May–mid-October, weather permitting.

Directions: From Grants Pass, drive north on I-5 for 3.5 miles to Exit 61 (Merlin-Galice Road). Take that exit and drive northwest for 12.5 miles to Forest Road 25. Turn left on Forest Road 25 and head southwest for 12.8 miles to the campground on the right.

Contact: Siskiyou National Forest, Galice Ranger District, 541-471-6500, fax 541/471-6514, www.fs.fed.us.

122 SAM BROWN

Scenic rating: 4

near Grants Pass in Siskiyou National Forest

This campground is located in an isolated area near Grants Pass along Briggs Creek in a valley of pine and Douglas fir. It is set at an elevation of 2,500 feet. Many sites lie in the shade of trees, and a creek runs along one side of the campground. Briggs Creek Trail, Dutchy Creek Trail, and Taylor Creek Trail are nearby and are popular for hiking and horseback riding. An amphitheater is available for small group presentations. Although the campground was spared, the Biscuit Fire of 2002 did burn nearby areas.

Campsites, facilities: There are 27 sites for tents or RVs of any length at Sam Brown and seven equestrian tent sites with small corrals across the road at Sam Brown Horse Camp. Picnic tables and fire rings or grills are provided. Drinking water and vault toilets are available. A picnic shelter, solar shower, and an amphitheater are available. Some facilities are wheelchair accessible. Leashed pets are permitted.

Reservations, fees: Reservations are not accepted. Sites are $5 per night, $2 per night per additional vehicle. Open late May–mid-October, weather permitting.

Directions: From Grants Pass, drive north on I-5 for 3.5 miles to Exit 61 (Merlin-Galice Road). Take that exit and drive northwest for 12.5 miles to Forest Road 25. Turn left on Forest Road 25 and head southwest for 14 miles to the campground.

Contact: Siskiyou National Forest, Galice Ranger District, 541/471-6500, fax 541/471-6514, www.fs.fed.us.

123 IRELAND'S OCEAN VIEW RV PARK

Scenic rating: 8

in Gold Beach

This spot is situated on the beach in the quaint little town of Gold Beach, only one mile from the famous Rogue River. The park is very clean and features blacktop roads and grass beside each site. Recreation options include beachcombing, boating, and fishing. Great ocean views are possible from the observatory/lighthouse.

Campsites, facilities: There are 33 sites with full hookups (20-, 30-, and 50-amp) for RVs up to 40 feet long; some sites are pull-through. Picnic tables are provided. No open fires are allowed. Cable TV, restrooms with showers, coin laundry, recreation room, horseshoe pits, and modem access are available. Leashed pets are permitted.

Reservations, fees: Reservations are recommended. Sites are $24 per night, $1 per person per night for more than two people. Monthly rates are available. Open year-round.

Directions: On U.S. 101, drive to the southern end of Gold Beach (U.S. 101 becomes Ellensburg Avenue). The park is located at 20272 Ellensburg Avenue, across from the U.S. Forest Service office.

Contact: Ireland's Ocean View RV Park, 541/247-0148, www.irelandsrvpark.com.

124 OCEANSIDE RV PARK

Scenic rating: 5

in Gold Beach

Set 100 yards from the ocean, this park is close to beachcombing terrain, marked bike trails, and boating facilities. The park is also adjacent to the mouth of the Rogue River, in the Port of Gold Beach.

Campsites, facilities: There are 80 sites with full or partial hookups for RVs up to 40 feet long and two yurts; some sites are pull-through. Drinking water and picnic tables are provided. Restrooms with flush toilets and showers, coin laundry, cable TV, a convenience store, picnic area, and ice are available. Propane gas, a store, and a café are within two miles. Boat docks, launching facilities, and rentals are nearby. Leashed pets are permitted.

Reservations, fees: Reservations are recommended. Sites are $25–29, $1 per person per night for more than two people; yurts are $35 per night. Some credit cards are accepted. Open year-round.

Directions: On U.S. 101, drive to central Gold Beach and the intersection with Moore Street. Turn west and drive two blocks to Airport Way. Turn right and drive three blocks to South Jetty Road. Turn left and look for the park on the left.

Contact: Oceanside RV Park, 541/247-2301, www.oceansiderv1.com.

125 WHALESHEAD BEACH RESORT

Scenic rating: 7

near Brookings

This resort, about 0.25 mile from the beach, is set in a forested area with a small stream nearby. Activities at and around the camp include ocean and river fishing, jet boat trips, whale-watching excursions, and a golf course (13 miles away). Each campsite has a deck, and many cabins have an ocean view. One unique feature, a tunnel connects the campground to a trail to the beach.

Campsites, facilities: There are 45 sites with full hookups for RVs up to 60 feet long and 36 cabins. Picnic tables are provided and fire rings are available on request. Cable TV, restrooms with showers, coin laundry, modem access, limited groceries, ice, snacks, RV supplies, propane gas, and a restaurant are available. A dump station is six miles away. Some facilities are wheelchair accessible. Leashed pets are permitted.

Reservations, fees: Reservations are recommended. Sites are $25 per night, $2 per person per night for more than two people; cable TV is $1.50 per night. Some credit cards are accepted. Open year-round.

Directions: From Brookings, drive seven miles north on U.S. 101 until you pass Harris Beach. Look for the resort on the right.

Contact: Whaleshead Beach Resort, 541/469-7446, fax 541/469-7447, www.whaleshead-resort.com.

126 ALFRED A. LOEB STATE PARK

Scenic rating: 8

near the Chetco River

This park is set in a canyon formed by the Chetco River. The campsites are set in a beautiful old myrtle grove. The 0.75-mile River View Trail follows the Chetco River to a redwood grove. Swimming, fishing, and rafting are popular activities. Nature programs and interpretive tours are available by request.

Campsites, facilities: There are 48 sites with partial hookups for tents or RVs up to 50 feet long and three log cabins. Picnic tables, drinking water, garbage bins, and fire grills are provided. Restrooms with flush toilets and showers and firewood are available. A camp host is on-site. Some facilities are wheelchair accessible. Leashed pets are permitted.

Reservations, fees: Reservations are accepted for cabins only at 800/452-5687 or www.oregonstateparks.org ($8 reservation fee). Sites are $12–20 per night, $5 per night per additional vehicle; cabins are $35–39 per night. Some credit cards are accepted. Open year-round.

Directions: On U.S. 101, drive south to

Brookings and County Road 784 (North Bank Chetco River Road). Turn northeast and drive eight miles northeast on North Bank Road to the park entrance on the right.

Contact: Harris Beach State Park, 541/469-2021 or 800/551-6949, www.oregonstateparks.org.

127 HARRIS BEACH STATE PARK

Scenic rating: 8

near Brookings

BEST (

This park is prime with wildlife-watching opportunities. Not only is it home to Bird Island, a breeding site for the tufted puffin and other rare birds, but gray whales, harbor seals, and sea lions can be spotted here as well. Tidepooling is also popular. Sites are shaded and well-spaced with plenty of beach and nature trails leading from the campground. In the fall and winter, the nearby Chetco River attracts good runs of salmon and steelhead, respectively.

Campsites, facilities: There are 63 sites for tents or RVs up to 50 feet (no hookups), 86 sites with full or partial hookups for RVs up to 60 feet long, a hiker/biker camp, and six yurts. Picnic tables, garbage bins, and fire grills are provided. Drinking water, cable TV, Wi-Fi, restrooms with flush toilets and showers, a dump station, coin laundry, and firewood are available. A camp host is on-site. Some facilities are wheelchair accessible. Leashed pets are permitted.

Reservations, fees: Reservations are accepted at 800/452-5687 or www.oregonstateparks.org ($8 reservation fee). RV sites are $17–26 per night, tent sites are $13–20 per night, $5 per night per additional vehicle, $4–5 per night per person for hikers/bikers, $17 per night for group tent sites, and $29–39 per night for yurts. Some credit cards are accepted. Open year-round.

Directions: From Brookings, drive north on U.S. 101 for two miles to the park entrance on the left (west side of road).

Contact: Harris Beach State Park, 541/469-2021, www.oregonstateparks.org.

128 BEACHFRONT RV PARK

Scenic rating: 8

near Brookings

Beachfront RV, located just this side of the Oregon/California border on the Pacific Ocean, makes a great layover spot. Oceanfront sites are available, and recreational activities include boating, fishing, and swimming. Beach access is available from the park. Plan your trip early, as sites usually book up for the entire summer season. Nearby Harris Beach State Park, with its beach access and hiking trails, makes a good side trip.

Campsites, facilities: There are 25 tent sites and 138 sites with full or partial hookups for RVs of any length; some sites are pull-through. Picnic tables and fire rings are provided. Restrooms with showers, dump station, public phone, modem access, coin laundry, restaurant, ice, and a marina with a boat ramp, boat dock, and snacks are available. Supplies are available nearby. Some facilities are wheelchair accessible. Leashed pets are permitted.

Reservations, fees: Reservations are accepted at 800/441-0856. Tent sites are $14 per night and RV sites are $22–28.28 per night. Some credit cards are accepted. Open year-round.

Directions: From Brookings, drive south on U.S. 101 for 2.5 miles to Benham Lane. Turn west on Benham Lane and drive 1.5 miles (it becomes Lower Harbor Road) to Boat Basin Road. Turn left and drive two blocks to the park on the right.

Contact: Beachfront RV Park, 541/469-5867 or 800/441-0856; Port of Brookings Harbor, 541/469-2218, www.port-brookings-harbor.org.

129 ATRIVERS EDGE RV RESORT

Scenic rating: 7

on the Chetco River

This resort lies along the banks of the Chetco River, just upstream from Brookings Harbor. A favorite spot for anglers, it features salmon and steelhead trips on the Chetco in the fall and winter. Deep-sea trips for salmon or rockfish are available nearby in the summer. This resort looks like the Rhine Valley in Germany, a pretty canyon between the trees and the river. A golf course is nearby.

Campsites, facilities: There are 110 sites with full hookups for RVs of any length; some are pull-through. Nine cabins are also available. Picnic tables are provided and fire rings are at most sites. Restrooms with flush toilets and showers, wireless Internet service, modem access, propane gas, dump station, recreation hall with exercise equipment, coin laundry, recycling station, small boat launch, and cable TV are available. Leashed pets are permitted.

Reservations, fees: Reservations are recommended at 888/295-1441. Sites are $30–33 per night, $2 per person per night for more than two people. Some credit cards are accepted. Open year-round.

Directions: On U.S. 101, drive to the southern end of Brookings (harbor side) and to South Bank Chetco River Road (a cloverleaf exit). Turn east on South Bank Chetco River Road and drive 1.5 miles to the resort entrance on the left (a slanted left turn, through the pillars, well signed).

Contact: AtRivers Edge RV Resort, 541/469-3356, www.atriversedge.com.

130 SEA BIRD RV PARK

🏃 🚴 🏊 🛶 🛥 🐎 🚐

Scenic rating: 5

near Brookings

Sea Bird is one of several parks in the area. Nearby recreation options include marked bike trails, a full-service marina, and tennis courts. A nice, neat park, it features paved roads and gravel/granite sites. There is also a beach for surfing near the park. In summer, most of the sites are reserved for the season. An 18-hole golf course is within 2.5 miles.

Campsites, facilities: There are 60 sites with full or partial hookups for RVs of any length; some are pull-through sites. Picnic tables are provided. No open fires are allowed. Restrooms with flush toilets and showers, dump station, high-speed modem access, recreation hall, and a coin laundry are available. Boat docks, launching facilities, and rentals are nearby. Leashed pets are permitted.

Reservations, fees: Reservations are accepted. Sites are $18 per night, $2 per person per night for more than two people. Open year-round.

Directions: In Brookings, drive south on U.S. 101 to the Chetco River Bridge. Continue 0.25 mile south on U.S. 101 to the park entrance on the left.

Contact: Sea Bird RV Park, 541/469-3512, www.seabirdrv.com.

OREGON COAST HIKING

© SEAN PATRICK HILL

BEST HIKES

HIKING

Oregonians go to "the coast," but never to

"the beach." Sure, there are beaches here, but forget your image of the West Coast. This is not your ordinary Los Angeles beach with surfers riding the waves – though you'll see them, too. Oregon's coastline is 363 miles of rugged, awe-inspiring, and unforgettable landscape. From enormous, cliff-lined capes to windswept sand dunes, from rhododendron-sheltered coves to forested mountains, from sandy spits to towering sea stacks teeming with wildlife, Oregon's coast runs the gamut. You can see ancient Sitka spruce and redwoods, climb lava flow headlands, explore tidal pools, or just sit on a beach watching the brown pelicans skirt the surf, making Oregon's coastline by far some of the most dramatic in the country.

The Oregon state parks on the coast are among the best in the state, and many are free. There are also scores of "waysides," simple turnouts with a picnic table or two that are often the site of amazing trailheads. Many parks offer camping, swimming, and historical sites in addition to trails and beaches. You will also find National Forest land with dense forests of Douglas fir, Western red cedar, Western hemlock, and Sitka spruce. Wildlife is plentiful, from elk to deer to shorebirds. Among the parks and forestlands is the Oregon Dunes National Recreation Area, a must-see for anyone, with its stupendous dunes rising hundreds of feet and covering nearly 36 miles of coastline.

But there is more than just ocean and sand; what Oregonians know of the coast also includes the Coast Range, mountains that separate the coastline proper from the Willamette Valley. In the Coast Range, you'll find incredible mountain hikes, flowering rhododendrons, and waterfall after waterfall. The southern portion of the Coast Range gives way to the Klamath and Siskiyou Mountains, a granite landscape that geographically is one of the oldest parts of the state. The sweeping forest fire known as the Biscuit Fire, among the largest in Oregon's history, swept through here in 2002, but the area is recovering nicely. Flowers bloom and many trees were spared. Cutting through these mountains are the Rogue and Illinois Rivers, destinations for river rats and wilderness aficionados.

Many of the trails in this area follow the 360-mile Oregon Coast Trail, extending from Brookings in the south to Astoria in the north. Following this trail, you'll cross rivers, follow rocky headlands, and pass through quaint towns. As with the more well-known Pacific Crest Trail, this path can be followed for the entire distance, backpacked for shorter sequences, or just make for some great day-tripping.

In the coastal area, towering, inaccessible cliffs often hem in beaches, so be sure to check tide charts and go at low tide. Be extra careful when atop the cliffs themselves, too. Though the many capes and cliffs make for great vistas, they can also be dangerous. Make sure you don't step on anything living around sea stacks and tidepools. Many areas, like Haystack Rock on Cannon Beach, are federally protected wildlife preserves, and it is against the law to intrude on these important nesting and breeding sites. When in doubt, check with local agencies and land management.

So don't go thinking "coast" means bathing suits and sand castles, though you'll see your share of those. Instead, think of it as a real wilderness. In this regard, it is valuable to not only check the weather before you go (Oregon weather anywhere, let alone the finicky coast, can change abruptly; believe me, I know), but check the tide charts. Oregon is famous for its "sneaker waves" that come up quite unexpectedly with little forewarning. Be safe on your adventures on the Oregon coast, and you'll remember it as the rugged adventure it has always been.

HIKING

HIKING

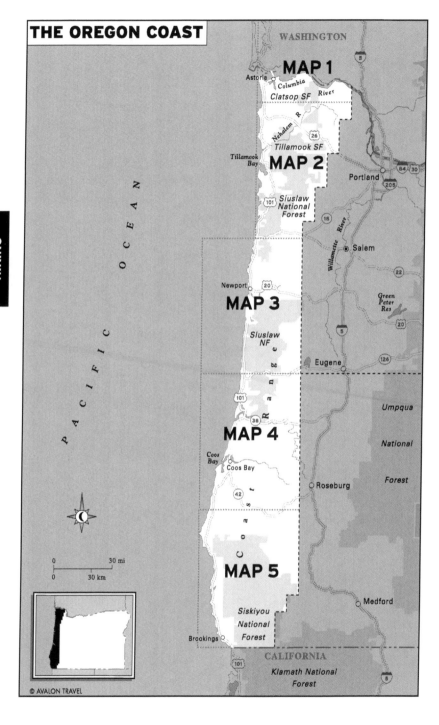

THE OREGON COAST

WASHINGTON

MAP 1

Astoria
Columbia River

Clatsop SF

Nehalem R.
26

Tillamook SF

Tillamook Bay

MAP 2

Portland

84 30

205

101 Siuslaw National Forest

18

Willamette River

Salem

22

Newport 20

MAP 3

Green Peter Res

20

Siuslaw NF

Range

Eugene

126

101

Umpqua

38

MAP 4

National

Coos Bay
Coos Bay

Forest

42

Roseburg

Coast

MAP 5

Medford

30 mi

30 km

Siskiyou National Forest

Brookings

CALIFORNIA

101

Klamath National Forest

© AVALON TRAVEL

PACIFIC OCEAN

Map 1

Hikes 1-2

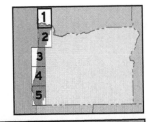

HIKING

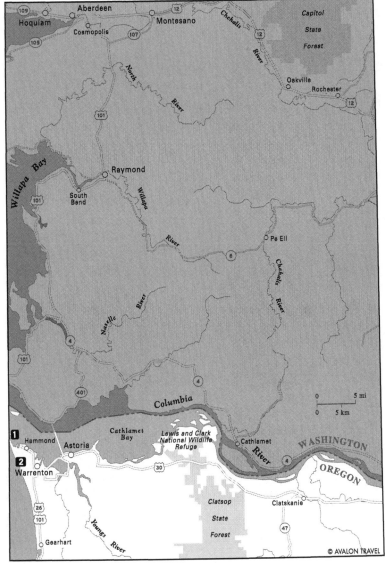

109
Aberdeen
Hoquiam
Cosmopolis
Montesano
12
Chehalis
12
Capitol
State
Forest
103
107
North
River
Oakville
Rochester
101
12
Willapa Bay
Raymond
101
South Bend
Willapa
River
Pe Ell
6
Chehalis River
River
Naselle
4
101
401
Columbia
4
0   5 mi
0   5 km
Hammond
Astoria
Cathlamet Bay
Lewis and Clark National Wildlife Refuge
Cathlamet
WASHINGTON
Warrenton
30
River
4
OREGON
26
101
Youngs River
Clatsop State Forest
Clatskanie
47
Gearhart

© AVALON TRAVEL

Map 2

Hikes 3-24

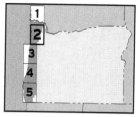

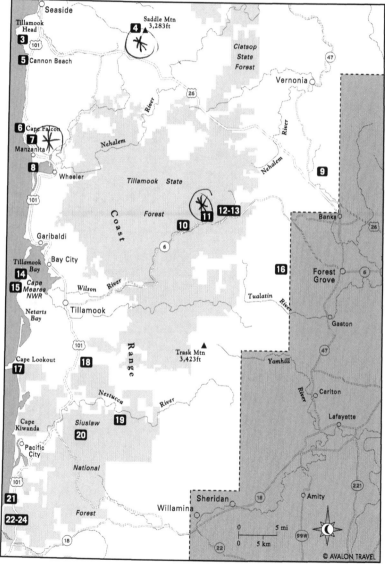

Seaside

Tillamook
Head
3
101

5 Cannon Beach

Saddle Mtn
4 ▲ 3,283ft

Clatsop
State
Forest

47

Vernonia

26

6 Cape Falcon
7
Manzanita

Nehalem

River

Nehalem

Nehalem

River

9

8

Wheeler

Tillamook   State

101

Forest

Banks

26

C o a s t

10

6

11 **12-13**

16

Forest
Grove

6

Garibaldi

Tillamook
Bay
14
15 Cape
Meares
NWR

Bay City

Wilson

River

Tualatin

River

Gaston

Netarts
Bay

Tillamook

101

R a n g e

Trask Mtn
▲ 3,423ft

47

Yamhill

Cape Lookout
17

18

Carlton

Lafayette

Cape
Kiwanda

Siuslaw

20

Nestucca

19

River

Pacific
City

National

221

101

21

99W

22-24

Forest

Willamina

Sheridan

18

Amity

18

22

0   5 mi
0   5 km

© AVALON TRAVEL

Map 3

Hikes 25-48

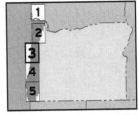

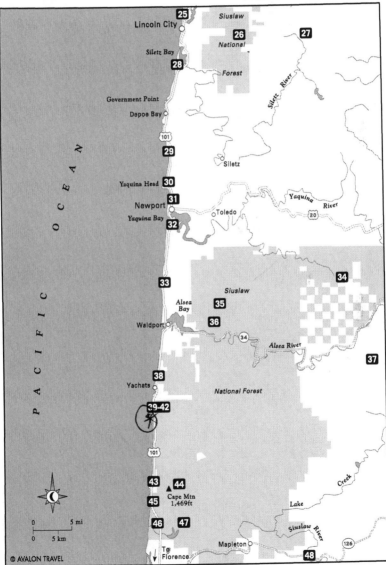

Map 4

Hikes 49-66

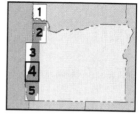

HIKING

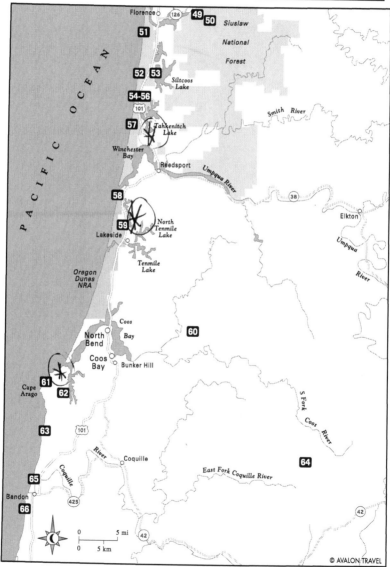

Map 5

Hikes 67-98

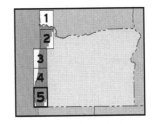

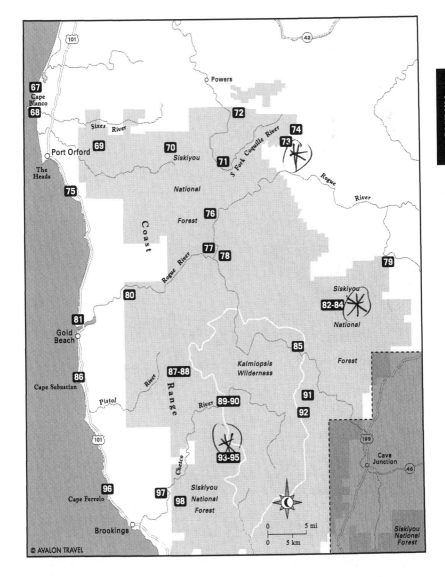

1 CLATSOP SPIT
4.5 mi/2.0 hr

on the Columbia River in Fort Stevens State Park

The Oregon coast begins at Clatsop Spit, where the Columbia River meets the Pacific Ocean. Here the fishing boats and towering barges butt their way inland, reckoning with the Columbia Bar and crazy tides. With all this water comes a lot of wildlife, too, and the Spit offers an easy way to see famous shorebirds. An easy hike begins in Area D of Fort Stevens State Park, with opportunities to get in a bit of both bird-watching and barge-watching, as enormous freighters and marine birds push against the tides and winds.

This easy exploration of the spit and the South Jetty begins at the Area D lot, with a short boardwalk leading to a bird blind overlooking Trestle Bay, an excellent place to spot coastal birds, and a trail leading through the dunes to the beach on the Columbia River. Follow the beach to the left for 2.3 miles to the massive jetty, then go left another 0.5 mile to a viewing platform. Continuing south along the top of the jetty 0.3 mile brings you to an X-junction; turn left here another 0.3 mile to the paved road, and follow it to the left, going 1.1 mile back to Area D.

User Groups: Hikers and dogs on leashes. No horses or mountain bikes. No wheelchair facilities.

Permits: Permits are not required. If you use the day-use area only, parking and access are free. Otherwise, a $3 day-use fee is collected at the camping entrance, or you can get an annual Oregon Parks and Recreation pass for $25; contact Oregon Parks and Recreation, 800/551-6949.

Maps: For a free park brochure, call Oregon Parks and Recreation, 800/551-6949, or download a free map at www.oregonstateparks. org. For a topographic map, ask the USGS for Clatsop Spit.

Directions: Drive south of Astoria on U.S. 101 for four miles and turn west at a sign for Fort Stevens State Park. Follow park signs for 4.9 miles, turning left at the day-use entrance. Drive at total of 3.9 miles, passing Battery Russell, to a fork. Go right to Area D.

Contact: Oregon Parks and Recreation Department, 1115 Commercial Street NE, Salem, OR, 97301, 800/551-6949, www.oregonstateparks.org.

2 FORT STEVENS STATE PARK
5.3 mi/2.5 hr

northwest of Astoria in Fort Stevens State Park

BEST (

The tip of the Oregon coast lies between the Pacific Ocean and the Columbia River, the "Gateway to the West," at least for ships. Explorers had been trying for years to find the elusive mouth of the Columbia, which more often than not was shrouded in fog. As you can imagine, this area was heavily guarded during World War II by no less than three military installations. Fort Stevens was in use for a total of 84 years, from the Civil War to the close of World War II. Today it is an 11-square-mile state park with campgrounds, miles of bike paths, a swimmable lake, and even the rusting remains of the *Peter Iredale*, a historic 1906 shipwreck. The network of paved trails makes it that much more accessible for everyone.

To begin your exploration, park in the loop lot for Battery Russell. Behind an exhibit board, climb a stairway and walk along the concrete bunkers, site of a battery that guarded the Columbia's mouth for 40 years. When you reach a sandy trail, follow it 1.3 miles, staying right at all junctions, to Picnic Area A and the loop trail around Coffenbury Lake. At the end of the loop, and to try a different way back, head to the nearby campground to the start of the Nature Trail behind campsite B5T. This 1.4-mile trail follows a creek and joins with a paved bike path, going left 0.2 mile back to the Battery Russell lot.

User Groups: Hikers and dogs on leashes.

Bikes on designated paths only. Paved paths are wheelchair accessible.

Permits: Permits are not required. If you use the day-use area only, parking and access are free. Otherwise, a $3 day-use fee is collected at the camping entrance, or you can get an annual Oregon Parks and Recreation pass for $25; contact Oregon Parks and Recreation, 800/551-6949.

Maps: For a free park brochure, call Oregon Parks and Recreation, 800/551-6949, or download a free map at www.oregonstateparks.org. For a topographic map, ask the USGS for Warrenton.

Directions: Drive south of Astoria on U.S. 101 for four miles and turn west at a sign for Fort Stevens State Park. Follow park signs for 4.9 miles, turning left at the day-use entrance. Drive one mile to Battery Russell.

Contact: Oregon Parks and Recreation Department, 1115 Commercial Street NE, Salem, OR, 97301, 800/551-6949, www.oregonstateparks.org.

🎦 TILLAMOOK HEAD

6.1 mi one-way/3.0 hr   🏃2   ⛰8

north of Cannon Beach in Ecola State Park

`BEST (`

The Oregon coast has some of the best state parks in Oregon, and this is by far one of the most scenic. The Tillamook Head, a remnant of a 15-billion-year-old Columbia River basaltic lava flow, rises over 1,000 feet above the Pacific Ocean, and it was on this headland that Lewis and Clark stood on their famous cross-country journey, their mission to find an overland route to the Pacific successful. In fact, they were crossing this head in 1806 to make their way down to nearby Cannon Beach to buy some blubber from a beached whale from some local Native Americans. No one said exploration was easy. You can re-create this journey, seeing things they never saw, like the abandoned military bunker and an unbelievable lighthouse on the island of

Tillamook Rock, which operated from 1881 to 1957. The only reason it is unmanned today is that winter storms tended to throw waves right over the top of the lighthouse. Today, it houses cremated remains taken ashore by helicopters. Consider bringing a backpack for this one—there's a handy camping area in a nook atop the head.

You can tour the entire head or take it in pieces. Start at the Ecola Point Picnic Area lot, where you can take a short walk out to the point to see a sea lion-populated rock. The hike begins in the trees at the edge of the lot, heading north on the Oregon Coast Trail. The first 1.5 miles breezes through some woods before dramatically following the cliffs over the ocean and dropping down to secluded Indian Beach, usually rife with surfers, which is a good turnaround for a short hike. If you continue on, the hike gets more difficult as it climbs 1.6 mile to a primitive campground (either on the road to the right or the trail to the left), complete with sheltered bunkhouses. From this camping area, follow a short trail toward the ocean for a look at the mossed-over bunkers. If you're up for more, you can continue as far as you like up the headland, but be ready to climb. The trail gains 200 feet in the next half-mile, then eases off for the next 2.1 miles to the summit. The remaining 1.7 miles of this stretch of the OCT descends to the beach at Seaside.

User Groups: Hikers and dogs on leashes only. No horses or mountain bikes permitted. No wheelchair facilities.

Permits: Permits are not required. A $3 day-use fee is collected at the camping entrance, or you can get an annual Oregon Parks and Recreation pass for $25; contact Oregon Parks and Recreation, 800/551-6949.

Maps: For a free park brochure, call Oregon Parks and Recreation, 800/551-6949 or download a free map at www.oregonstateparks.org. For a topographic map, ask the USGS for Tillamook Head.

Directions: From U.S. 101, take the north exit for Cannon Beach and follow Ecola State Park signs, keeping right for two miles to the entrance booth. To shuttle, drive north from the north exit to Cannon Beach on U.S. 101 toward Seaside for 5.8 miles. Turn left on Avenue U for 0.2 mile and take the first left on Edgewood Street for 0.4 mile. Continue on Edgewood Street until becomes Ocean Vista Drive, and follow it for 0.2 mile. Ocean Vista Drive turns into Sunset Boulevard. Follow Sunset Boulevard for 0.7 mile to its end at the trailhead.

Contact: Oregon Parks and Recreation Department, 1115 Commercial Street NE, Salem, OR, 97301, 800/551-6949, www.oregonstateparks.org.

© SEAN PATRICK HILL

Saddle Mountain

4 SADDLE MOUNTAIN
5.0 mi/3.0 hr

east of Seaside in Saddle Mountain State Natural Area

BEST (

Aptly named for its dipping peak, Saddle Mountain is the highest point in northwestern Oregon. It has a commanding 360-degree view reaching from the Pacific to five Cascade peaks ranging from Rainier to Jefferson. To earn that view, you must endure the difficult hike up a steep trail, though it is comforting to know that the trail has been drastically improved of late. On the other hand, the flower show here is famous: trilliums, bleeding hearts, goatsbeard, chocolate lily, candyflower, larkspur, Indian paintbrush, fawn lily, purple iris, and phlox are some of the 300-odd blooms you'll see along the trail, particularly in spring, and the peak offers refuge to the rare crucifer and Saddle Mountain bittercress, a mustard-family flower found virtually nowhere else on earth.

The first 0.2-mile portion of the Saddle Mountain Trail passes through an alder forest, passing a short side trail to the right that climbs 0.2 mile to a rocky viewpoint of the mountain itself—a worthy side trip. The next 1.1 miles climbs steeply up a series of switchbacks to the long wall of a basalt dike formed from lava poured into cracks in the ground and cooled, the ground having slowly eroded away around it leaving a wall that resembles stacked wood. The next 0.9 mile crosses the wild-flowered meadows populated by Ice Age species (stay on the trail) before reaching the saddle itself. The remaining 0.4 mile is a steep pitch lined with cables that ascends to an awe-inspiring viewpoint at the 3,283-foot peak, with vistas reaching as far as the Pacific Ocean, Cape Disappointment, the Columbia River, and the Cascades.

User Groups: Hikers and dogs on leash only. No horses or mountain bikes allowed. No wheelchair facilities.

Permits: Permits are not required. Parking and access are free.

Maps: For a topographic map, ask the USGS for Saddle Mountain.

Directions: From Portland, take U.S 26 west of Portland 66 miles and turn north at a state park sign. This winding, paved road climbs seven miles to its end at a picnic area and campground.

Contact: Oregon Parks and Recreation Department, 1115 Commercial Street NE, Salem, OR, 97301, 800/551-6949, www.oregonstateparks.org.

5 CANNON BEACH TO HUG POINT
8.6 mi/4.0 hr

in the Tolovana Beach State Recreation Site in Cannon Beach on the Pacific Ocean

BEST (

If you wonder why the town of Cannon Beach is so named, it dates back to 1846 when a Navy ship broke up crossing the infamous Columbia River bar. An entire piece of the deck, with the cannon mounted to it, washed ashore. The town is known especially for Haystack Rock, the 235-foot sea stack that ends up on quite a few calendars.

This stretch of beach was, for the longest time, the main travel route for motorists. Getting around Hug Point during even low tide required motorists to "hug" the cliff; they decided the easiest way around it was over it, and so they dynamited their own road into the sandstone. An easy beachside stroll visits all these points, plus other sea stacks, tidepools, and a waterfall pouring right onto the beach.

Start at the Haystack Rock Parking Area, within view of Haystack Rock. Head south along the sandstone cliffs for 1.2 miles to the Tovana Beach Wayside. For the next 1.8 miles, watch for a number of sea stacks, including Silver Point, Jockey Cap, and Lion Rock. Round Humbug Point, aptly named because it is not the fabled Hug Point, and arrive at the Arcadia Wayside. Continuing another 1.3 miles brings you to Hug Point itself, with its powder-blasted road, a cave, the falls of Fall Creek, and the Hug Point Wayside.

User Groups: Hikers, dogs, and horses. No wheelchair facilities.

Permits: Permits are not required. Parking and access are free.

Maps: For a topographic map, ask the USGS for Arch Cape.

Directions: From U.S. 101 take the southern Cannon Beach exit, heading west on East Sunset Boulevard 0.2 mile to Hemlock Street. Go right on Hemlock to the Haystack Rock parking area.

Contact: Oregon Parks and Recreation Department, 1115 Commercial Street NE, Salem, OR, 97301, 800/551-6949, www.oregonstateparks.org.

6 CAPE FALCON
5.0 mi/2.5 hr

south of Cannon Beach in Oswald West State Park

BEST (

Oswald West is a certain kind of hero in Oregon. As the 14th governor of Oregon, his lasting contribution was to designate the entire length of the Oregon coast as a public highway, thus forever protecting it from development. His legacy shows, in particular at the state park named for him. Dense with old-growth Sitka spruce forests, with Neahkahnie Mountain and Cape Falcon cupping the wide Smuggler Cove and a sandy beach, Oswald West State Park brings a hiker close to a coastal wilderness area. The Oregon Coast Trail goes either direction from Short Sands Beach: to the south, it climbs the cliffs and continues on to Neahkahnie Mountain (see *Neahkahnie Mountain* listing in this chapter), and to the north it climbs to raptor-shaped Cape Falcon.

For an easy exploration, follow Short Sand Creek from the parking area to the coast for 0.4 paved miles. If the view here isn't staggering enough, just wait. A moderate 2.1-mile trail following the OCT route leads up from the beach and into groves of Sitkas that rival the fabled redwoods. The trail skirts a cliff above the cove with views to lofty Neahkahnie Mountain. Watch for the side trail to the left

HIKING

HIKING

traveling 0.2 mile out the headland of rocky Cape Falcon, the peak a dense cover of leathery salal. This makes a good turnaround point, but to add another 2.4 miles on for more rewarding views, keep going up the OCT to three astonishing viewpoints of the wave-pounded inlets. When the trail begins to steeply ascend away from the ocean, turn back.

User Groups: Hikers, dogs, horses. No mountain bikes allowed. The paved trail to Short Sands Beach is wheelchair accessible.

Permits: Permits are not required. Parking and access are free.

Maps: For a free park brochure, call Oregon Parks and Recreation, 800/551-6949, or download a free map at www.oregonstateparks.org. For a topographic map, ask the USGS for Arch Cape.

Directions: Drive 10 miles south of Cannon Beach on U.S. 101. Park in the lot on the east side of the highway a bit south of milepost 39.

Contact: Oregon Parks and Recreation Department, 1115 Commercial Street NE, Salem, OR, 97301, 800/551-6949, www.oregonstateparks.org.

7 NEAHKAHNIE MOUNTAIN
3.0 mi/2.0 hr 🏃 ♿3 ⛺8

south of Cannon Beach in Oswald West State Park

Rising above the surf and breezy ocean air, Neahkahnie Mountain in Oswald West State Park is a panoramic dream. As far as climbing mountains goes, this one is fairly easy, at 1,600 feet above sea level, but enough of a haul to get your heart going. It was a coastal Indian tribe, probably the Tillamook, who named this peak to mean, roughly, "place of the gods." The hike can be extended, too, out onto a ridge with red huckleberry bushes that fan out overhead like green umbrellas, and if you're really daring, a descent down the west slope leads to Highway 101 and farther to an oceanic cliff-edge view of the Devil's Cauldron.

The hike follows the Oregon Coast Trail, an easy, single trail, that steeply switchbacks up the first 0.9 mile before leveling out on the wooded peak for 0.6 mile, arriving at the summit meadows and an easy view down to the town of Manzanita. Turning around here makes for a three-mile round-trip, though the trail continues down another two miles to Highway 101, where it crosses the roadway and continues about 100 yards to two good viewpoints over the rugged cliffs to the Pacific.

User Groups: Hikers and dogs. No mountain bikes or horses. No wheelchair facilities.

Permits: Permits are not required. Parking and access are free.

Maps: For a free park brochure, call Oregon Parks and Recreation, 800/551-6949, or download a free map at www.oregonstateparks.org. For a topographic map, ask the USGS for Nehalem.

Directions: Drive south of Cannon Beach on U.S. 101 about 13 miles to a brown hiker symbol between mileposts 41 and 42. Turn east onto a gravel road for 0.4 mile to a Trailhead Parking sign. The trail begins at a post.

Contact: Oregon Parks and Recreation Department, 1115 Commercial Street NE, Salem, OR, 97301, 800/551-6949, www.oregonstateparks.org.

8 NEHALEM BAY
5.2 mi/2.5 hr ♿1 ⛺6

south of Manzanita in Nehalem Bay State Park

BEST (

The beach that lies between Neahkahnie Mountain and Nehalem Spit has seen its share of bad luck: In 1913, a drunk captain steered the British *Glenesslin*, with an astoundingly inexperienced crew, into the nearby cliffs, and rumors still abound of a wrecked Spanish galleon heavy with treasure, most of which is believed to have been buried by survivors somewhere in the area. Needless to say, people are still looking for it. There's other treasure to be found here today in a trove of seals and seabirds along the Nehalem Spit. Formed by tidal patterns, the Oregon spits make for ideal wildlife-viewing, especially of seabirds. This hike visits two distinct zones: the beach and the bay, seemingly worlds apart.

From the Nehalem Bay State Park picnic area, head out along the ocean 2.3 miles to the North Jetty, and turn right for 0.5 mile to a beach where harbor seals tend to lay around and sun themselves. It's illegal to harass them, though they'll quickly disperse if you approach at all. Return along the bay for a 2.2-mile walk, turning left at the boat ramp for a quick 0.2-mile return to the picnic area.

User Groups: Hikers, dogs, and horses. Mountain bikes allowed on loop path only. A 1.5-mile loop is wheelchair accessible.

Permits: Permits are not required. A $3 day-use fee is collected at the entrance, or you can get an annual Oregon Parks and Recreation pass for $25; contact Oregon Parks and Recreation, 800/551-6949.

Maps: For a free park brochure, call Oregon Parks and Recreation, 800/551-6949, or download a free map at www.oregonstateparks.org. For a topographic map, ask the USGS for Nehalem.

Directions: From Manzanita, follow U.S 101 to milepost 44. Turn right on Necarney City Road and follow signs for two miles to Nehalem Bay State Park. Park at the picnic area after the fee booth

Contact: Oregon Parks and Recreation Department, 1115 Commercial Street NE, Salem, OR, 97301, 800/551-6949, www.oregonstateparks.org.

9 BANKS-VERNONIA RAILROAD

5.3 mi one-way/2.5 hr   🏃1 ⛰7

northwest of Portland in Banks Vernonia Linear Park

BEST (

Oregon has many fine examples of "rails-to-trails" paths, and this is certainly one of

them. Totaling 21 miles in all, the former grade of this 1920s Burlington-Northern Railroad Line used primarily for lumber and, later, excursion trains, has been converted to a great pathway through the Coast Range foothills. Though there are plenty of options for journeys along the old route, a good day trip can be made by going between two old wooden trestles, either as a longer hike or with a car shuttle. The trail can accommodate just about anyone on foot, horses, bikes, and wheelchair users.

Start at the Buxton Trestle just outside the town of Buxton. An easy loop explores the area around the trestle spanning Mendenhall Creek, which is now open to trail use. From there the trail stretches north 5.3 miles to a second trailhead beneath Horseshoe Trestle, which is not to be crossed—but is a good place for a shuttle. Along the way, you'll cross Logging and Williams Creeks and stay largely out of sight of Highway 43.

User Groups: Hikers, dogs, mountain bikes, and horses. Parts of the paved path are wheelchair accessible.

Permits: Permits are not required. Parking and access are free.

Maps: For a free park brochure, call Oregon Parks and Recreation, 800/551-6949, or download a free map at www.oregonstateparks.org. For a topographic map, ask the USGS for Buxton.

Directions: From Portland, drive 28 miles west on U.S. 26 and turn right on Fisher Road. In 0.7 mile, the road becomes Baconia Road and leads to the Buxton Trailhead on the right. To shuttle to the Horseshoe Trestle, return to Highway 47 and drive 5.5 miles north to the Tophill Trailhead on the left.

Contact: Oregon Parks and Recreation Department, 1115 Commercial Street NE, Salem, OR, 97301, 800/551-6949, www.oregonstateparks.org.

HIKING

HIKING

10 KINGS MOUNTAIN
5.4 mi/3.5 hr 🏃4 ⛰8

east of Tillamook in the Tillamook State Forest

Between 1933 and 1951, four massive fires swept through this area of the Coast Range in what is known as the Tillamook Burn. With the help of determined locals, an equally massive campaign was waged to replant the area into what is now the Tillamook State Forest. Kings Mountain bears both the scars of the fire (those emblematic snags testify to that) and also the regrowth capable with the help of humans and nature. This hike passes through that history and ultimately rises above it to views of the Wilson River Valley and the Cascade Mountains. Granted, this hike is difficult: You'll have to climb more than 2,500 feet in 2.5 miles, but because of the burned trees—known as "gray ghosts"—it makes for good views. You'll even pass a picnic table before the last pitch, and you can leave your name in a summit registry at the top. A 1.3-mile extension connects to nearby Elk Mountain, potentially making this a daunting day.

The first mile of the Kings Mountain Trail threads through red alder and maple woods and wildflowers and then steepens dramatically for the next 1.4 miles. At the top of the 2.7-mile climb is the 3,226-foot peak of Kings Mountain, having passed through meadows of summer beargrass plumes (a type of lily). This hike can be stretched to nearby pinnacles and Elk Mountain (see *Elk Mountain* listing in this chapter) but only for the exceptionally hardy. Otherwise, return as you came.

User Groups: Hikers and dogs only. No wheelchair facilities.

Permits: Permits are not required. Parking and access are free.

Maps: For a Tillamook Forest Visitor Map & Guide, contact the Forest Grove District Office, 503/357-2191, egov.oregon.gov/ODF/TSF/about_us.shtml. For a topographic map, ask the USGS for Rogers Peak.

Directions: From Portland, drive U.S. 26 west 20 miles to Highway 6. Go west on Highway 6 for 22 miles to the trailhead and parking area near milepost 25, on the north side of the road.

Contact: Tillamook State Forest, Forest Grove District Office, 801 Gales Creek Road, Forest Grove, OR, 97116, 503/357-2191, egov.oregon.gov/ODF/TSF/about_us.shtml.

11 ELK MOUNTAIN
3.0 mi/2.5 hr ✳ 🏃3 ⛰8

east of Tillamook in the Tillamook State Forest

Because the route to loop this hike with Kings Mountain can prove arduous, it is easiest to climb Elk Mountain by its own trail. Did I say "easy"? This is also a strenuous hike, but ultimately a rewarding one, with views on a clear day as far as the Pacific Ocean and Mounts Adams, Hood, and Jefferson, due in part to the massive Tillamook Burn that swept much of this mountain clear of living trees, leaving the ghostly white snags behind. This trail is narrower than Kings Mountain, gaining 1,900 feet in 1.5 miles.

Starting from the Elk Creek Campground, the Wilson River Trail heads 0.1 mile to the junction with the Elk Mountain Trail, which climbs steeply through alder forests and onto the rocky trail for 1.4 miles to the 2,788 peak. Be sure to watch your footing and wear good boots, as much of the trail can be loose scree. Crossing four saddles, as well as vaunting a false summit, you'll arrive at the peak, which bears white Washington lilies in spring.

User Groups: Hikers and dogs only. No wheelchair facilities.

Permits: Permits are not required. Parking and access are free.

Maps: For a Tillamook Forest Visitor Map & Guide, contact the Forest Grove District Office, 503/357-2191, egov.oregon.gov/ODF/TSF/about_us.shtml. For a topographic map, ask the USGS for Cochran.

Directions: From Portland, drive U.S. 26 west

20 miles to Highway 6. Go west on Highway 6 for 19 miles to the Elk Creek Campground near milepost 28, on the north side of the road. Turn right into the campground, driving 0.6 mile to the far end of the campground and crossing a bridge. The trailhead is behind the information board.

Contact: Tillamook State Forest, Forest Grove District Office, 801 Gales Creek Road, Forest Grove, OR, 97116, 503/357-2191, egov. oregon.gov/ODF/TSF/about_us.shtml.

12 GALES CREEK
3.6 mi/1.5 hr

east of Tillamook in the Tillamook State Forest

In the deep green forests of the Coast Range, Gales Creek glides swiftly in its bed. To find this creek from the highway, visiting two picturesque fern-draped creeks, begin at the Summit Trailhead and descend sharply on the Gales Creek Trail, following Low Divide Creek 1.9 miles along an old 1930s railroad grade to the Gales Creek Campground (which is suitable for picnics, as there are plenty of tables amidst the trees). Near the end of the trail, a spur trail to the left leads to the parking area and the Gales Creek Trail. Granted, the return trip to the highway will be uphill, a little more than 600 feet elevation gain, but either way this trail is remarkably wild in comparison to much of the devastation resulting from decades of forest fires.

Gales Creek, too, is entirely explorable, with a trail leading out of the campground and following Gales Creek up into the hills. Beginning from the junction with the Low Divide Creek Trail, head upstream 0.8 mile, staying right at a junction with the Storey Burn Trail. The remaining trail follows Gales Creek through forest for 5.2 miles farther, meeting Bell Camp Road; this section may be closed due to storm damage. Once open, you will be able to continue on another 3.4 miles from Bell Camp Road to the terminal trailhead at Reehers Camp.

User Groups: Hikers, dogs, and mountain bikes. Horses allowed on parts of Gales Creek Trail north of the campground. No wheelchair facilities.

Permits: Permits are not required. Parking and access are free.

Maps: For a Tillamook Forest Visitor Map & Guide, contact the Forest Grove District Office, 503/357-2191, egov.oregon.gov/ODF/TSF/about_us.shtml. For a topographic map, ask the USGS for Cochran and Timber.

Directions: From Portland, drive U.S. 26 west 20 miles to Highway 6. Go west on Highway 6 for 21 miles to milepost 33 at the Coast Range Summit. The parking area for Low Divide Creek and the Summit Trailhead is on the north side of the highway. To enter the Gales Creek Campground parking area, open mid-May through October, follow Highway 6 west of Portland 39 miles to a sign near milepost 35 reading "Gales Creek CG" and turn north through a yellow gate. If the gate is locked, park to the side and walk in 0.7 mile.

Contact: Tillamook State Forest, Forest Grove District Office, 801 Gales Creek Road, Forest Grove, OR, 97116, 503/357-2191, egov.oregon.gov/ODF/TSF/about_us.shtml.

13 UNIVERSITY FALLS
8.6 mi/4.5 hr

east of Tillamook in the Tillamook State Forest

Despite the massive Tillamook Fires—particularly the 1933 fire, which torched 240,000 acres—the forest has been reborn. Now there's second-growth Douglas fir, western hemlock, red alder, and red cedar, with a sturdy undergrowth of sword ferns, Oregon grape—the state flower—and leathery salal. Wildlife has returned; you can hear grouse on occasion in the underbrush. This loop, sometimes following an old wagon road, tours the reborn forest with University Falls as the destination high in the headwaters of the Wilson River. The 65-foot falls on Elliott Creek just southwest of the Coast Range summit suffers from off-road vehicle use, particularly the motorcycles whining in the distance. You'll leave them behind eventually on this small epic tour of the rain forest.

From the Rogers Camp RV parking area, briefly follow the Fire Break 1 road uphill to the Nels Rogers Trail. The first 1.3 miles crosses two roads and reaches a junction on the Devils Lake Fork of the Wilson River. Turn left over a footbridge, cross the creek, and turn left again, staying on Nels Rogers, which ends in 0.3 mile at the Beaver Dam Road and continues as the Wilson River Wagon Road Trail on the opposite side. This trail wanders three miles, crossing roads, ducking under power lines, crossing clear-cuts and Deyoe Creek, where you'll find a bench near a footbridge, before ending at University Falls Road and another trailhead. From here follow the Gravelle Brothers Trail, arriving in 0.4 mile at the wispy University Falls, where a left-hand junction comes to a viewpoint. To complete the loop, follow the Gravelle Trail two miles to an old road, going right toward Rogers Camp. Follow a gravel road to the right to the top of the hill and a maintenance shed. Go behind the cement barriers on the Elliott Creek OHV Trail, then follow Beaver Dam Road 0.2 miles back to the trailhead.

User Groups: Hikers, dogs, mountain bikes, horses. No wheelchair facilities.

Permits: Permits are not required. Parking and access are free.

Maps: For a Tillamook Forest Visitor Map & Guide, contact the Forest Grove District Office, 503/357-2191, egov.oregon.gov/ODF/TSF/about_us.shtml. For a topographic map, ask the USGS for Woods Point.

Directions: From Portland, drive U.S. 26 west 20 miles to Highway 6. Go west on Highway 6 for 21 miles to milepost 33 at the Coast Range Summit. Watching for signs to Rogers Camp, turn left on Beaver Dam Road and go 250 feet to a T-junction. Turn left 0.1 mile to the trailhead.

Contact: Tillamook State Forest, Forest Grove District Office, 801 Gales Creek Road, Forest Grove, OR, 97116, 503/357-2191, egov. oregon.gov/ODF/TSF/about_us.shtml.

14 BAYOCEAN SPIT
8.1 mi/4.0 hr

west of Tillamook in Cape Meares State Park

Cradling Tillamook Bay like a mother's arm, the Bayocean Spit is the site of a ghost town that is more ghost than town. The town formerly known as Bayocean, the "Atlantic City of the West," sold some 600 lots for excited resort types, in addition to having a bowling alley, hotel, dance hall, and grocery store. The developer apparently went mad one fateful night and disappeared. And that, as they say, was that. But what really did the town in was the construction of the South Jetty, which altered currents so that the town slowly eroded into the sea. Now it's a great place to spot wading birds in Tillamook Bay. Being a spit, you'll be able to enjoy both bird-watching and beach-strolling, and there is even the opportunity for camping. In the center of the spit, a large forested rock formation makes for a short cut and exploration, and makes a good turnaround point if you want to cut this hike in half.

Start out by following the old road for 1.6 miles. About halfway out, a well-marked trail cuts 0.5 mile through a forested bluff to the left. Follow this route to the beach, and head left 1.9 miles to the South Jetty. Watch for tufted puffins and brown pelicans. Continuing onward toward the bay for another 2.8 miles will bring you past Crab Harbor, a primitive campsite, and back to the beginning of the loop. Follow the road back 1.6 miles to your car.

User Groups: Hikers, dogs, horses. Bikes allowed on the old road. No wheelchair facilities.

Permits: Permits are not required. Parking and access are free.

Maps: For a topographic map, ask the USGS for Garibaldi.

Directions: From U.S 101 in downtown Tillamook, follow signs for Three Capes Scenic Route for seven miles. On the right, near a large wooden sign about Bayocean Spit, turn right on a gravel road along the dike for 0.9 mile to a parking area.

Contact: Oregon Parks and Recreation Department, 1115 Commercial Street NE, Salem, OR, 97301, 800/551-6949, www.oregonstateparks.org.

15 CAPE MEARES
0.6–4.0 mi/0.5–3.0 hr

west of Tillamook in Cape Meares State Park

Cape Meares is a great place to take the grandparents when they come for a visit. There are a number of short trails, making it easy to experience wonders like the historic lighthouse or the Octopus Tree, a giant Sitka spruce that has to be seen to be believed. But it is also a fine place to take a longer hike over a magnificent Oregon cape, visiting a 400-year-old, 16-foot-thick spruce and descending to a pleasant cove on the Pacific. Keep an eye on those cliffs, which are home to peregrine falcons. There's also the Three Arch Rocks, an offshore wildlife refuge home to common murres, black oystercatchers, Leach's storm-petrels, and pigeon guillemots.

For two easy hikes to the lighthouse and the Octopus Tree, start at the main parking lot on Cape Meares. The 0.4-mile round-trip to the lighthouse is paved and easy, and the 0.2-mile round-trip to the Octopus Tree is mostly level dirt but just as easy. For a more challenging hike on the Big Spruce Tree Trail, park at a small lot just before the entrance to the park off Three Capes Loop Drive. From here the trail quickly splits; 0.2 mile to the left is the giant spruce, and to the right a 0.9-mile descent, dropping 500 feet, to a cove on the ocean only passable at low tide. It's a good way to get down to the beach and watch for seabirds, and provides views out to Bayocean Spit.

User Groups: Hikers and dogs only. No horses or mountain bikes allowed. Paved portions of the park are wheelchair accessible.

Permits: Permits are not required. Parking and access are free.

Maps: For a free park brochure, call Oregon Parks and Recreation, 800/551-6949, or download a free map at www.oregonstateparks.org. For a topographic map, ask the USGS for Netarts.

Directions: From U.S 101 in downtown Tillamook follow signs for Three Capes Scenic Route for 10 miles. The park entrance is on the right. Follow the paved road 0.6 mile to a parking lot turnaround.

Contact: Oregon Parks and Recreation Department, 1115 Commercial Street NE, Salem, OR, 97301, 800/551-6949, www.oregonstateparks.org.

16 HAGG LAKE
13.1 mi/6.5 hr

southwest of Forest Grove in Scoggins Valley Park

Hagg Lake has been a destination for boaters and fishermen since 1975, when the Scoggins Valley Dam was built. Now hikers can get in on Hagg's unique landscape and spend anywhere from an hour to an entire day exploring the lake's weaving inlets and meadows from a plethora of access points. There are a number of creeks tumbling over smooth rock beds, and a variety of forest types from Douglas fir to white oak. Watch for poison oak along some trails. Also be aware that at times the trail joins the road for short intervals. All trails are marked by posts and along the way there are opportunities to stop at picnic areas and explore side creeks in shaded coves.

Should you decide to have a go at the entire 13.1-mile loop, you can start from the "free parking" lot by climbing the earth dam to the road, and following it to the left for 0.8 mile past a fishing dock to a lot where the official shoreline trail begins. The first 3.6 miles to Boat Ramp "C" crosses long span footbridges and scenic picnic areas. The next 1.3 miles follows the lake well past the "buoy line," thus moving away from the motorized boats and into the quieter areas of the park. The trail follows the road 0.6 mile over Scoggins Creek and another picnic area, then follows the lake 3.7 miles through grasslands and forest, over Tanner Creek and out to a grassy promontory on the lake. The remaining 3.1 miles returns along the north shore to the dam, passing more picnic areas and Boat Ramp "A."

User Groups: Hikers, dogs, and mountain bikes. Horses are not allowed. There is wheelchair access on some trails, boat ramps, and picnic areas.

Permits: Permits are not required. A $5 day-use fee is collected at the park entrance unless parking at the free parking lot beside the fee booth.

Maps: For a map, contact Washington County Facilities Management, 169 North 1st Avenue, MS 42, Hillsboro, OR, 97124, 503/846-8715. For a topographic map, ask the USGS for Gaston.

Directions: From Portland, drive U.S. 26 west 20 miles to Highway 6. Go west on Highway 6 for 2.3 miles and take the ramp for NW OR-47, following this highway south for 12.2 miles. Turn right at SW Scoggins Valley Road for 3.2 miles to the park.

Contact: Washington County Facilities Management, 169 North 1st Avenue, MS 42, Hillsboro, OR, 97124, 503/846-8715.

⓱ CAPE LOOKOUT

5.0 mi/2.5 hr   🏃2 ⛺9

south of Tillamook in Cape Lookout State Park

Of all the capes on the Oregon coast, this one stands out by sheer length: it extends two full miles to sea like an accusing finger, making it one of the best places to whale-watch and, of course, hike. Numerous viewpoints scan north, south, and west, including one viewpoint over the spot where a patrolling B-17 bomber crashed into the cliffs on a foggy 1943 day. You'll see Cape Kiwanda, Cape Foulweather, the Cascade Head, and Cape Meares from this promontory—all on a single trail that boasts enormous trees and boggy microclimates. The destination is a sheer cliff viewpoint where the shoreline tidal sounds are a distant echo.

Beginning at the main parking area, take the left-hand Cape Lookout Trail (the right descends 2.3 miles to the day-use area on Netarts Spit) and just ahead stay straight at a second junction (this left-hand trail descends two miles to a beach) and continue 2.5 miles overland, descending into a hollow and back up and crossing several wooden bridges. The trail can be muddy. At the tip of the cape, the ocean hovers 400 feet below, and the surf against the mainland is a distant white noise. Each year, 20,000 gray whales migrate around this cape between December and June. Return as you came.

User Groups: Hikers and dogs. No mountain bikes or horses allowed. No wheelchair facilities.

Permits: Permits are not required. A $3 day-use fee is collected at the camping entrance, or you can get an annual Oregon Parks and Recreation pass for $25; contact Oregon Parks and Recreation, 800/551-6949.

Maps: For a free park brochure, call Oregon Parks and Recreation, 800/551-6949, or download a free map at www.oregonstateparks.org. For a topographic map, ask the USGS for Sand Lake.

Directions: From Tillamook, drive 3rd Street west following signs for Cape Lookout State Park for 13 miles. Head 2.7 miles past the campground turnoff to the trailhead lot on the right.

Contact: Oregon Parks and Recreation Department, 1115 Commercial Street NE, Salem, OR, 97301, 800/551-6949, www.oregonstateparks.org.

18 MUNSON CREEK FALLS
0.6 mi/0.25 hr   🏃₁ ⛰₇

south of Tillamook in Munson Creek State
Natural Site

At 366 feet, the five-tiered Munson Creek Falls, named for early pioneer Goran Munson, is the tallest in the Coast Range. Munson settled near here, coming all the way from Michigan in 1889. Today, visitors have easy access and a short walk through old-growth Western red cedars and Sitka spruce to see the falls, and even eat from a picnic table viewpoint. At the right time of year, you may see salmon spawning here. In fact, these trails are good any time of year, even winter when ice crystallizes around the falls.

The 0.3-mile trail begins in Munson Creek State Natural Site and follows an easy path to the falls. Along the way, the trail is shaded by a variety of trees, hung heavy with mosses and lichens. The gravel path makes this one good for a good family trip.

User Groups: Hikers and dogs. No wheelchair facilities.

Permits: Permits are not required. Parking and access are free.

Maps: For a topographic map, ask the USGS for Beaver.

Directions: Drive south of Tillamook eight miles on U.S. 101. Just before milepost 73, turn left at a sign for Munson Creek Falls, following a paved road for one mile and forking right on a 0.4-mile gravel road to a small turnaround lot.

Contact: Oregon Parks and Recreation Department, 1115 Commercial Street NE, Salem, OR, 97301, 800/551-6949, www.oregonstateparks.org.

19 NIAGARA FALLS
2.0 mi/1.0 hr   🏃₁ ⛰₇

southeast of Tillamook in the Siuslaw National Forest

Well, it may not be as grand as *the* Niagara Falls we all know, but then *those* Niagara Falls don't plunge 107 feet over a magnificent lava wall into a lush box canyon of vine maples and yellow monkeyflower, either. Sometimes, smaller is better. This trail also passes shimmering Pheasant Creek Falls, another 112-foot cascade, along the way. This easy one-mile trail crosses a gurgling creek several times to a picnic table overlooking the amphitheatre wall over which the falls pour. The trail makes use of four wooden bridges and an observation deck overlooking the lush creeks.

User Groups: Hikers and dogs. No wheelchair facilities.

Permits: Permits are not required. Parking and access are free.

Maps: For a map of the Siuslaw National Forest, contact the Siuslaw National Forest headquarters, 4077 SW Research Way, P.O. Box 1148, Corvallis, OR, 97339, 541/750-7000. For a topographic map, ask the USGS for Niagara Creek.

Directions: Drive U.S. 101 south of Tillamook 15 miles to the village of Beaver near milepost 80. Turn east on Blaine Road for 6.7 miles. At Blaine Junction, turn right on Upper Nestucca River Road for 5.8 miles to Forest Service Road 8533. Go south on this road 4.3 miles to FS 8533-131. Turn right at the junction and continue 0.7 mile to the trailhead.

Contact: Siuslaw National Forest, Hebo Ranger District, 31525 Highway 22, Hebo, OR, 97122, 503/392-5100.

HIKING

HIKING

🔟 MOUNT HEBO
6.5 mi/4.0 hr   🏃2 ⛰7

east of Pacific City in the Siuslaw National Forest

The Pioneer-Indian Trail is so named because this trail, if you can believe it, was the first developed route between the Willamette Valley and the Tillamook Valley. Why wouldn't you believe it? Because this is a mountain, and one tall enough to be buried in snow, a rarity for these elevations so close to the ocean and sea level. Native Americans first used it, likely figuring it easier to cross this meadow plateau rather than fighting through the deep forests. Later, Hiram Smith and some Tillamook settlers improved the trail in 1854. This route remained the main thoroughfare over the Coast Range until a new wagon road was built in 1882. The trail went forgotten until the Forest Service reopened it as an 8-mile trail over Mount Hebo. This 3,174-foot summit commands a view of the Coast Range, extending to the Cascade volcanoes from Rainier to Jefferson. And, of course, the Pacific Ocean. Locals say the best time to see the view is late summer, though even the valleys may be bottomed out in fog. All this is likely what helps designate the area as the Mount Hebo Special Interest Area.

Starting at a signboard at Hebo Lake, the Pioneer-Indian Trail climbs 2.9 miles, crossing both a gravel road and a meadow of bracken fern, which can grow to five feet tall, before reaching a saddle and Road 14. Cross the road and take a side trail on an abandoned road to the right leading 0.3 mile up to the peak. Here there was once a Cold War–era radar station, but now only a bulldozed site surrounded by steep meadows of edible thimbleberry. For those in the mood for a 16-mile day, the Pioneer-Indian Trail continues along the plateau, paralleling Road 14 to a primitive campground before descending to North and South Lakes.

User Groups: Hikers, dogs, and horses.

Mountain bikes not allowed. The trail around Hebo Lake is wheelchair accessible.

Permits: Permits are not required. A federal Northwest Forest Pass is required to park here; the cost is $5 a day or $30 for an annual pass. You can buy a day pass at the trailhead, at ranger stations, or through private vendors.

Maps: For a map of the Siuslaw National Forest, contact the Siuslaw National Forest headquarters, 4077 SW Research Way, P.O. Box 1148, Corvallis, OR, 97339, 541/750-7000. For a topographic map, ask the USGS for Niagara Creek and Hebo.

Directions: Drive U.S. 101 south of Tillamook 19 miles to Hebo and turn east on Highway 22 for 0.3 mile. Turn left at a sign for Hebo Lake just before the Hebo Ranger Station. Follow Road 14 for 4.7 miles, taking the right-hand fork at the Hebo Lake campground entrance. Keep right for 0.2 mile to the trailhead parking area. From November to mid-April, the campground is gated closed, so you'll need to walk in 0.2 mile to the trailhead.

Contact: Siuslaw National Forest, Hebo Ranger District, 31525 Highway 22, Hebo, OR, 97122, 503/392-5100.

🔢 KIWANDA BEACH AND PORTER POINT
9.2 mi/3.5 hr   🏃3 ⛰7

at Neskowin on the Pacific Ocean

It's always interesting to see the estuaries where a coastal river flows into the ocean; sometimes they argue, each pushing against the other, creating a unique landscape amenable to birds and other wildlife. This lovely beach trek heads up Kiwanda Beach to the mouth of the Nestucca River. Along the way it passes climbable Proposal Rock, where an 1800s sea captain was said to have rowed his beloved to ask her hand, and continues to the cliffs of Porter Point and the river mouth opposite the Nestucca Spit.

From the Neskowin Wayside, hike 0.3 mile along Neskowin Creek to Proposal Rock. To the south, the Cascade Head looms up. Hike 3.3 miles along a sandy beach to the base of Winema Road and Camp Winema. From there, it is one mile to the mouth of the Nestucca. Return as you came.

User Groups: Hikers, dogs, and horses. No wheelchair facilities.

Permits: Permits are not required. Parking and access are free.

Maps: For a topographic map, ask the USGS for Neskowin.

Directions: Drive south of Tillamook on U.S. 101 for 33 miles and turn west at a "Neskowin" pointer. Head straight about 100 yards to the Neskowin Wayside.

Contact: Oregon Parks and Recreation Department, 1115 Commercial Street NE, Salem, OR, 97301, 800/551-6949, www.oregonstateparks.org.

22 HARTS COVE
5.4 mi/2.5 hr   🥾3   ⛰9

on Cascade Head in the Siuslaw National Forest

The Cascade Head is a unique landform, a massive headland rising above the ocean like a fortress, capped with forests and swaths of meadow. Harts Cove is a trek that requires you to climb down 900 feet, and then back up, to see the spectacle. It's worth it: With views of the Cascade Head's jaggy cliffs, the Chitwood Creek waterfall plunging into a towering ocean cove, and a Sitka spruce and western hemlock forest, you'll see what the fuss is about. But note that the road to the trailhead is closed from January 1 to July 15 to protect endangered butterflies and rare wildflowers that thrive here. This area is part of the Cascade Head Scenic Research Area for just this reason.

Harts Cove Trail begins from the road on a series of switchbacks dropping 0.7 mile to Cliff Creek then meanders through the forest of giants another 1.4 miles before reaching a bench looking down to Harts Cove's head. Continue on the main trail 0.5 mile to Chitwood Creek, then another 0.6 mile to a former homestead meadow. A path on the left overlooks Harts Cove and its waterfall. Like many places on the coast, you can sometimes hear the sea lions barking below.

User Groups: Hikers and dogs. No horses or mountain bikes allowed. No wheelchair facilities.

Permits: Permits are not required. Parking and access are free.

Maps: For a map of the Siuslaw National Forest, contact the Siuslaw National Forest headquarters, 4077 SW Research Way, P.O. Box 1148, Corvallis, OR, 97339, 541/750-7000. For a topographic map, ask the USGS for Neskowin.

Directions: From the junction of U.S. 101 and Highway 18 north of Lincoln City, drive north on 101 for 4 miles. Just before the crest, turn left on Cascade Head Road (Road 1861) and follow Hart's Cove signs down this 4.1-mile gravel road to road's end.

Contact: Siuslaw National Forest, Hebo Ranger District, 31525 Highway 22, Hebo, OR, 97122, 503/392-5100.

23 CASCADE HEAD INLAND TRAIL
6.0 mi one-way/3.0 hr   🥾2   ⛰6

north of Lincoln City in Cascade Head Experimental Forest

The Cascade Head is a veritable museum, preserved and protected from development because of its unique ecosystem and importance to education and study. The inland trail over the head does not visit the ocean, but certainly does tour the rainforests of coastal Oregon. A path leads into the Cascade Head Experimental Forest, an area studied by foresters since 1934. It shelters a grove of six-foot-thick Sitka spruce on the headwater springs of Calkins Creek, but it's a less-traveled trail because of its lack of views. Check with the Siuslaw National Forest before heading out, as this trail may be closed due to tree hazards.

From the trailhead at Three Rocks Road, the path switchbacks up a hill of elderberry, salmonberry, and thimbleberry. The Sitka grove is 2.9 miles along the trail where a boardwalk path crosses a marsh of skunk cabbage. In another 0.7 mile the trail meets Road 1861. Go right 100 yards to find the remainder of the trail, a 2.4-mile stretch that ends at U.S. 101.

User Groups: Hikers and dogs. No horses or mountain bikes allowed. No wheelchair facilities.

Permits: Permits are not required. Parking and access are free.

Maps: For a map of the Siuslaw National Forest, contact the Siuslaw National Forest headquarters, 4077 SW Research Way, P.O. Box 1148, Corvallis, OR, 97339, 541/750-7000. For a topographic map, ask the USGS for Neskowin.

Directions: From the junction of U.S. 101 and Highway 18 north of Lincoln City, drive north on U.S. 101 for one mile and turn left on Three Rocks Road and immediately park on the right by a trail sign. To shuttle, continue north on U.S. 101 toward Neskowin for about five miles and park at a trailhead sign on the left, one mile south of Neskowin on U.S. 101.

Contact: Siuslaw National Forest, Hebo Ranger District, 31525 Highway 22, Hebo, OR, 97122, 503/392-5100.

24 CASCADE HEAD NATURE CONSERVANCY TRAIL

3.4 mi/1.5 hr   🏃2 ⛰8

north of Lincoln City in Cascade Head Preserve

The steep and undulating meadows atop Cascade Head are the home of a rare

the Pacific Ocean from Cascade Head

© SEAN PATRICK HILL

checkermallow and an equally rare caterpillar of the Oregon silverspot butterfly. Because of this, this trail is considered a delicate area, and with the support of locals, the area was purchased by the non-profit Nature Conservancy. The road to the upper trailhead is closed from January 1 to July 15 to protect this fragile habitat, but the lower trailhead is open year-round. Be sure to stay on the trail and respect nature, and pay attention to seasonal closure signs. The trail is steep at times, but the expansive views are rewarding beyond belief—the ocean surges forth hundreds of feet below, and the coastline stretches out to the south as far as the eye can see.

From the boat ramp trailhead, follow the trail along the Three Rocks Road then uphill along Savage Road for 0.6 mile, passing the Sitka Arts Center. From this road, the well-marked trail climbs steadily through old-growth spruce and over several creeks for 1.1 miles to the first viewpoint down to the Salmon River estuary and Cape Foulweather. The next 0.6 mile to the top is breathtaking—both for its views and for its steepness. A marker points out the actual peak at 1,200 feet; relax and enjoy the view and the play of light on the surf in the distance. From here, the trail continues an easy mile through more woods to the trailhead on the 1861 road.

User Groups: Hikers and horses. Mountain bikes and dogs are not allowed. No wheelchair facilities.

Permits: Permits are not required. Parking and access are free.

Maps: For a map of the Siuslaw National Forest, contact the Siuslaw National Forest headquarters, 4077 SW Research Way, P.O. Box 1148, Corvallis, OR, 97339, 541/750-7000. For a topographic map, ask the USGS for Neskowin.

Directions: From the junction of U.S. 101 and Highway 18 north of Lincoln City, drive north on 101 for one mile and turn left on Three Rocks Road and immediately park on the right by a trail sign.

Contact: Siuslaw National Forest, Hebo Ranger District, 31525 Highway 22, Hebo, OR, 97122, 503/392-5100.

25 ROADS END WAYSIDE
2.8 mi/1.5 hr 🏃1 △6

north of Lincoln City on the Pacific Ocean

BEST (

An easy stroll along the beach from the hidden town of Roads End leads 1.4 miles north to rough basalt cliffs and tidepools alive with barnacles, sea stars, and anemones. This is a great hike for kids, who'll enjoy poking around the lakes of seawater in the bowls of black rock. You might even see a few old guys panning for gold. If the tide is low, make your way farther north to a secret cove where stones of just about every color are washed up alongside polished agates on the beach in droves. The entire cove is hemmed in by rugged sea stacks and overhanging cliffs—there's even a cave to

poke around in. Bring the kids; they'll stay entertained for a long time. Just be sure to check the tide charts, since isolated spots like this can quickly become inundated with waves. Go at low tide and be safe.

User Groups: Hikers, dogs, and horses. No wheelchair facilities.

Permits: Permits are not required. Parking and access are free.

Maps: For a topographic map, ask the USGS for Neskowin OE W.

Directions: From Lighthouse Square on U.S. 101 in Lincoln City, turn onto Logan Road and follow it one mile to Roads End Wayside.

Contact: Oregon Parks and Recreation Department, 1115 Commercial Street NE, Salem, OR, 97301, 800/551-6949, www.oregonstateparks.org.

26 DRIFT CREEK FALLS
3.0 mi/1.5 hr 🏃1 △7

east of Lincoln City in the Siuslaw National Forest

It's all about the numbers: Here you can overlook a 75-foot horsetail waterfall from a 240-foot-long swaying suspension bridge hung 100 feet over Drift Creek. Sound perilous? It's actually quite easy, a three-mile walk through ferns, salal, red huckleberry, and vine maple. The best time to go is in the spring and fall when the rains have powered the flow, making for a great show in this rain-forested chasm. The bridge itself is one of the more popular features of the trail, and in and of itself is an engineering marvel. Whether you dare to step foot on it is entirely up to you.

The first mile on the Drift Creek Falls Trail is an easy descent through forest to a 20-foot creek crossing. In the next 0.3 mile, the trail briefly traverses an old clear-cut before entering an old-growth grove and reaching the suspension bridge. The last 0.2 mile heads down to the waterfall's misty pool.

User Groups: Hikers and dogs. Part of the gravel trail is wheelchair accessible.

Permits: Permits are not required. A federal Northwest Forest Pass is required to park here; the cost is $5 a day or $30 for an annual pass. You can buy a day pass at the trailhead, at ranger stations, or through private vendors.

Maps: For a map of the Siuslaw National Forest, contact the Siuslaw National Forest headquarters, 4077 SW Research Way, P.O. Box 1148, Corvallis, OR, 97339, 541/750-7000. For a topographic map, ask the USGS for Devils Lake.

Directions: From Lincoln City, follow Highway 101 south of town to milepost 119 and turn east on Drift Creek Road for 1.5 miles, turn right at a T-junction and go 0.3 mile to another fork, heading uphill to the left onto Road 17/Drift Creek Camp Road. After 0.8 mile, turn uphill to the left. Go 9.1 miles to a large parking area on the right.

Contact: Siuslaw National Forest, Hebo Ranger District, 31525 Highway 22, Hebo, OR, 97122, 503/392-5100.

27 VALLEY OF THE GIANTS
4.7 mi/2.0 hr ﷯1 ﷯7

west of Falls City in the Coast Range

BEST (

At one point, Oregon was renowned for its old-growth trees. Nowadays finding a trail that really brings out the big guys is not as easy as it was, say, 100 years ago. Though the drive to the Valley of the Giants requires navigating a maze of old logging roads, the end is an easy trail through some of Oregon's oldest and largest trees. This 51-acre forest preserve receives more than 180 inches of rain a year, and it shows. Douglas firs and Western hemlocks dominate the sky here. In spring and early summer, marbled murrelets roost high in these trees but build no nests, instead laying their eggs on flat branches a good 150 feet above the forest floor. They spend the rest of their lives at sea, but stands of trees like this are crucial to the birds' survival. To get here, it is crucial to get the directions right, and it is in your best interest to call the BLM's Salem District Office (503/375-5646). The route is best traveled on weekends to avoid log truck traffic.

Begin your descent into 450-year-old trees following the Valley of the Giants Trail 0.4 mile, crossing the river on a six-foot thick log. The main portion of the trail loops 0.7 mile through the area's biggest and most impressive stand of Oregon-style old-growth and wildflowers. Go right or left, either way you'll miss nothing.

User Groups: Hikers and dogs. No wheelchair facilities.

Permits: Permits are not required. Parking and access are free.

Maps: For a topographic map, ask the USGS for Warnicke Creek.

Directions: From the intersection of U.S. 99 West and OR 22, follow signs for Dallas for four miles. From Dallas, follow signs nine miles to Falls City. At the far end of town, curve left across a bridge onto Bridge Street, which becomes gravel in 0.7 mile, then becomes a one-lane log road. A total of 14.9 miles from Falls City, the road turns left at a locked gate with a Keep Out sign. At another 200 yards past this gate, turn right at a T-junction. Travel 8.2 miles past this gate, keeping right around an old lakebed, until you reach a wooden bridge over the South Fork Siletz River. At 0.2 mile past the bridge, head uphill to the right. In another 0.3 mile, go left at a fork. For the remaining 4.9 rough and potholed miles, keep left at all junctions to a bridge over the North Fork Siletz River. Continue 1.1 miles to a fork, going right 0.5 mile to the trailhead.

Contact: Bureau of Land Management, Salem District Office, 1717 Fabry Road SE, Salem, OR, 97306, 503/375-5646.

28 SALISHAN SPIT
8.0 mi/4.0 hr

north of Gleneden Beach on the Pacific Ocean

Of all the sandy peninsulas in Oregon, the "spits" that guard the bays of every coastal river mouth, only the Salishan Spit has been developed for houses. Well, actually it's a resort. Though storms threatened the stability of this community and did indeed do some damage, the land has been stabilized. Why hike here? Because people aren't the only inhabitants: Harbor seals and sea otters frequent the more wild tip of the spit, away from the everyday human world. Views extend to the Cascade Head in the north and up to a gaggle of strange houses lining the ocean.

From the Gleneden Beach Wayside, a short paved trail leads down the sandstone bluffs to the beach. From here head north—that is, to the right—up the beach for a casual four-mile walk to the tip of the Salishan Spit. Be prepared for a moderately difficult hike not only for the distance, but because you'll be walking through sand.

User Groups: Hikers, dogs, and horses. No wheelchair facilities.

Permits: Permits are not required. Parking and access are free.

Maps: For a topographic map, ask the USGS for Lincoln City.

Directions: Head south from Lincoln City on U.S. 101 about 3.8 miles and turn west on Wessler Street at a sign for Gleneden Beach State Park, driving 0.2 mile to the parking lot.

Contact: Oregon Parks and Recreation Department, 1115 Commercial Street NE, Salem, OR, 97301, 800/551-6949, www.oregonstateparks.org.

29 DEVILS PUNCH BOWL
4.1 mi/2.0 hr

north of Newport in Devils Punch Bowl State Natural Area

Surfers, tidepools, whale-watching, and thundering tides pounding into a series of sea caves beneath Otter Rock. Need I say more? There's a lot to see at the Devils Punch Bowl, and a number of ways to do it. An easy hike out the headland, a short saunter to its base within view of the Marine Gardens, and a hike down Beverly Beach are all possibilities at this state wayside. Winter storms are a great time to visit, as the ocean becomes vehement as it crashes into the sea-carved bowl, thundering and exploding like the devil himself. From the town of Newport, you can also spend some time on nearby Beverly Beach, going from violent to mellow in the space of a mile.

The first easy hike (0.3 mile round-trip) begins from the day-use lot and heads to a picnic area atop the rock. From a fenced overlook, you can see the churning Punch Bowl, waves pounding against sandstone and basalt. The second hike (0.4 mile one-way) goes down to the Punch Bowl itself and a series of tidepools called the Marine Gardens. To get here, return to the lot and walk C Street for two blocks to a Dead End sign and take the trail to the left to a hidden beach. Be sure to try this one at low tide, when anemones, mussels, and starfish are revealed. At the southern edge of the beach, at low tide you can slip into two caves. To access Beverly Beach, return to the lot and cross the road to a long staircase descending Otter Rock to a 1.5-mile walk along the beach to Spencer Creek.

User Groups: Hikers and dogs. No wheelchair facilities.

Permits: Permits are not required. Parking and access are free.

Maps: For a topographic map, ask the USGS for Newport North.

Directions: Drive north of Newport eight miles on U.S. 101 to the turnoff for the Otter

HIKING

Crest Loop between mileposts 132 and 133. Follow signs 0.7 mile to the day-use parking area.

Contact: Oregon Parks and Recreation Department, 1115 Commercial Street NE, Salem, OR, 97301, 800/551-6949, www.oregonstateparks.org.

30 YAQUINA HEAD LIGHTHOUSE
0.1-2.6 mi/0.25-1.0 hr 🏃1 ⛰7

north of Newport on Yaquina Head

With a name like Yaquina Head Outstanding Natural Area, it ought to be good. With a historic 1873 lighthouse, whale-watching opportunities, colonies of seals, and views to seabird-populated Colony Rock, it really is one-of-a-kind. Five trails in all explore the head, with an interpretive center and viewpoints suitable for binoculars and cameras.

The centerpiece, of course, is the 93-foot lighthouse, the tallest in Oregon. The 200-yard paved Yaquina Head Lighthouse Trail

leads to its base. This trail begins at the parking area located at the end of Lighthouse Drive, where the 0.4-mile Salal Hill Trail also begins. From the Quarry Cove parking area, the Quarry Cove Trail dives down 0.5 mile to a series of low-tide tidepools and the 0.5-mile Communications Hill Trails climbs to excellent viewpoints. There's even a stairway leading down to Cobble Beach. Bring a picnic and spend a day here.

User Groups: Hikers and mountain bikes. No dogs or horses allowed. There is wheelchair access to the tidepools.

Permits: Permits are not required. A $7 day-use fee is collected at the camping entrance, or you can get an annual Yaquina Head Vehicle Pass for $15; contact Bureau of Land Management, Salem District Office, 503/375-5646.

Maps: For a brochure and map, contact the Bureau of Land Management, 503/375-5646, or download a free map and brochure at www.blm.gov/or/resources/recreation/picbrochures.php. For a topographic map, ask the USGS for Newport North.

Directions: From Newport, drive two miles north on U.S. 101 to the park entrance. All

Yaquina Head Lighthouse

© SEAN PATRICK HILL

trailheads start from the parking areas and are well labeled.

Contact: Bureau of Land Management, Salem District Office, 1717 Fabry Road SE, Salem, OR, 97306, 503/375-5646.

31 NYE AND AGATE BEACH
4.0 mi one-way/2.0 hr   🥾2 ⛰6

in Newport on the Pacific Ocean

The 93-foot Yaquina Head Lighthouse is not the original lighthouse for this area; in fact, it is the Yaquina Bay Lighthouse that originally steered ships into the bay at Newport. This unique lighthouse is actually a lighthouse atop a house, making for an easy workday for past lighthouse keepers. You can visit this lighthouse and explore two beaches divided by an eroded sea stack called Jumpoff Joe; it used to have an arch beneath it, but it's been worn away by the surging tides.

Beginning from the Yaquina Bay Lighthouse picnic area, head down the stone steps to the North Jetty and views of the massive Yaquina Bay Bridge. Head to the right, going as far as you like. After 1.8 miles, you'll reach Jumpoff Joe, a good turnaround point. If you're up for more, continue along the 2.2-mile stretch of Agate Beach, so named for its abundance of agates and jaspers washed up by the tides, especially in winter.

User Groups: Hikers, dogs, and horses. No wheelchair facilities.

Permits: Permits are not required. Parking and access are free.

Maps: For a topographic map, ask the USGS for Newport North.

Directions: From the north end of Newport's Yaquina Bay Bridge (U.S. 101), follow state park signs to a picnic area at the Yaquina Bay Lighthouse. To shuttle from the Agate Beach State Wayside, drive 2.2 miles north of Yaquina Bay State Park on U.S. 101. Turn left on NW 26th Street for 0.2 mile, then right on NW Oceanview Drive for 0.2 mile

to the Agate Beach pullout. From here, you can walk 1.2 miles north along the beach to its end at the Yaquina Head, or south 2.8 miles to Yaquina Bay.

Contact: Oregon Parks and Recreation Department, 1115 Commercial Street NE, Salem, OR, 97301, 800/551-6949, www.oregonstateparks.org.

32 SOUTH JETTY TRAIL
2.1 mi/1.0 hr   🥾1 ⛰6

south of Newport in South Beach State Park

If you're looking for the perfect place to let the kids run off their energy without running off yours, South Beach State Park across the Yaquina Bay from Newport is perfect. In the course of a single hour (or more, depending on how much those kids may run in and out of the sand dunes), you'll cross a golden beach, skirting a foredune to a view of an old railroad route, and cross a deflation plain, a lowland area where the winds have stripped the sand down to hard ground.

From the day-use area, cross the foredune to the ocean shore. From here, walk to the right 0.9 mile toward the South Jetty on the Yaquina River. Climb the jetty for a look at the nearby Yaquina Bay Lighthouse and a series of pilings marking the long-lost railroad that brought the rocks here. Follow the jetty road back inland 0.3 mile, watching for a trail sign on the right. Follow the left fork path 0.2 mile to a paved trail. Go left a short distance on the paved path, then go right on a bark dust path across the deflation plain for 0.7 mile back to the day-use lot.

User Groups: Hikers, dogs, and horses. Bicycles on marked trails only. Paved paths are wheelchair accessible.

Permits: Permits are not required. Parking and access are free.

Maps: For a topographic map, ask the USGS for Newport South.

Directions: Drive U.S. 101 south of the

Yaquina Bay Bridge 1.4 miles and turn right at a sign for South Beach State Park. Drive straight on this road 0.5 mile to the day-use parking area.

Contact: Oregon Parks and Recreation Department, 1115 Commercial Street NE, Salem, OR, 97301, 800/551-6949, www.oregonstateparks.org.

33 SEAL ROCK
4.2 mi/2.5 hr

south of Newport in Ona Beach State Park

This rock, recognized in the Chinook language as "seal home," is just that. You can reach Seal Rock, one of the southernmost remnants of a 15-million-year-old lava flow that originated somewhere near Hells Canyon, by car. You could have a sandwich in the neat little picnic area in a grove of spruce and shore pine. There's another way to enjoy it, though: For a more rewarding adventure, try a 2.1-mile beach walk from Ona Beach State Park and twisting Beaver Creek. It will make the sight of those seals, and sea lions, all the more spectacular.

From the Ona Beach State Park turnout, take the large paved trail toward the ocean. Cross the footbridge over Beaver Creek and head south toward Seal Rock. At a small creek, about 0.3 mile short of the cape, take a side trail up the bluff to the highway, and continue south about 300 yards to the Seal Rock Wayside. From there, you can descend another trail to a beach on the other side of the cape.

User Groups: Hikers and dogs. Paved paths are wheelchair accessible.

Permits: Permits are not required. Parking and access are free.

Maps: For a topographic map, ask the USGS for Newport South.

Directions: Follow U.S. 101 south of Newport seven miles to the parking area near milepost 149.

Contact: Oregon Parks and Recreation

Department, 1115 Commercial Street NE, Salem, OR, 97301, 800/551-6949, www.oregonstateparks.org.

34 MARY'S PEAK
4.0-10.0 mi/2.0-6.0 hr

west of Philomath in the Siuslaw National Forest

From summer daisy fields to trees bowed down by winter snow, Mary's Peak is accessible all year long to some degree. Even better, it's the highest point in the Coastal Range, with views from the ocean to the Cascade Mountains. The Kalapuya sent their young men here on vision quests, naming the mountain Chateemanwi, the "place where spirits dwell." In fact, native legend has it that an angry coyote dammed up the Willamette, flooding all the world but this sole peak, which he spared as a refuge for all living things.

Mary's Peak is a designated Scenic Botanical Area, boasting a unique noble fir forest that rings many Ice Age flower species (more than 200 in all) dating back an estimated 6,000 years. A number of trails explore this unique vista, fanning out over the North and East Ridges with an easy, hikeable road to the summit.

From the observation point parking lot, an easy hike follows the East Ridge Trail out 1.2 miles, connecting to a 1.1-mile tie trail and returning on a 0.7-mile section of the North Ridge Trail. The East Ridge Trail in all is 2.2 miles, dropping 1,200 feet to a lower trailhead. The North Ridge Trail in its entirety is a more difficult 3.7 miles, switchbacking down nearly 2,000 feet to a trailhead and gate on Woods Creek Road.

The easier trails are the 4,097-foot summit, accessible from the observation point by climbing the gated road 0.6 mile to the top. From the campground, the easy Meadow Edge Trail loops 2.2 miles and connects to the summit as well.

User Groups: Hikers, dogs, mountain bikes,

and horses. The summit is wheelchair accessible.

Permits: Permits are not required. A federal Northwest Forest Pass is required to park here; the cost is $5 a day or $30 for an annual pass. You can buy a day pass at the trailhead, at ranger stations, or through private vendors.

Maps: For a map of the Siuslaw National Forest, contact the Siuslaw National Forest headquarters, 4077 SW Research Way, P.O. Box 1148, Corvallis, OR, 97339, 541/750-7000. For a topographic map, ask the USGS for Mary's Peak.

Directions: Drive U.S. 20 west of Corvallis through Philomath, then follow OR 34 for 8.8 miles and turn right onto Mary's Peak Road for 9.5 miles to its end at the observation point. For the Meadow Edge Trail, drive Mary's Peak Road from OR 34 8.8 miles up to the campground on the right, forking left to a picnic area and the trailhead.

Contact: Siuslaw National Forest, Waldport Ranger District, 1130 Forestry Lane, P.O. Box 400, Waldport, OR, 97122, 541/563-3211.

35 HORSE CREEK TRAIL
8.0 mi/4.0 hr   🚶2 ⛰7

northeast of Waldport in Drift Creek Wilderness

Welcome to the northernmost and largest wilderness area in the Oregon Coastal Range: the Drift Creek Wilderness. Dropping 1,000 feet to this wilderness's namesake creek, the Horse Creek Trail wanders under moss-draped maples, passing huge and substantially bigger trees along the way, including hemlock, fir, and spruce. In spring, queen's-cup dots the forest floor, and in autumn chanterelle mushrooms poke from the duff.

From the trailhead, the path remains level the first mile or so, then descends 2.6 miles to a ford with a view of the ocean along the way. Turn right and follow the creek downstream one mile to another ford. Take the right-hand path, an unofficial trail to a campsite

and continue uphill 0.4 mile to return to the Horse Creek Trail.

User Groups: Hikers, dogs, and horses. No mountain bikes allowed. No wheelchair facilities.

Permits: Permits are not required. Parking and access are free.

Maps: For a map of the Siuslaw National Forest, contact the Siuslaw National Forest headquarters, 4077 SW Research Way, P.O. Box 1148, Corvallis, OR, 97339, 541/750-7000. For a map of Drift Creek Wilderness, ask the USFS for Drift Creek Wilderness. For a topographic map, ask the USGS for Tidewater.

Directions: Drive seven miles north of Waldport on U.S. 101 to Ona Beach State Park and turn right on North Beaver Creek Road for one mile. At a fork, head left for 2.7 miles to another junction and turn right onto the paved, one-lane North Elkhorn Road/Road 51 for 5.8 miles. At the next junction, turn left on Road 50 for 1.4 miles. Take a right fork onto gravel Road 5087 for 3.4 miles to the trailhead at a gate.

Contact: Siuslaw National Forest, Waldport Ranger District, 1130 Forestry Lane, P.O. Box 400, Waldport, OR, 97122, 541/563-3211.

36 HARRIS RANCH TRAIL
4.4 mi/2.5 hr   🚶2 ⛰7

northeast of Waldport in Drift Creek Wilderness

Like the hike along Horse Creek Trail (see previous listing), this trail leads down to Drift Creek in its namesake wilderness area, though this trail is shorter and less difficult. To boot, it visits a meadow overgrown with bracken fern and blackberry and the site of an old homestead. For further adventuring, you can easily ford the creek here (especially in summer) and continue on to the Horse Creek Trail and the unmaintained Boulder Ridge Trail. Watch for wildlife in the meadow, including elk and black bear. This is also a good place to watch for bald eagles and the northern spotted owl.

In fall, the creek teems with spawning chinook and coho salmon, as well as steelhead and cutthroat trout.

From the trailhead, descend a whopping 1,200 feet on the Harris Ranch Trail, which is actually an abandoned road, down 2.2 miles to some small meadows and the remains of the pre–World War II ranch along Drift Creek. If the water is low, you can ford the creek 0.3 mile past the meadows and join the Horse Creek Trail, which connects to the Boulder Ridge Trail in one mile.

User Groups: Hikers, dogs, and horses. No mountain bikes allowed. No wheelchair facilities.

Permits: Permits are not required. Parking and access are free.

Maps: For a map of the Siuslaw National Forest, contact the Siuslaw National Forest headquarters, 4077 SW Research Way, P.O. Box 1148, Corvallis, OR, 97339, 541/750-7000. For a map of Drift Creek Wilderness, ask the USFS for Drift Creek Wilderness. For a topographic map, ask the USGS for Tidewater.

Directions: Drive east of Waldport on OR 34 for 6.9 miles to a bridge over the Alsea River. Turn north on Risley Creek Road/Road 3446 for 4.1 miles, staying on the larger road at each junction. Veer left on Road 346 for 0.8 mile to the Harris Ranch Trailhead.

Contact: Siuslaw National Forest, Waldport Ranger District, 1130 Forestry Lane, P.O. Box 400, Waldport, OR, 97122, 541/563-3211.

37 ALSEA FALLS

3.5 mi/1.5 hr

east of Waldport on the South Fork Alsea River

If you've never seen a fish launch itself into the air to get itself over a waterfall, this is the place to do it. The 20-foot Alsea Falls are a bit off the beaten path on a scenic route over the Coast Range. A Boy Scout–constructed loop trail circles the South Fork Alsea River, while providing access to another span to another nearby waterfall in a lush side canyon. Along the way are the enormous stumps left from old-time logging, though the forest has had a long time to recover.

Starting from the Alsea Falls Recreation Area, take the left-hand trail beginning at a sign behind a maintenance garage. This trail follows the creek through second-growth woods for 0.6 mile to the first look at Alsea Falls and continues 0.3 mile down to the creek and over a logjam and boulder crossing beneath the pool at the base of the falls. Now the old-growth begins, as does the poison oak. At a junction, the right-hand trail continues the loop back one mile upstream and over a footbridge back to the car, but save that for the return; instead, take the left-hand trail, which joins a road to McBee Park. From here it's a short, 0.8-mile walk to Green Peak Falls. Stay on the gravel road until reaching the entrance road; turn right on that road, then take a quick right through a picnic site and follow that path to the 60-foot falls. A steep path can be scrambled down to reach a pool at the base.

User Groups: Hikers, dogs, and mountain bikes. No wheelchair facilities.

Permits: Permits are not required. Day-use fee is $3.

Maps: For a brochure and map, contact the Bureau of Land Management, Salem District Office, 503/375-5646, or go to www.blm.gov/or/resources/recreation/files/brochures/Alsea_Falls_Trail_System.pdf. For a topographic map, ask the USGS for Glenbrook.

Directions: Drive 16 miles south of Corvallis on U.S. 99W and turn west on South Fork Road at a sign for Alpine, and follow Alsea Falls signs to the camping area entrance on the right. Keep left to the trailhead.

Contact: Bureau of Land Management, Salem District Office, 1717 Fabry Road SE, Salem, OR, 97306, 503/375-5646.

38 SMELT SANDS WAYSIDE
1.4 m/0.75 hr   🏃1 ▲7

north of Yachats on the Pacific Ocean

Smelt are a family of small fish found in many waters, including the Pacific. Just offshore of the quaint town of Yachats, a landowner blocked access to some traditional fishing rocks in the 1970s. Some locals went to the books and discovered a long-forgotten, 19th-century right of way for a road that was never built. A decade-long court battle went all the way to the Oregon Supreme Court and left us the 0.7-mile 804 Trail in a State Park wayside. You'll have the opportunity to see some "spouting horns" (waves crashing upward through cracks in the lava) and a long beach with running creeks and grassy dunes.

From the wayside, strike out on the gravel trail that eventually heads north, passing a motel and crossing a driveway before descending steps to the beach. From here, Tillicum Beach Campground is 2.7 miles ahead and Patterson State Park is 6.3 miles ahead.

User Groups: Hikers and dogs. No wheelchair facilities.

Permits: Permits are not required. Parking and access are free.

Maps: For a topographic map, ask the USGS for Yachats.

Directions: On the north end of Yachats on U.S. 101, turn west onto Lemwick Lane, driving to the end at a turnaround and parking area.

Contact: Oregon Parks and Recreation Department, 1115 Commercial Street NE, Salem, OR, 97301, 800/551-6949, www.oregonstateparks.org.

39 CAPE PERPETUA ⚲
1.0-6.8 mi/0.5-3.5 hrs   🏃2 ▲8

south of Yachats in Cape Perpetua Scenic Area

The Cape Perpetua Scenic Area is one of the jewels of the Oregon coast. A network of trails radiates from the visitors center, offering access to a giant spruce, an ancient Native American midden, the Devil's Churn, Cooks Chasm and a spouting horn, and the centerpiece: a wonderful stone shelter atop 746-foot Cape Perpetua itself, built in 1933 by the Civilian Conservation Corps. It's easy to do three interesting trails in a single day and visit the top spots.

All trails begin at the visitors center lot. For the ocean hike, follow the "Tidepools" pointer on a paved trail, which goes 0.2 mile and under U.S. 101, then forks. The left fork circles 0.2 mile for a view to the spouting horns at Cooks Chasm, named for Captain Cook, who in turn named this cape for St. Perpetua in 1778. You'll also walk over the midden, a staggering mound of white mussel shells left by Native Americans (possibly as long as 6,000 years ago). The right fork heads out 0.5 mile to a loop around the Devil's Churn, a wave-pounded chasm in the lava.

For two inland hikes, return to the lot. First, follow "Giant Spruce" and "Viewpoint" pointers. In 0.2 mile, the trail splits: To see the 15-foot-thick, 600-year-old Sitka spruce, an Oregon Heritage Tree whose roots form a small tunnel, go to the right on the Giant Spruce Trail 0.8 mile. To climb Cape Perpetua, head left at this junction over Cape Creek to cross two paved roads and climb the switchbacks 1.3 miles up the Saint Perpetua Trail to the stone shelter, which affords views 37 miles to sea and 104 miles south to Cape Blanco. It's an excellent place to whale-watch, and you can consider how the CCC men endured winter storms and lugged buckets of sand up from the shore to make the mortar for the shelter.

User Groups: Hikers and dogs. Paved paths are wheelchair accessible.

Permits: Permits are not required. A federal Northwest Forest Pass is required to park here; the cost is $5 a day or $30 for an annual pass. You can buy a day pass at the visitors center, at ranger stations, or through private vendors.

Maps: For a map of the Siuslaw National Forest, contact the Siuslaw National Forest headquarters, 4077 SW Research Way, P.O. Box 1148, Corvallis, OR, 97339, 541/750-7000. For a topographic map, ask the USGS for Yachats.

Directions: Drive U.S. 101 south of Yachats three miles to the Cape Perpetua Visitor Center turnoff between mileposts 168 and 169.

Contact: Cape Perpetua Visitor Center, 2400 Highway 101, Yachats, OR, 97498, 541/547-3289, or Siuslaw National Forest, Waldport Ranger District, 1130 Forestry Lane, P.O. Box 400, Waldport, OR, 97122, 541/563-3211.

40 GWYNN CREEK
6.7 mi/3.5 hr   🏃2 ⛰7

south of Yachats in Cape Perpetua Scenic Area

Sitka spruce thrive on the foggy ocean climate and can only survive within three miles of the coastline. It so happens that some of the best spruce forests on the entire coast are in the canyons south of Cape Perpetua. This loop trail spans Cooks Ridge, drops into Gwynn Creek's canyon, and follows the Oregon Coast Trail back to the visitors center. Mushrooms love it here, too, including the delectable chanterelle and the poisonous panther amanita. Parts of the trail follow old logging roads and an 1895 wagon road between Yachats and Florence that ran until about 1910.

From the visitors center upper parking lot, follow signs for the Cooks Ridge Trail. In 0.4 mile, the path forks but rejoins, forming the Discovery Loop. Take either side and continue 0.3 mile to where the paths meet and continue on the Cooks Ridge Trail two

miles to a junction. Turn right on the Gwynn Creek Trail, descending 3.3 miles and 1,000 feet down the canyon. At the Oregon Coast Trail, go right for a 0.7-mile return to the visitors center.

User Groups: Hikers, dogs, and horses. No wheelchair facilities.

Permits: Permits are not required. A federal Northwest Forest Pass is required to park here; the cost is $5 a day or $30 for an annual pass. You can buy a day pass at the visitors center, at ranger stations, or through private vendors.

Maps: For a map of the Siuslaw National Forest, contact the Siuslaw National Forest headquarters, 4077 SW Research Way, P.O. Box 1148, Corvallis, OR, 97339, 541/750-7000. For a topographic map, ask the USGS for Yachats.

Directions: Drive U.S. 101 south of Yachats three miles to the Cape Perpetua Visitor Center turnoff between mileposts 168 and 169.

Contact: Cape Perpetua Visitor Center, 2400 Highway 101, Yachats, OR, 97498, 541/547-3289, or Siuslaw National Forest, Waldport Ranger District, 1130 Forestry Lane, P.O. Box 400, Waldport, OR, 97122, 541/563-3211.

41 CUMMINS CREEK
8.0 mi/4.0 hr   🏃3 ⛰7

south of Yachats in Cape Perpetua Scenic Area

Traversing the edge of the Cummins Creek Wilderness and connecting to the network of trails in the Cape Perpetua Scenic Area, this little-known trail itself never comes near the creek, but a small user trail will get you there nonetheless. A moderate-length loop offers a good tour of this area with opportunities for even longer hikes if you wish.

Beginning at the barricade, the initial part of the Cummins Creek Trail is an abandoned road. In the first 300 yards, an unofficial side trail to the right leads to two spots on the canyon, about 1.8 miles out and back. But the main Cummins Creek Trail ascends gradually up a forested ridge 1.4 miles to a junction. The Cummins Creek Loop Trail continues to the left 1.2 miles to the next junction; turn right for 0.5 mile, watching for a short spur trail to the left that offers a view. At the next junction, follow the Cummins Creek Trail to the right 1.4 miles back to the first junction, then stay to the left on the Cummins Creek Trail 1.4 miles back to the barricade.

User Groups: Hikers, dogs, and horses. No wheelchair facilities.

Permits: Permits are not required. A federal Northwest Forest Pass is required to park here; the cost is $5 a day or $30 for an annual pass. You can buy a day pass at the visitors center, at ranger stations, or through private vendors.

Maps: For a map of the Siuslaw National Forest, contact the Siuslaw National Forest headquarters, 4077 SW Research Way, P.O. Box 1148, Corvallis, OR, 97339, 541/750-7000. For a topographic map, ask the USGS for Yachats.

Directions: Drive U.S. 101 south of the Cape Perpetua Visitors Center one mile to a sign for Cummins Creek Trailhead. Turn left and drive gravel road 1050 for 0.3 mile to the barricade.

Contact: Cape Perpetua Visitor Center, 2400 Highway 101, Yachats, OR, 97498, 541/547-3289, or Siuslaw National Forest, Waldport Ranger District, 1130 Forestry Lane, P.O. Box 400, Waldport, OR, 97122, 541/563-3211.

42 CUMMINS RIDGE
12.0 mi/6.0 hr   🚶3 ⛰7

south of Yachats in Cummins Creek Wilderness

With only 9,173 acres, Cummins Creek Wilderness is not huge. It has, in fact, only one trail. On the other hand, it has the only old-growth Sitka spruce forest in the entire wilderness system of Oregon, so why not visit? You'll find not only Cummins Creek but Bob Creek, both overhung with droopy maple and alder. The Cummins Ridge tops out at 2,200 feet

and bisects the wilderness. Wild salmon and trout spawn in the cold waters, and flowers like yellow monkeyflower, white candyflower, purple aster, and the tall spikes of foxglove thrive here. With 80–100 inches of rain a year here, it's no wonder that spruce in this rainforest sometimes reach nine feet in diameter.

From the barricade on the dirt road, the Cummins Ridge Trail begins at 1,000 foot elevation. Follow the abandoned road up three miles, gaining 750 feet in elevation, to a cairn, then follow the trail to the right another three miles to trail's end on Forest Service Road 5694-515. Return the way you came.

User Groups: Hikers, dogs, and horses. No mountain bikes allowed. No wheelchair facilities.

Permits: Permits are not required. A federal Northwest Forest Pass is required to park here; the cost is $5 a day or $30 for an annual pass. You can buy a day pass at the visitors center, at ranger stations, or through private vendors.

Maps: For a map of the Siuslaw National Forest, contact the Siuslaw National Forest headquarters, 4077 SW Research Way, P.O. Box 1148, Corvallis, OR, 97339, 541/750-7000. For a topographic map, ask the USGS for Yachats.

Directions: From Yachats, drive four miles south on U.S. 101 and turn inland on gravel Road 1051 for 2.2 miles to the end at a barricade.

Contact: Siuslaw National Forest, Waldport Ranger District, 1130 Forestry Ln., P.O. Box 400, Waldport, OR, 97122, 541/563-3211.

43 HECETA HEAD
6.9 mi/3.0 hr   🚶2 ⛰8

north of Florence in Carl Washburne State Park

BEST (

A plethora of fantastic landscapes nearly assaults the senses in this everything-and-the-kitchen-sink hike. From beaver ponds to a lighthouse on a surf-pounded rock to the strange "Hobbit Trails," there is plenty to discover here. There is even, if you believe in this sort of thing, a supposedly haunted light keeper's house. All in all, you'll get the best of all worlds in this meandering loop.

From the day-use area, follow the beach south 1.2 miles, crossing Blowout Creek, toward the looming Heceta Head, where starfish and mollusks cling in the booming waves. Piles of gravel near the base are a good place to dig around for agates. You'll spot a trail leading into the woods; take this up 0.4 mile through a network of paths called the Hobbit Trails (tunnels of a sort made by hollowed-out sand chutes and arching rhododendrons). At the top of the climb, nearing the highway, go right on the next trail, which climbs 1.3 mile over the Heceta Head itself, coming down to the lighthouse and an overlook. Just offshore, Parrot Rock and other sea stacks are roosting areas for thousands of Brandt's cormorants; it's the largest nesting colony in Oregon. Walk the last 0.5 mile toward the Heceta House, an 1893 Queen Anne–style home for the lighthouse keepers that is supposedly haunted; it's a bed-and-breakfast now, so you can find out for yourself.

To complete the loop, head back over the head to the U.S. 101 Hobbit Trail trailhead and cross the highway to the continuation of the Valley Trail, which in the course of 1.1 miles passes a number of ponds and a beaver lake before forking to the left (though you could hike a bit down China Creek if you head right). This trail returns to the Washburne Campground, where you can follow the entrance road out and across the highway to return to the day-use area.

User Groups: Horses and dogs. No wheelchair facilities.

Permits: Permits are not required. Parking and access are free.

Maps: For a free park brochure, call Oregon Parks and Recreation, 800/551-6949, or download a free map at www.oregonstateparks. org. For a topographic map, ask the USGS for Heceta Head.

Directions: Drive U.S. 101 north of Florence

one mile to milepost 176 and turn left into the Washburne State Park day-use area, parking at the far end of the picnic area. The trail begins past the restrooms.

Contact: Oregon Parks and Recreation Department, 1115 Commercial Street NE, Salem, OR, 97301, 800/551-6949, www.oregonstateparks.org.

44 CAPE MOUNTAIN
2.0 mi/1.0 hr   1 7

north of Florence in the Siuslaw National Forest

In a joint venture between the Forest Service and equestrian club volunteers, a network of trails was built on and around Cape Mountain. The Coast Horse Trail system is open to hikers, too. An easy two-mile loop leads to the peak, the site of a 1932 fire watchtower. Once you've done this easy loop, you can fan out into the wild network of trails going every which way, exploring Nelson and Scurvy Ridge and a number of loops. Much of the forest here was spared by previous wildfires, leaving habitat for old-growth trees and wildlife.

From the Dry Lake Trailhead, head behind the stables for the Princess Tasha Trail, climbing 0.4 mile through old-growth Douglas fir and coastal spruce to a four-way junction. Turn left on the Cape Mountain spur for 0.5 mile, keeping left at all junctions to attain the summit. For a loop option, follow the old road down, keeping left at all junctions to return directly to the car.

User Groups: Hikers, dogs, mountain bikes, and horses. No wheelchair facilities.

Permits: Permits are not required. Parking and access are free.

Maps: For a map of the Siuslaw National Forest, contact the Siuslaw National Forest headquarters, 4077 SW Research Way, P.O. Box 1148, Corvallis, OR, 97339, 541/750-7000. For a topographic map, ask the USGS for Mercer Lake.

Directions: Drive U.S, 101 north of Florence

seven miles and go right on Herman Peak Road for 2.8 miles to the Dry Lake Trailhead on the left.

Contact: Siuslaw National Forest, Mapleton Ranger District, 4480 Highway 101, Building G, Florence, OR, 97439, 541/902-8526.

45 BAKER BEACH
0.5-6.5 mi/0.25-3.5 hr

north of Florence in the Siuslaw National Forest

BEST (

Baker Beach's windswept dunes sure look a lot like something from *Lawrence of Arabia,* and standing amid such colossal waves it's hard to believe we're still in Oregon. Interspersed with Sutton Creek, grassy hummocks, and perhaps even a little lupine flower or wild strawberry, it doesn't seem like other beaches. Nearby Lily Lake provides an easy 1.4-mile loop, and the beach itself is explorable (with trails and dunes). Hike from the lot 0.4 mile toward the ocean, then strike out in any direction; heading north three miles will land you at the estuary of Sutton Creek, a great place to bird-watch. But you may just want to go striding over the dunes themselves, finding a big one and rolling down the other side. Kids love this area, as do horseback riders.

User Groups: Hikers and horses. Dogs allowed on leash only. Bikes prohibited. No wheelchair facilities.

Permits: Permits are not required. A federal Northwest Forest Pass is required to park here; the cost is $5 a day or $30 for an annual pass. You can buy a day pass at the visitors center, at ranger stations, or through private vendors.

Maps: For a map of the Siuslaw National Forest, contact the Siuslaw National Forest headquarters, 4077 SW Research Way, P.O. Box 1148, Corvallis, OR, 97339, 541/750-7000. For a topographic map, ask the USGS for Mercer Lake.

Directions: Drive U.S. 101 north of Florence seven miles and turn west on gravel Baker Beach Road for 0.5 miles to its end.

Contact: Siuslaw National Forest, Mapleton Ranger District, 4480 Highway 101, Building G, Florence, OR, 97439, 541/902-8526.

46 SUTTON CREEK DUNES
4.4 mi/2.0 hr

north of Florence in the Siuslaw National Forest

If you've never seen the famous Oregon rhododendrons, this is the place to do it. In the Sutton Creek Recreation Area, jungles of these sweet flowering trees line the meandering Sutton Creek, easy and warm to wade in the summer. Patches of spiny salal rustle in the wind, and blue herons wade in the water. A loop trail courses through the dunes and follows the creek. If you go to the shore, keep out of designated snowy plover nesting sites, as these birds are endangered and protected. A variety of dunes punctuate the landscape, making for a geographically and biologically diverse area. Look for the rare *Darlingtonia,* the insect-munching cobra lily.

From the Holman Vista lot, start at the trail behind the kitchen shelter in the picnic area. This trail curves 0.8 mile along the creek, passing a number of fords, to a bench and footbridge. Follow a sign upstream to the right for the Sutton Campground, following the Sutton Creek Trail. In 0.5 mile, you'll reach the campground's A Loop. Turn left along the road and cross a footbridge over the creek and stay to the left at the next two junctions (part of a 0.4-mile loop), continuing 1.4 miles out along the dunes (a right-hand trail leads to the Alder Dune Campground) before dropping down to the footbridge to Boldac's Meadow. Turn right along the creek, then left at the next junction to return the half-mile back to Holman Vista.

User Groups: Hikers, dogs on leash only, and horses. No bikes allowed. The Holman Vista Observation Deck is wheelchair accessible.

Permits: Permits are not required. A federal Northwest Forest Pass is required to park

HIKING

HIKING

here; the cost is $5 a day or $30 for an annual pass. You can buy a day pass at the visitors center, at ranger stations, or through private vendors.

Maps: For a map of the Siuslaw National Forest, contact the Siuslaw National Forest headquarters, 4077 SW Research Way, P.O. Box 1148, Corvallis, OR, 97339, 541/750-7000. For a topographic map, ask the USGS for Mercer Lake.

Directions: From Florence, drive U.S. 101 north for five miles, turning west at the Sutton creek Recreation Area sign. Follow this paved road 2.2 miles to the Holman Vista lot.

Contact: Siuslaw National Forest, Mapleton Ranger District, 4480 Highway 101, Building G, Florence, OR, 97439, 541/902-8526.

47 ENCHANTED VALLEY
5.0 mi/2.5 hr

north of Florence in the Siuslaw National Forest

This former dairy farm has been abandoned, and a host of wildlife (including deer and elk) has taken the place of the cows. The bed of Bailey Creek shimmers with bits of iron pyrite and is being restored for native coho salmon, thus making this a place to see both silver salmon and fool's gold: a real treasure. This fairly easy hike follows the creek 2.5 miles from a feeder creek for Mercer Lake along meadows teeming with horsetail and skunk cabbage, visiting an old farmhouse site and an upper homestead meadow, site of an old apple orchard. Following an old road converted to a path, there's really no way to lose your way. Return as you came.

User Groups: Hikers, dogs, and horses. No wheelchair facilities.

Permits: Permits are not required. Parking and access are free.

Maps: For a map of the Siuslaw National Forest, contact the Siuslaw National Forest headquarters, 4077 SW Research Way, P.O. Box 1148, Corvallis, OR, 97339, 541/750-

7000. For a topographic map, ask the USGS for Mercer Lake.

Directions: Drive five miles north of Florence on U.S. 101 and turn right on Mercer Lake Road for 3.7 miles. Fork left on Twin Fawn Drive for 0.3 mile to a parking area at the end of the road.

Contact: Siuslaw National Forest, Mapleton Ranger District, 4480 Highway 101, Building G, Florence, OR, 97439, 541/902-8526.

48 SIUSLAW RIDGE
2.6 mi/1.0 hr

west of Eugene in Whittaker Creek Recreation Site

From the campground at the Whittaker Creek Recreation Site deep in the Coastal Range, you can watch the annual salmon run. Chinook, coho, and steelhead all push upstream to their spawning grounds. Just off the road, the Siuslaw River cuts its way through the mountains heading for the sea, and here the Siuslaw Ridge rises above it with a trail leading to a truly large Douglas fir: seven-feet thick and 500-years-old. The trail is just steep enough to give your heart a workout.

From the parking area near a dam, head across a footbridge spanning Whittaker Creek and down the campground road to a sign reading Old Growth Ridge Trail. This one-mile climb rockets up 800 feet to a junction at the peak of the ridge. Take a left for a short 0.1-mile jaunt to the giant fir, and a right for a short 0.2-mile walk to a river viewpoint.

User Groups: Hikers and dogs. No wheelchair facilities.

Permits: Permits are not required. Parking and access are free.

Maps: For a topographic map, ask the USGS for Roman Nose Mountain.

Directions: Drive west of Eugene 33 miles on OR 126 to a junction between mileposts 26 and 27. Turn south on Siuslaw River Road, following signs for "Whittaker Cr. Rec. Area" for 1.5 miles, turn right for 0.2 mile, then right again into the campground.

Contact: Bureau of Land Management, Eugene District Office, 2890 Chad Dr., Eugene, OR, 97440, 541/683-6600.

49 SWEET CREEK FALLS
5.2 mi/2.5 hr   🚶1 ⛰7

east of Florence in the Siuslaw National Forest

This hike would be quite epic if not for lack of a bridge spanning the gorge at Sweet Creek Falls. No matter. Two trailheads will do fine to visit not just two different views of Sweet Creek, but Beaver Creek Falls, which is—to my understanding—the only double waterfall in Oregon made of two completely different creeks. One section of the trail follows an old wagon road through the Zarah T. Sweet homestead, the path now pioneered only by red alders, which thrive in disturbed ground. The other fans out toward both sets of waterfalls and stunning views. Rain or shine, it's beautiful. A total of four trailheads break these trails up into easy segments that pass a dozen waterfalls in all. To make it easy and worthwhile, try these two. Part of the trail, by the way, is a dramatic catwalk on a metal walkway hugging the canyon wall.

The Homestead Trailhead sets out into Punchbowl Falls Canyon 0.7 mile, joining up with the trail from the Sweet Creek Falls Trailhead for the final 0.4-mile walk to Sweet Creek Falls. It's easiest to return the way you came, though in very low water a ford is possible over slippery boulders. Instead, proceed by car to the Wagon Road Trailhead, where two trails begin. Directly across the road from the parking area, one 0.8-mile trail, a stretch of the old Sunset Wagon Road, leads down to a viewpoint of Sweet Creek Falls opposite the previous trails. The second route, Beaver Creek Trail, begins over the roadway bridge from the parking area for a 0.6-mile trail to Beaver Creek Falls.

User Groups: Hikers and dogs only. No wheelchair facilities.

Permits: Permits are not required. Parking and access are free.

Maps: For a map of the Siuslaw National Forest, contact the Siuslaw National Forest headquarters, 4077 SW Research Way, P.O. Box 1148, Corvallis, OR, 97339, 541/750-7000. For a topographic map, ask the USGS for Goodwin Peak.

Directions: Drive 15 miles east of Florence on OR 126 to Mapleton to the Siuslaw River Bridge. Cross the bridge and turn right on Sweet Creek Road for 10.2 miles. Take a paved turnoff to the right for the Homestead Trail. To get to the Wagon Road Trailhead, drive 1.3 miles farther to a parking area on the left.

Contact: Siuslaw National Forest, Mapleton Ranger District, 4480 Highway 101, Building G, Florence, OR, 97439, 541/902-8526.

50 KENTUCKY FALLS AND NORTH FORK SMITH RIVER
4.4-17.4 mi/2.0 hr-1 day   🚶2 ⛰7

west of Eugene in the Siuslaw National Forest

 BEST (

Eugenians certainly know about Kentucky Falls. It boasts an upper and lower fall, both dropping 100 feet, and this short trail visits both. The roads here may be twisty, and the hike may require you to climb back out of this rainforest canyon, but it's a must at any time of year. These falls are among the most famous in the entire Coast Range, and among the biggest. Because the drive to get here is so long, it's tempting to extend the hike along the North Fork Smith River, a trail that is only accessible in summer's low water.

From the trailhead, descend the Kentucky Falls Trail 0.8 mile to Upper Kentucky Falls, and continue another 1.4 miles to an observation deck overlooking Lower Kentucky Falls. From here, a newer trail follows the North Fork Smith River 6.5 miles. Head downstream two miles to a switchbacking descent, and in another 1.5 miles the trail fords the river for the first time, and in another 1.5 miles fords a second time. The trail leaves the river and ends at another trailhead after the last 1.5 miles. Note that this trail is accessible in summers only, and as of July 2008, there is an impassable slide about four miles north of the North Fork Smith Trailhead; contact the Mapleton Ranger District (541/902-8526) for up-to-date information.

User Groups: Hikers and dogs. No wheelchair facilities.

Permits: Permits are not required. Parking and access are free.

Maps: For a map of the Siuslaw National Forest, contact the Siuslaw National Forest headquarters, 4077 SW Research Way, P.O. Box 1148, Corvallis, OR, 97339, 541/750-7000. For a topographic map, ask the USGS for Baldy Mountain.

Directions: Drive west of Eugene 33 miles on OR 126 to a junction between mileposts 26 and 27. Turn south on Siuslaw River Road, following signs for "Whittaker Cr. Rec. Area" for 1.5 miles, then turn right over a bridge at another Whittaker sign. Follow this one-lane, paved road back into the hills 1.5 miles and fork left onto Dunn Ridge Road. Follow this fork 6.7 miles uphill to a junction at pavement's end and turn left on Knowles Creek Road for 2.7 miles, then right on Road 23 for 1.6 miles, then right on paved Road 919 for 2.6 miles to trailhead parking on the right. To make this hike an 8.7-mile one-way trip, shuttle a car at the North Fork Smith River Trailhead. From the junction of Forest Service Road 23 and Road 919, go 5.7 miles south on Road 23 to the trailhead.

Contact: Siuslaw National Forest, Mapleton Ranger District, 4480 Highway 101, Building G, Florence, OR, 97439, 541/902-8526.

51 HONEYMAN STATE PARK DUNES

1.6 mi/1.0 hr

south of Florence in Honeyman State Park

The Oregon Dunes, the jewel of the Northwest, begin just south of historic Florence. With nearly 40 miles of rippling coastline, this is an otherworldly place of massive sand dunes, tree islands, and quiet estuaries reached only by rugged hikes over sort and shifting sand. Honeyman State Park is the second-largest overnight camp in the state, and with its two freshwater lakes, pink rhododendrons, and fall huckleberries, there is more to the park than just sand. Yet sand is why they come in droves, and an easy loop allows you to get your first glimpse of what wind and weather can do to a landscape.

From the day-use lot, a sand trail leads out along lovely Cleawox Lake. At the edge of the lake, turn left and crest a grassy dune. Looking ahead and to the left of a tree island, you'll spot the biggest of the dunes here at 250 feet. Strike out on the trail-less dunes 0.5 mile toward that big one. Spend some time up top, as the views are extensive. Head down the slope opposite the ocean and head into one of the sandy trails that emerges in a sandy bowl circled by forest. Cross the bowl and head for a gap on the ridge which leads to the campground on the "I" loop. Go left on the paved road and left again on the main campground road, 0.4 mile in all. Just past the campground fee booth, go left on a paved trail for 0.2 mile to return to the day-use area.

User Groups: Hikers, dogs, and horses. Paved areas of the park are wheelchair accessible.

Permits: Permits are not required. A $3 day-use fee is collected at the camping entrance, or you can get an annual Oregon Parks and Recreation pass for $25; contact Oregon Parks and Recreation, 800/551-6949.

Maps: For a free park brochure, call Oregon Parks and Recreation, 800/551-6949, or download a free map at www.oregonstateparks.

org. For a topographic map, ask the USGS for Florence.

Directions: Drive south of Florence three miles on U.S. 101 and turn right into the park entrance, following signs 0.3 mile to the Sand Dunes Picnic Area.

Contact: Oregon Parks and Recreation Department, 1115 Commercial Street NE, Salem, OR, 97301, 800/551-6949, www.oregonstateparks.org.

52 SILTCOOS RIVER
2.6 mi/1.0 hr

In the Oregon Dunes National Recreation Area

BEST (

A small estuary at the mouth of the Siltcoos River is home to nesting snowy plovers, among other water-loving birds. The Waxmyrtle Beach Trail sets out toward the coastline with views of the estuary along a meandering river where kayakers glide by quietly. Note: The Estuary Trail is closed March 15 through September 15 to protect snowy plover nesting sites.

From the Stagecoach Trailhead, start out on the Waxmyrtle Trail, which runs 0.2 mile between the river and road, then turn right on the campground road over the river. After crossing the bridge, turn right on the trail and follow the river 0.7 mile (if it's snowy plover season, you'll have to instead take a sandy, gated road to the left and follow it 0.8 mile). At a junction, continue toward the ocean 0.3 mile on the sandy old road. Turn right 0.2 mile to the river's mouth.

User Groups: Hikers, dogs on a leash, and horses. No wheelchair facilities.

Permits: Permits are not required. A federal Northwest Forest Pass is required to park here; the cost is $5 a day or $30 for an annual pass. You can buy a day pass at the visitors center, at ranger stations, or through private vendors.

Maps: For a map of the Siuslaw National Forest, contact the Siuslaw National Forest headquarters, 4077 SW Research Way, P.O.

Box 1148, Corvallis, OR, 97339, 541/750-7000. For a topographic map, ask the USGS for Tahkenitch Creek.

Directions: Drive U.S. 101 south of Florence eight miles to the Siltcoos Recreation Area turnoff at milepost 198. Turn west and drive 0.9 mile to the Stagecoach Trailhead on the left.

Contact: Siuslaw National Forest, Mapleton Ranger District, 4480 Highway 101, Building G, Florence, OR, 97439, 541/902-8526, or the Oregon Dunes National Recreation Area, 855 Highway Avenue, Reedsport, OR, 97467, 541/271-6019.

53 SILTCOOS LAKE
4.3 mi/2.0 hr

In the Oregon Dunes National Recreation Area

At 3,500 acres, Siltcoos Lake is the largest freshwater lake on the Oregon coast. A loop trail visits two isolated campsites on the lake's shore facing forested Booth Island.

From the highway, hike inland and downhill on the Siltcoos Lake Trail 0.8 mile to a junction. Go right 0.7 mile to another junction, then right 0.2 mile to South Camp on the lake. Head back up this spur trail to the junction, then go right 0.5 mile to access North Camp, which has more spots to pitch a tent. In the jumble of trails, continue on the main one to complete the loop and return 1.1 miles back to the first junction, then right the remaining 0.8 mile to the highway.

User Groups: Hikers, dogs, horses, and mountain bikes. No wheelchair facilities.

Permits: Permits are not required. A federal Northwest Forest Pass is required to park here; the cost is $5 a day or $30 for an annual pass. You can buy a day pass at the visitors center, at ranger stations, or through private vendors.

Maps: For a map of the Siuslaw National Forest, contact the Siuslaw National Forest headquarters, 4077 SW Research Way, P.O. Box 1148, Corvallis, OR, 97339,

541/750-7000. For a topographic map, ask the USGS for Florence.

Directions: Drive U.S. 101 south of Florence eight miles and park on the east side of 101 opposite the Siltcoos Recreation Area turnoff at milepost 198.

Contact: Siuslaw National Forest, Mapleton Ranger District, 4480 Highway 101, Building G, Florence, OR, 97439, 541/902-8526, or the Oregon Dunes National Recreation Area, 855 Highway Avenue, Reedsport, OR, 97467, 541/271-6019.

54 CARTER LAKE DUNES
2.7 mi/1.5 hr

in the Oregon Dunes National Recreation Area

Two lakes, Carter and Taylor, sit atop a forested ridge overlooking the Oregon Dunes. In some spots, the ocean is far away and a slogging walk just to reach the shore. From here, it's pretty easy, actually, and you can walk along beautiful Taylor Lake on your way to the big dunes. You'll have to follow blue-striped posts out over the dunes, over the deflation plain with its shore pine and Scotch broom forest and down to the beach. Just keep an eye on that trail once you reach the beach, so as not to wander off and lose it. Also keep in mind that sand-hiking can be tiring and slow-going.

The first 0.4 mile passes Taylor Lake to two view decks and a bench before dropping 0.5 mile to the dunes to join with the Carter Lake Trail. From here, follow posts 0.5 mile to the ocean. For a loop possibility, you could well follow the Carter Lake Trail back to the road, then head 0.4 mile left along the road to the Taylor Dunes Trailhead.

User Groups: Hikers, dogs, and horses. The first 0.5 mile is wheelchair accessible.

Permits: Permits are not required. A federal Northwest Forest Pass is required to park here; the cost is $5 a day or $30 for an annual pass. You can buy a day pass at the visitors center, at ranger stations, or through private vendors.

Maps: For a map of the Siuslaw National Forest, contact the Siuslaw National Forest headquarters, 4077 SW Research Way, P.O. Box 1148, Corvallis, OR, 97339, 541/750-7000. For a topographic map, ask the USGS for Tahkenitch Creek.

Directions: Drive U.S. 101 south of Florence nine miles, or north of Reedsport 12 miles, and turn west into the Carter Lake Campground entrance. The Taylor Dunes Trailhead is on the left just after the entrance.

Contact: Siuslaw National Forest, Mapleton Ranger District, 4480 Highway 101, Building G, Florence, OR, 97439, 541/902-8526, or the Oregon Dunes National Recreation Area, 855 Highway Avenue, Reedsport, OR, 97467, 541/271-6019.

55 OREGON DUNES OVERLOOK
2.2 mi/1.0 hr

in the Oregon Dunes National Recreation Area

What a great view these overlooks afford: a vast sea of sand, massive tree islands swelling between the dunes, and beyond a shore pine forest, the rolling tides. Want a closer look? Then hike right past those decks and down to the sand, where blue-striped posts lead hikers to a long beach with opportunities to explore the wild-flowered deflation plain, where deer wander and the hummocks of sand cradle deep valleys where kids can play and dogs can run. This is one of the easier, meaning shorter, paths through the dunes to the shoreline.

The main trail begins as a paved path that drops 0.3 mile to the sand, though another trail begins just past the observation decks, briefly passing through the scrubby trees and out onto the peak of a dune. Once you get down to the flatter ground, the posts lead 0.8 mile to the shore.

User Groups: Hikers, dogs, and horses, No mountain bikes allowed. Viewing decks are wheelchair accessible.

Permits: Permits are not required. A federal Northwest Forest Pass is required to park here; the cost is $5 a day or $30 for an annual pass. You can buy a day pass at the visitors center, at ranger stations, or through private vendors.

Maps: For a map of the Siuslaw National Forest, contact the Siuslaw National Forest headquarters, 4077 SW Research Way, P.O. Box 1148, Corvallis, OR, 97339, 541/750-7000. For a topographic map, ask the USGS for Tahkenitch Creek.

Directions: The Oregon Dunes Overlook entrance is on the west side of U.S. 101, 10 miles south of Florence or 11 miles north of Reedsport.

Contact: Siuslaw National Forest, Mapleton Ranger District, 4480 Highway 101, Building G, Florence, OR, 97439, 541/902-8526, or the Oregon Dunes National Recreation Area, 855 Highway Avenue, Reedsport, OR, 97467, 541/271-6019.

HIKING

Tahkenitch Creek

56 TAHKENITCH CREEK
4.2 mi/2.0 hr   👫2 ⛰8

in the Oregon Dunes National Recreation Area

The Oregon Dunes are more than just sand, as the Tahkenitch Creek Trail amply demonstrates. This lazy creek, forested with Douglas fir and flowering rhododendrons, drifts toward the sea, meeting the tides at a lonely and largely unvisited estuary frequented by brown pelicans frequent and nesting snowy plovers. Thorny gorse, a particularly nasty invasive bush, grows here as well. Be mindful that winter often brings flooding in certain areas, making some of the loops impossible.

The first 0.3 mile of the Tahkenitch Creek Trail is in a coastal forest, crossing the creek on a long footbridge with views of the creek along the way. At a junction, a short loop is possible by heading to the right, hugging the creek a short distance until the next junction, where a left turn brings you to another left turn: a 1.6-mile loop in all. But continuing

on along the creek to another junction, as well as a view of the estuary, taking the same two left turns, then keeping right at the next two junctions represents another loop, 2.6 miles in all. The longest loop follows the creek out a full mile past this first junction, eventually passing a few marshy lakes to a four-way junction with the Tahkenitch Dunes Trail; going hard left here to return to the Tahkenitch Creek Trail and keeping to the right at each consecutive junction makes a 4.2-mile loop. If you feel like you've got a bit more oomph, you could head right on the Tahkenitch Dunes Trail from this last junction an extra 0.3 mile, then take a right for another 0.3 mile to reach the beach; remember, though, that this much sand makes for a tiring hike, so save your energy.

User Groups: Hikers, dogs, and horses. No mountain bikes allowed. No wheelchair facilities.

Permits: Permits are not required. A federal Northwest Forest Pass is required to park here;

the cost is $5 a day or $30 for an annual pass. You can buy a day pass at the visitors center, at ranger stations, or through private vendors.

Maps: For a map of the Siuslaw National Forest, contact the Siuslaw National Forest headquarters, 4077 SW Research Way, P.O. Box 1148, Corvallis, OR, 97339, 541/750-7000. For a topographic map, ask the USGS for Tahkenitch Creek.

Directions: The Tahkenitch Creek Trailhead is located on the west side of U.S. 101 between mileposts 202 and 203, about 12 miles south of Florence or nine miles north of Reedsport.

Contact: Siuslaw National Forest, Mapleton Ranger District, 4480 Highway 101, Building G, Florence, OR, 97439, 541/902-8526, or the Oregon Dunes National Recreation Area, 855 Highway Avenue, Reedsport, OR, 97467, 541/271-6019.

57 TAHKENITCH DUNES
6.5 mi/3.0 hr

in the Oregon Dunes National Recreation Area

For those who want to explore the Oregon Dunes on a far more rugged expedition, the Tahkenitch Dunes offer this kind of epic journey in excess. Along the way, you can view the Tahkenitch Creek estuary and a beach along Threemile Lake, and cross over a forested summit above the sand. Be aware that long hikes through sand can be tiring and slow-going, so plan on plenty of time and pack plenty of water.

The first 0.2 mile of the Tahkenitch Dunes Trail climbs into the forest to a junction. Go right for 1.1 miles across the open dunes, eventually entering a brushy forest of shore pine—also known as lodgepole pine. At a junction, go left for 0.3 mile along a marsh, then right for 0.3 mile to the beach. Note that ORV vehicles are allowed on this beach, so don't be surprised by the dune buggies. Heading to the right 0.9 mile will take you to the estuary,

but for a longer hike head to the left instead, going north 1.3 miles along the beach. Watch for a trail sign on the foredune, then head inland 0.4 mile to a viewpoint over a beach on Threemile Lake. Follow the Threemile Lake Trail 2.7 miles up and over a 400-foot summit of second-growth woods back to the first junction, and head right the remaining 0.2 mile back to the campground.

User Groups: Hikers, dogs, and horses, No mountain bikes allowed. No wheelchair facilities.

Permits: Permits are not required. A federal Northwest Forest Pass is required to park here; the cost is $5 a day or $30 for an annual pass. You can buy a day pass at the visitors center, at ranger stations, or through private vendors.

Maps: For a map of the Siuslaw National Forest, contact the Siuslaw National Forest headquarters, 4077 SW Research Way, P.O. Box 1148, Corvallis, OR, 97339, 541/750-7000. For a topographic map, ask the USGS for Tahkenitch Creek.

Directions: The Tahkenitch Dunes Trailhead is located in the Tahkenitch Campground on the west side of U.S. 101 about 13 miles south of Florence or eight miles north of Reedsport. Keep left at the loop and park at a small picnic area.

Contact: Siuslaw National Forest, Mapleton Ranger District, 4480 Highway 101, Building G, Florence, OR, 97439, 541/902-8526, or the Oregon Dunes National Recreation Area, 855 Highway Avenue, Reedsport, OR, 97467, 541/271-6019.

58 LAKE MARIE
1.4 mi/1.0 hr

south of Reedsport in Umpqua Lighthouse State Park

High atop a bluff over Winchester Bay and the mouth of the Umpqua River stands the 65-foot lighthouse blinking its read and white warning to boats. Also beneath the fog-piercing light lie the beginning of the seven-mile stretch of the Umpqua Dunes and little Lake Marie. An easy hike around this forested lake begins at a picturesque picnic area, and proceeds to a viewpoint of the dunes themselves, a worthy goal for exploration.

From the shoreline, head on the right-hand trail following the lakeside 0.2 mile. At a junction, follow the right trail 0.2 mile to a view of the Umpqua Dunes. Head back and continue an easy 0.8 mile back to the picnic area.

User Groups: Hikers, dogs, and horses. No wheelchair facilities.

Permits: Permits are not required. Parking and access are free.

Maps: For a free park brochure, call Oregon Parks and Recreation, 800/551-6949, or download a free map at www.oregonstateparks.org. For a topographic map, ask the USGS for Winchester Bay.

Directions: Drive U.S 101 south of Reedsport five miles to milepost 217 and follow signs for Umpqua Lighthouse State Park. Travel one mile west, passing the campground entrance, and park at a picnic area on the left on the shore of Lake Marie.

Contact: Oregon Parks and Recreation Department, 1115 Commercial Street NE, Salem, OR, 97301, 800/551-6949, www.oregonstateparks.org.

59 UMPQUA DUNES
5.0 mi/2.5 hr 🏃3 ⛰9

In the Oregon Dunes National Recreation Area

BEST (

The sheer enormity of the Umpqua Dunes is staggering. This stretch of sand, nearly unreal in its proportions, makes this one of Oregon's most outstanding and beautiful areas. If you're going to pick any area of the Dunes to hike, make it this one. That being said, reaching the ocean on the John Dellenback Dunes Trail, named for the U.S. congressman who helped establish this recreation area, is one of the most difficult hikes on the coast. These towering

© SEAN PATRICK HILL

Umpqua Dunes in the Oregon Dunes National Recreation Area

dunes south of the Umpqua River are the largest and the broadest, stretching over two miles to the distant ocean. Blue-striped trail posts seem lonely in the vast waves of sand, following a valley between massive oblique dunes, sloping on one side and sharply carved by wind on the other. The otherworldly beauty is so tremendous that it's worth a day's journey just to get here, let alone hike this area.

From Eel Creek Campground, follow the 0.2-mile trail through twisting red-barked madrones to an impressive overlook, the sea a far-off rumble. Head for the long, high dune for a sweeping view to a massive tree island and mile after mile of cascading sand. Look toward the ocean to spot the tiny trail markers marching off into the sand. Follow these posts a total of 2.2-miles to reach the ocean.

User Groups: Hikers, dogs, and horses. No wheelchair facilities.

Permits: Permits are not required. A federal Northwest Forest Pass is required to park here; the cost is $5 a day or $30 for an annual pass.

HIKING

You can buy a day pass at the visitors center, at ranger stations, or through private vendors.

Maps: For a map of the Siuslaw National Forest, contact the Siuslaw National Forest headquarters, 4077 SW Research Way, P.O. Box 1148, Corvallis, OR, 97339, 541/750-7000. For a topographic map, ask the USGS for Lakeside.

Directions: Drive 11 miles south of Reedsport on U.S. 101. Near milepost 222, turn west into Eel Creek Campground and keep left for 0.3 mile to a parking lot. The trailhead begins at a large signpost.

Contact: Siuslaw National Forest, Mapleton Ranger District, 4480 Highway 101, Building G, Florence, OR, 97439, 541/902-8526, or the Oregon Dunes National Recreation Area, 855 Highway Avenue, Reedsport, OR, 97467, 541/271-6019.

60 GOLDEN AND SILVER FALLS

3.0 mi/1.5 hr 🏃1 ⛰8

east of Coos Bay in Golden and Silver Falls State Park

Not to be confused with Silver Falls State Park just outside of the Willamette Valley, this state park has two falls that topple hundreds of feet into two canyons, the creeks joining a short distance below. Three different trails fan out here, following Glenn and Silver Creeks, and it's worth it to take them all, as they afford multiple views of both plunging falls. Along the way you'll see myrtlewood trees, common to this part of the state.

To start, go to the trailhead and take the farthest left-hand trail up 0.3 mile to a view of 160-foot Silver Falls, a good warm-up. Return to the lot and take the right-hand trail, which crosses Silver Creek. Here the trail splits. The left trail goes 0.4 mile up Silver Creek to another breathtaking view of Silver Falls, and continues up the canyon walls on a dizzying climb up 0.5 mile to a couple overlooks

over 200-foot Golden Falls. Return the way you came, and take the last of the trails, the right-hand junction after the footbridge, which heads through groves of myrtlewood along Glenn Creek to a lower view of Golden Falls.

User Groups: Hikers and dogs. No wheelchair facilities.

Permits: Permits are not required. Parking and access are free.

Maps: For a topographic map, ask the USGS for Golden Falls.

Directions: Follow U.S. 101 to the south end of Coos Bay and follow signs for Alleghany, eventually turning east on Coos River Highway. In 13.5 miles, arrive at Alleghany, then follow state park signs 9.4 miles on East Millicoma Road and Glen Creek Road to the end of the road at a picnic area.

Contact: Oregon Parks and Recreation Department, 1115 Commercial Street NE, Salem, OR, 97301, 800/551-6949, www.oregonstateparks.org.

61 SUNSET BAY TO CAPE ARAGO

9.4 mi/4.5 hr 🏃3 ⛰9

west of Coos Bay in Sunset Bay/Shore Acres State Parks

BEST (

Leave it to the Oregon State Parks to hold onto history. Cape Arago, hovering above a series of reefs, islands, and barking sea lions, was first spotted by Sir Francis Drake in the 1500s. Later, the land in what is now Shore Acres State Park was the estate for lumber baron Louis Simpson, including an unforgettable garden that is still blooming to this day. Today you can see all of this history and migrating whales, too, thanks to a stretch of the Oregon Coast Trail that passes along this rugged and wild coastline. You can pay a fee to enter the main part of the park, or you can hike your way in on a stunning trip along one of Oregon's best seaside trails.

For the full day's walk, start at Sunset Bay State Park parking area and follow an 0.8-mile stretch of the Oregon Coast Trail overlooking Sunset Bay and the Norton Gulch. The path briefly heads to the right along the road, then parallels the road before heading back into the woods for 1.3 miles before arriving in the core of Shore Acres State Park, site of the Botanical Gardens and the 1906 Simpson mansion, with an observation building suitable for whale-watching. Stay right at a sign for Simpson Beach. The next 0.3 mile leads to this beach in Simpson's Cove. In 0.2 mile, continue right on the Oregon Coast Trail one mile, crossing a creek and heads up a gully to an intersection. Go right on the OCT toward the stunning cliff viewpoints. The trail meets the road, follows it for a brief stretch before passing through a coastal forest and rejoining the road at the Sea Lion Viewpoint, where you can look out a quarter-mile to Shell Island where masses of the sea lions congregate. From here, you'll need to follow the paved road 0.7 mile to Cape Arago, where a short 0.3 mile trail leads out to views over North Cove, the Simpson Reef, and Shell Island. It is possible to arrange a shuttle from this point.

User Groups: Hikers only. Dogs are not allowed in Shore Acres State Park. No horses or mountain bikes allowed. Paved paths in Shore Acres State Park are wheelchair accessible.

Permits: Permits are not required. Parking and access are free.

Maps: For a free park brochure, call Oregon Parks and Recreation, 800/551-6949, or download a free map at www.oregonstateparks.org. For a topographic map, ask the USGS for Charleston and Cape Arago.

Directions: From Coos Bay, drive 12 miles south on Cape Arago Highway, following signs to Sunset Bay State Park. Park in the day-use area on the right. The trailhead is marked as the Oregon Coast Trail.

Contact: Oregon Parks and Recreation Department, 1115 Commercial Street NE, Salem, OR, 97301, 800/551-6949, www.oregonstateparks.org.

62 SOUTH SLOUGH ESTUARY
5.0 mi/2.0 hr   👥1 ⛰7

south of Coos Bay in South Slough Reserve

BEST (

The South Slough National Estuarine Research Reserve is a 4,800-acre mix of freshwater and tidal wetlands, open-water channels, riparian areas, and coastal forest. Egrets perch in the trees, mudflats are exposed at low tide, and Pacific wax myrtle and Port Orford cedar populate the uplands. Salt marshes, sand flats, the list goes on. So why not visit?

There are a number of trails throughout the park, eight miles altogether. To try a loop trail, begin at the Interpretive Center and follow the 0.5-mile Middle Creek Trail. Cross a road and follow the 1.2-mile Hidden Creek Trail to a boardwalk over a skunk cabbage grove and a tide flats observation deck. From here, the 0.4-mile Tunnel Trail heads out a peninsula between the South Slough and Rhodes Marsh right out to the tip, near some old pilings. Head back from the point to a right-hand junction over the Rhodes Dike to the Bog Loop, continuing straight on the 2.5-mile North Creek Trail (where dogs are not permitted). This trail completes the loop, connecting with the 0.2-mile Ten-Minute Trail loop.

User Groups: Hikers. Leashed dogs are admitted on some trails. Some trails are wheelchair accessible.

Permits: Permits are not required. Parking and access are free.

Maps: A downloadable brochure and map is available at www.oregon.gov/DSL/SSNERR/maps.shtml. For a topographic map, ask the USGS for Charleston.

Directions: From U.S. 101 in Coos Bay, take the Cape Arago Highway nine miles west to Charleston. Turn left on Seven Devils Road and go 4.3 miles, turning left into the South Slough Reserve entrance road. In 0.2 mile, park on the left by the interpretive center.

Contact: South Slough Reserve, P.O. Box 5417, Charleston, OR, 97420, 541/888-5558.

63 SEVEN DEVILS WAYSIDE
3.0 mi/1.5 hr 🏃1 ⛰6

north of Bandon on the Pacific Ocean

Some towns have all the luck—and some don't. One of the ones that didn't was Randolph, a gold-rush town that once sat on Whiskey Run Beach and was all but gone in two years. The nearby town of Bandon was burned twice by fires feeding on spiny gorse, a nasty, thorny shrub that blankets areas of the Oregon coast, including the ravines above Whiskey Run Beach and the Seven Devils Wayside. The beaches, though, are thankfully free of it, and this excursion escapes the bristling bush in favor of a hike beneath sandstone cliffs around Fivemile Point. From the Seven Devils Wayside, strike out south along the ocean for 1.4 miles along Merchants Beach to the headland of Fivemile Point, easily passable if the tide is low. Another 0.8 mile beyond this leads along Whiskey Run Beach to another ravine with a beach access road.

User Groups: Hikers, dogs, and horses. No wheelchair facilities.

Permits: Permits are not required. Parking and access are free.

Maps: For a topographic map, ask the USGS for Bullards.

Directions: From Bandon, go north on U.S. 101 for five miles and turn left on Randolph Road, which becomes Seven Devils Road. Follow signs 4.2 miles to Seven Devils State Park.

Contact: Oregon Parks and Recreation Department, 1115 Commercial Street NE, Salem, OR, 97301, 800/551-6949, www.oregonstateparks.org.

64 THE DOERNER FIR
1.0 mi/0.5 hr 🏃1 ⛰7

east of Coos Bay in the Coast Range

Sometimes when you're passing through an area, or taking a nearby hike, it's worth it to get in a little side trip to see something special. The Doerner Fir is one such spectacle, and at 329 feet tall and 11 feet in diameter, maybe this side trip isn't so "small." It is, in fact, the world's largest Douglas fir—and it's somewhere between 500 and 700 years old. This is an opportunity to see how trees grow; you'll notice that on a true old-growth fir, the limbs don't even begin until hundreds of feet up, having been lost over the course of time as they grew in the darkness of other big trees' crowns. Now its own crown is about 10 stories up in the atmosphere. This easy half-mile hike is also a good tour of a coastal rainforest considered to be pristine, with abundant undergrowth of ferns, salmonberry, and vine maple. The trail begins across the road from the parking area, descending into a drainage only 200 feet to visit the massive fir.

User Groups: Hikers and dogs. No wheelchair facilities.

Permits: Permits are not required. Parking and access are free.

Maps: For a topographic map, ask the USGS for Sitkum.

Directions: From Coos Bay, take U.S. 101 south five miles then go left on OR 42 toward Roseburg 11 miles. Just before Coquille, turn left on West Central Boulevard for one mile and go left toward Fairview for 8.1 miles. At a junction, go right onto the Coos Bay Wagon Road for 3.7 miles and turn left on Middle Creek Road for 6.3 miles. At a fork go left toward the Park Creek Recreation Site for 6.6 miles, then turn to the right heading uphill on Burnt Mountain-Middle Creek Tie Road for 4.4 miles to a junction. Turn left, following a "Burnt Ridge Road" sign for 4.6 miles, then go right on gravel Road 27-9-21.0 for 4.3 miles to the trailhead.

Contact: Bureau of Land Management, Coos Bay District, 1300 Airport Lane, North Bend, OR, 97459, 541/756-0100.

65 BULLARDS BEACH STATE PARK
5.0 mi/2.0 hr   🏃1 ⛰7

north of Bandon on the Pacific Ocean

BEST (

The scenic tip of the Bullards Beach peninsula passes an 1896 lighthouse, a view of Bandon (the "Storm Watching Capitol of the World"), and the estuary of the Coquille River, with views to the Bandon Marsh Wildlife Refuge. This state park even has a horse camp, so be prepared to see equestrians passing over the sand at sunset. Anglers and crabbers find this to be one of the best places to ply their trade. You'll get plenty of beach exploration here, both along the ocean and the bay.

From the beach parking area, head to the beach and go left 1.7 miles toward the north jetty and the 47-foot lighthouse. An easy 0.6-mile round-trip walk extends to the tip of the jetty. Then head east from the lighthouse along the river 0.4 mile on an old road and follow the beach 1.9 mile farther along the river to the road. Turn left along the road for 0.4 mile to return to the parking area.

User Groups: Hikers, dogs, and horses. The 1.3-mile bike trail is wheelchair accessible.

Permits: Permits are not required. Parking and access are free.

Maps: For a free park brochure, call Oregon Parks and Recreation, 800/551-6949, or download a free map at www.oregonstateparks.org. For a topographic map, ask the USGS for Bullards.

Directions: Drive U.S. 101 north of Bandon three miles and turn west at a Bullards Beach State Park sign. Drive past the campground entrance and picnic areas 1.4 miles to a junction. Turn right into the beach parking area.

Contact: Oregon Parks and Recreation Department, 1115 Commercial Street NE, Salem, OR, 97301, 800/551-6949, www.oregonstateparks.org.

66 FACE ROCK
3.8 mi/2.0 hr   🏃1 ⛰8

in Bandon at Face Rock Wayside

A Coquille tribal legend says that a maiden named Ewauna, daughter of Chief Siskiyou, decided to sneak off for a late-night swim. Unfortunately, an evil spirit named Seatka who lived in the ocean grabbed her. But she was bright enough to know that to look into his eyes was to be caught forever; to this day, she looks instead to the sky. Looking at Face Rock, the resemblance is, to say the least, uncanny. This maiden is only one of many sea stacks and rocks jutting from the ocean offshore of Bandon-by-the-Sea, and some easy hiking brings one close to this jumble of tide-worn stone.

A staircase descends down Grave Point from the Face Rock Wayside. Turn right at the beach to view Cat and Kittens Rocks, Face Rock, and Elephant Rock. Continue to jutting Coquille Point; by now you've gone 0.9 mile. The next mile continues to the south jetty, with views to the Coquille River Lighthouse and Table Rock.

User Groups: Hikers and dogs. Overlook is wheelchair accessible.

Permits: Permits are not required. Parking and access are free.

Maps: For a topographic map, ask the USGS for Bandon.

Directions: From U.S. 101 in Bandon, head west on 11th Avenue for 0.9 mile, then go left on Beach Loop Road 0.6 mile to the Face Rock Wayside on the right.

Contact: Oregon Parks and Recreation Department, 1115 Commercial Street NE, Salem, OR, 97301, 800/551-6949, www.oregonstateparks.org.

HIKING

HIKING

67 BLACKLOCK POINT
3.8 mi/1.5 hr   🏃1 ⛰7

north of Port Orford in Floras Lake State
Natural Area

On the way to Blacklock Point, you'll pass
through a whole litany of shore shrubbery and
coastal trees, including Sitka spruce and Sitka
alder, pygmy shore pine, evergreen huckleberry, wax myrtle and juniper, black twinberry,
salal, and wild azalea, rhododendron and black
crowberry. All this leads to some serious cliffs
atop Blacklock Point. In this largely undevel-
oped natural area, you may find some solitude;
being off the beaten path, not many people
even know about it. On the grassy headland,
you can spot the Cape Blanco Lighthouse, a
waterfall, and a number of islands.

The trail begins to the left of the gate on a
dirt road that becomes a trail. Follow this 0.8
mile to a creek and trail junction, going left
for 0.6 mile. Then fork left again, then right
for 0.5 mile to the sheer headland of Blacklock
Point. From here, trails fan out into Floras
Lake State Natural Area—following the trail
north along the coast leads to Floras Lake,
and two side trails to the left lead back to the
runway. Taking the first left after a waterfall
makes for a 4.4-mile loop, and taking the next
left at Floras Lake makes a 7.6-mile loop.

User Groups: Hikers, dogs on leash, horses,
and mountain bikes. No wheelchair facilities.

Permits: Permits are not required. Parking
and access are free.

Maps: For a topographic map, ask the USGS
for Floras Lake.

Directions: Go seven miles north of Port
Orford on U.S. 101 and between mileposts
293 and 294, turn west at an "Airport" sign.
Follow County Road 160 for 2.8 miles to a
parking area on the right at the gated entrance
to the airport.

Contact: Oregon Parks and Recreation
Department, 1115 Commercial Street NE,
Salem, OR, 97301, 800/551-6949, www.or-
egonstateparks.org.

68 CAPE BLANCO
4.0 mi/2.0 mi   🏃1 ⛰8

north of Port Orford in Cape Blanco State Park

Standing at the tip of Cape Blanco, you are
at the westernmost point in the state of Oregon. An 1870 lighthouse still functions here,
throwing its light from a cape named on a
1602 Spanish exploration (in which the major-
ity of the ship's crew died of scurvy). There are
many trails here to explore, as well as a historic
1898 Victorian house-turned-museum. For a
good opening exploratory route, a looping tour
of the headland and the North Beach passes
within view of islands, the Sixes River, and
over the headland.

From the boat ramp, and beyond a gate,
take the left-hand path 0.3 mile across a pas-
ture, then fork to the right for 0.4 mile to the
beach. Head left 1.2 miles along North Beach
toward the lighthouse. Just before the end of
the beach, take a trail up a slope 0.3 mile to
the parking area for the lighthouse. Head left
down the road 0.2 mile, then cut to the left at
a trailpost, crossing a meadow 1.3 miles along
the cliff's edges to return to the boat ramp.

User Groups: Hikers, dogs, horses, mountain
bikes. Paved portions of the park are wheelchair accessible.

Permits: Permits are not required. Parking
and access are free.

Maps: For a free park brochure, call Oregon
Parks and Recreation, 800/551-6949, or download a free map at www.oregonstateparks.
org. For a topographic map, ask the USGS
for Bullards.

Directions: Drive U.S 101 north of Port Orford four miles and turn west at a Cape Blanco
State Park sign for four miles to a fork. Go
right, passing the Hughes House Museum,
and park at the Sixes River Boat Ramp.

Contact: Oregon Parks and Recreation
Department, 1115 Commercial Street NE,
Salem, OR, 97301, 800/551-6949, www.or-
egonstateparks.org.

69 GRASSY KNOB

2.4 mi/1.0 hr   👥1 ⛺7

east of Port Orford in Grassy Knob Wilderness

From an old fire watchtower that once stood atop Grassy Knob during World War II, lookouts spotted a Japanese airplane that dropped an incendiary bomb into the forest, hoping to start a fire. The bomb never went off and was never found. The watchtower is now gone, and what remains in this corner of the Siskiyou Mountains is a 17,200-acre Wilderness Area designated by Congress in 1984. The area remains short on trails, but this one trail, actually an old road, leads to a peak overlooking the mountains and the ocean.

From the end of Grassy Knob Road, follow the road behind the gate up 0.4 mile to a side trail on the right leading 0.1 mile up to Grassy Knob's summit. Then continue up the road another 0.7 mile to a gravel turnaround, with views along the way.

User Groups: Hikers and dogs. No wheelchair facilities.

Permits: Permits are not required. Parking and access are free.

Maps: For a map of the Siskiyou National Forest, contact the Rogue River–Siskiyou National Forest headquarters, 3040 Biddle Road, Medford, OR, 97504, 541/618-2200. For a topographic map, ask the USGS for Father Mountain.

Directions: From Port Orford, drive U.S. 101 north four miles and turn east on Grassy Knob Road for 3.9 paved miles and 3.8 more gravel miles to a gate and parking area. The trail begins on the road beyond the gate.

Contact: Siskiyou National Forest, Powers Ranger District, 42861 Highway 242, Powers, OR, 97466, 541/439-6200.

70 BARKLOW MOUNTAIN

2.0 mi/1.0 hr   👥1 ⛺7

northeast of Gold Beach in Siskiyou National Forest

Due to budget cuts, many of the classic fire watchtowers have been abandoned and unmanned for a long time. Many of the relics of that age remain, including a shelter here atop Barklow Mountain. Of course, many of these sites have "remote" as their middle name. Still, if it's solitude you're looking for, you'll find it here.

The short 0.6-mile Barklow Mountain Trail climbs only 500 feet through a forest to the former lookout site here atop the 3,579-foot peak, with views over the Siskiyou Range; a 0.4-mile spur trail leads to the long-collapsed shelter at Barklow Camp. The Barklow Mountain Trail, in all, is six miles and wanders along the north ridge of the mountain, though this stretch is unmaintained, thus making for more opportunity to explore.

User Groups: Hikers and dogs. No horses or mountain bikes allowed. No wheelchair facilities.

Permits: Permits are not required. Parking and access are free.

Maps: For a map of the Siskiyou National Forest, contact the Rogue River–Siskiyou National Forest headquarters, 3040 Biddle Road, Medford, OR, 97504, 541/618-2200. For a topographic map, ask the USGS for Barklow Mountain.

Directions: From Gold Beach, drive Jerrys Flat Road 32 miles along the Rogue River to a bridge near Agness, and continue on Road 33 to Powers for 15.6 miles. From Powers, drive 11.5 miles south on Road 33 and turn right on Road 3353 for 11 miles to the trailhead just past milepost 11.

Contact: Siskiyou National Forest, Powers Ranger District, 42861 Highway 242, Powers, OR, 97466, 541/439-6200.

HIKING

71 COQUILLE RIVER FALLS
1.0 mi/0.5 hr

northeast of Gold Beach in Siskiyou National Forest

The Coquille River Falls Natural Area was established in 1945 to provide examples of the Port Orford cedar, and this rugged mountain canyon also plays host to the Douglas fir, myrtle, Pacific yew, grand fir, and sugar pine. Salamanders, voles, and secretive mammals like the bobcat, martin, and ermine all thrive here. The destination is the double falls on the Coquille River pouring over a bedrock edge into a stony bowl scoured into pockmarked mortars.

From the parking area, the trail abruptly switchbacks down 0.5 mile to a viewpoint of the Coquille River Falls and a series of cascades on Drowned Out Creek. It is possible to scramble around to a higher viewpoint and around the falls themselves, but it should only be attempted in the dry season. Mossy stones and wet leaves on the rocks around the base of the falls beg disaster—care should be taken on the slick rock.

User Groups: Hikers and dogs. No wheelchair facilities.

Permits: Permits are not required. Parking and access are free.

Maps: For a map of the Siskiyou National Forest, contact the Rogue River–Siskiyou National Forest headquarters, 3040 Biddle Road, Medford, OR, 97504, 541/618-2200. For a topographic map, ask the USGS for Illahe.

Directions: From Gold Beach, drive Jerrys Flat Road 32 miles along the Rogue River to a bridge near Agness, and continue on Road 33 to Powers for 15.6 miles. From Powers, travel south on FS 33 for 17 miles to paved FS 3348, turning left. Go 1.5 miles to a pullout on the left.

Contact: Siskiyou National Forest, Powers Ranger District, 42861 Highway 242, Powers, OR, 97466, 541/439-6200.

72 ELK CREEK FALLS
2.4 mi/1.0 hr

northeast of Gold Beach in Siskiyou National Forest

By the time you've come this far south into Oregon, the landscape begins to change along with the trees. Here, the Port Orford cedar is impressive, and the trail past 60-foot Elk Creek Falls goes on to arrive at the world's largest Port Orford, as well as other big tree varieties. But you'll realize you're lucky to see such trees, as logging and a kind of root fungus have seriously jeopardized the survival of the handsome Port Orford.

The trail forks at the trailhead, with the left-hand fork heading a scant 0.1 mile to Elk Creek Falls, a lovely cascade in a fern-lined grotto. Then head up the right-hand fork for 1.2 miles, switchbacking up a steep ridge through flowering rhododendrons. When the trail hits an old dirt road at the one-mile mark, head to the right and watch for the continuation of the path on the left. Here you'll see big Douglas firs and bigleaf maples, and when you turn left at the next junction, you'll easily spot Big Tree, the 239-foot-tall, 12-foot-thick cedar.

User Groups: Hikers and dogs. No wheelchair facilities.

Permits: Permits are not required. Parking and access are free.

Maps: For a map of the Siskiyou National Forest, contact the Rogue River–Siskiyou National Forest headquarters, 3040 Biddle Road, Medford, OR, 97504, 541/618-2200. For a topographic map, ask the USGS for China Flat.

Directions: From Gold Beach and U.S. 101, take Jerrys Flat Road for 32 miles to the bridge over the Rogue River, then continue on Road 33, which eventually turns to gravel, toward Powers another 25.6 miles. The trailhead is between mileposts 57 and 58.

Contact: Siskiyou National Forest, Powers

Ranger District, 42861 Highway 242, Powers, OR, 97466, 541/439-6200.

73 PANTHER RIDGE
4.0 mi-11.2 mi one-way/2.0 hr-1 day
👣3   △8

northeast of Gold Beach in Wild Rogue Wilderness

Here is your introduction to the Siskiyou Mountains: the classic Oregon trees like cedar and Douglas fir augmented by knobcone pine and tanoak, manzanita and chinquapin, and an amazing display of springtime rhododendrons. A wilderness ridge offers unparalleled views over the Rogue River Valley and its associated drainages. Most of this trail traverses the Wild Rogue Wilderness, which cradles the roaring river below. Here is a great opportunity for backpacking, but be sure to bring plenty of water. There's even a rentable lookout at Bald Knob where you may spot early morning elk and black bear. An easy way to start is to visit Hanging Rock, a dizzying edge above the canyon of the Wild Rogue, where the Devil's Backbone descends to Paradise Bar on the Rogue River.

From the Buck Point Trailhead, the Panther Ridge Trail climbs a mile-long ridge to Buck Point, and just around that point is a camping spot around the cedar-shaded spring of Buck Creek. The trail switchbacks up 0.6 mile to a junction. To the left, and 0.4 mile away, is the Hanging Rock. Returning to the trail, you could call it a day or continue on 2.3 miles through what becomes a maze of faint paths—stick to the lowest path to stay on the Panther Ridge Trail. A junction on the right leads 0.3 mile to Panther Camp, another backpacking site. From this junction, the trail continues 1.3 miles to a gravelly spot, where

you'll want to be careful to watch for the right trail. After this, the trail follows an old and overgrown road for 0.2 mile before meeting another road; follow this road to the left 0.2 mile to return to the forest path. In another 0.3 mile pass a spur trail, and enter a denser understory of rhododendron and wildflowers. The next 1.5 miles are a rough descent, then skirts clear-cuts for 1.3 miles. The trail then turns right along an abandoned road for 0.2 mile, then cuts left into the dense forest again. The Panther Ridge Trail ends at Forest Service Road 5520.020 near a gate. Go left on this road for 0.3 mile to arrive at the Bald Knob Lookout, with its expansive views.

User Groups: Hikers, dogs, and horses. No mountain bikes allowed in the wilderness area. No wheelchair facilities.

Permits: Permits are not required. Parking and access are free.

Maps: For a map of the Siskiyou National Forest and the Wild Rogue Wilderness, contact the Rogue River–Siskiyou National Forest headquarters, 3040 Biddle Road, Medford, OR, 97504, 541/618-2200. For a topographic map, ask the USGS for Marial.

Directions: From Gold Beach, drive Jerrys Flat Road 32 miles along the Rogue River to a bridge near Agness, and continue on Road 33 toward Powers for 15.6 miles. Go right on FS Road 3348 for 8.7 miles and turn right on gravel Road 5520 for 1.2 miles, then left on Road 230 to its end at the trailhead. To leave a shuttle at the Bald Knob Lookout, follow Road 3348 for two miles from the junction with Forest Service Road 33, then turn right on Road 5520. Follow this gravel road two miles to the spur road 020 on the right, and take it two miles to the Bald Knob Trailhead.

Contact: Siskiyou National Forest, Powers Ranger District, 42861 Highway 242, Powers, OR, 97466, 541/439-6200.

HIKING

HIKING

74 MOUNT BOLIVAR
2.8 mi/2.0 hr 🚶2 ⛰8

northeast of Gold Beach in Wild Rogue
Wilderness

For whatever reason, this mountain seems to be named for Simón Bolívar, though his conquests were thousands of miles away in South America. If you are of the conquistador spirit, then you'll spot your goal from the trailhead itself, a steep climb to 4,319-foot Mount Bolivar in the Wild Rogue Wilderness. Though it is a notoriously long drive to get here, it's comforting to know that from the peak you will have the commanding view from the Cascades to the California Siskiyous in a 360-degree panoramic view. The trail switchbacks up through open meadows, a Douglas fir forest, and finally onto the wildflower-covered rocky slopes, and all within 1.4 miles and over the course of 1,200 feet elevation gain. At the top, the site of a former lookout, you'll find a plaque commemorating Bolívar.

From the trailhead, begin on the Mount Bolivar Trail. The first mile meanders easily through dense woods and into a drier, sparser pine-fir forest intermingled with manzanita. The trail circles around the north face of the mountain, then begins to climb in the next 0.5 mile, growing steeper as the summit is neared. Return as you came.

User Groups: Hikers and dogs. No horses or mountain bikes allowed. No wheelchair facilities.

Permits: Permits are not required. Parking and access are free.

Maps: For a map of the Siskiyou National Forest, contact the Rogue River–Siskiyou National Forest headquarters, 3040 Biddle Road, Medford, OR, 97504, 541/618-2200. For a topographic map, ask the USGS for Mount Bolivar.

Directions: From Gold Beach, drive Jerrys Flat Road 32 miles along the Rogue River to a bridge near Agness, and continue on Road 33 to Powers for 15.6 miles. From Powers,

turn right on Road 3348 for 18.7 miles to a trailhead on the right, with the final 0.9 mile in BLM land.

Contact: Siskiyou National Forest, Powers Ranger District, 42861 Highway 242, Powers, OR, 97466, 541/439-6200.

75 HUMBUG MOUNTAIN
5.5 mi/3.0 hr 🚶3 ⛰8

south of Port Orford in Humbug Mountain
State Park

This trail has been popular ever since settlers arrived in 1851 looking for gold. They were told that if they climbed this mountain, they would see the mountains filled with gold. Instead, what the scouts saw was more ocean, and they named the peak accordingly. On a sunny day, expect to see the hordes still arriving, looking for that as-good-as-gold view. You will earn that gold in a breathtaking 1,700 foot ascent conveniently, if not mockingly, marked every half-mile up the slope from myrtlewood groves to old-growth Douglas fir. Humbug Mountain also holds the last uncut grove of old-growth trees on the southern Oregon coast. You can even, surprisingly, take this trail as a loop.

After a mile, the path forks. The right-hand fork proves shorter but a bit steeper, and climbs 1.4 mile with views to Cape Blanco. Near the top, a short spur leads 0.1 mile to the summit. Descend by taking the opposite fork, this time to the right, descending 1.9 mile back to the first junction. Continue to the right to return to the trailhead.

User Groups: Hikers and dogs. No horses or mountain bikes allowed. No wheelchair facilities.

Permits: Permits are not required. Parking and access are free.

Maps: For a free park brochure, call Oregon Parks and Recreation, 800/551-6949, or download a free map at www.oregonstateparks.org. For a topographic map, ask the USGS for Port Orford.

Directions: Drive U.S. 101 south of Port Orford six miles and park at a large sign for "Humbug Mountain Trail Parking."

Contact: Oregon Parks and Recreation Department, 1115 Commercial Street NE, Salem, OR, 97301, 800/551-6949, www.oregonstateparks.org.

76 ROGUE RIVER TRAIL
40.0 mi one-way/4-5 days 🏃5 ⛺10

northeast of Gold Beach in Wild Rogue Wilderness

In the heart of the Wild Rogue Wilderness, this 40-mile National Recreation Trail follows a stretch of the Wild and Scenic Rogue River into some serious canyonlands. Give yourself a week to do the entire length, travel time included. There are numerous opportunities for backpacking camps along the river, usually near creeks and sometimes equipped with toilets; there are even lodges along the way where you can make reservations. You'll pass rapids, waterfalls, and nice areas to relax, like Solitude Bar and the Coffeepot. If you're not up for a 40-mile journey, there are plenty of day-hike options in the first 15-mile wilderness stretch. This first portion can be hot and dry, particularly in summer, so be sure to pack enough water.

From the trailhead at Foster Bar, the first 4.3 miles rounds the river opposite Big Bend and continues to Flora Dell Falls, a good day-hike in itself. In another 1.7 miles you'll reach Clay Hill Lodge just above a series of rapids, with a primitive campsite on Tate Creek 0.8 mile beyond that. The next two miles passes a vista at Solitude Bar and another campground at Brushy Bar, beneath the long ridge of the Devil's Backbone. The next 2.9 miles rounds a bend to the Paradise Lodge and an airstrip and a primitive campsite at Blossom Bar beyond that. Another 1.4 miles climbs to a view at Inspiration Point, and the remaining 0.7 mile before a dirt road trailhead passes over the

churning Coffeepot, a boiling cauldron on the river where boaters often face disaster.

Walking along the road to Marial and the Rogue River Ranch for 1.8 miles connects to the remaining 23.2 miles of the Rogue River Trail to its end at Grave Creek, including a cabin at Winkle Bar (5.5 more miles), and campsites at Kelsey Creek (7.6 miles), Meadow Creek (9.4 miles), Copsey Creek (11.1 miles), Russian Creek (17.2 miles), Big Slide (19.3 miles), and Rainie Falls (23 miles). You'll also pass the Tyee Rapids, a narrow stretch appropriately called Slim Pickins, and the Whiskey Creek Cabin museum.

As of April 2009, the Bunker Creek Bridge nine miles downriver from Grave Creek is closed indefinitely, though a detour is in place. A slide in the Dulog area 14 miles downriver from Grave Creek has been deemed difficult to cross or impassable by managing agencies. Contact the Medford office of the BLM (503/808-6001) for updates.

User Groups: Hikers and dogs only. No mountain bikes and horses allowed. No wheelchair facilities.

Permits: Permits are not required. Parking and access are free.

Maps: For a map of the Siskiyou National Forest and the Wild Rogue Wilderness, contact the Rogue River–Siskiyou National Forest headquarters, 3040 Biddle Road, Medford, OR, 97504, 541/618-2200. For a topographic map, ask the USGS for Agness, Marial, Bunker Creek, Quosatana Butte, and Mount Reuben.

Directions: From U.S. 101, at the south end of the Gold Beach Bridge, follow Jerrys Flat Road for 32 miles along the Rogue River; the road becomes Road 33. Just after a river crossing, take a right fork at a sign for Illahe and follow this road for 3.5 paved miles to a trailhead spur on the right. To leave a shuttle at the trailhead, the Grave Creek Trailhead is located north of Galice. From Grants Pass, follow SW G Street/OR 260 west 1.2 miles, then continue on Upper River Road 2.4 miles. Turn right on Azalea Drive Cutoff 0.4 mile, and continue

HIKING

right on Azalea Drive 5.8 miles. Turn left on Galice Road, which becomes Merlin-Galice Road, for 10.7 miles to the town of Galice. Go about 7 miles north of Galice on BLM Road 35-8-13 to the Grave Creek Trailhead.

Contact: Siskiyou National Forest, Gold Beach Ranger District, 29279 Ellensburg Avenue, Gold Beach, OR, 97444, 541/247-3600.

77 COPPER CANYON ON THE ROGUE RIVER

12.6 mi one-way/7.0 hr

northeast of Gold Beach in Siskiyou National Forest

Though the Lower Rogue River Trail can be dauntingly long and laborious, there are options for taking it easier. Or at least, shorter. For a look at a lower section of the Rogue, crossing creek after creek, dipping down to a beach, passing viewpoints of Copper Canyon and crossing the lower reaches of Adams Prairie and a camping spot on Dog Creek, try this section of trail out of the town of Agness. You'll get the best of this region's dramatic canyon scenery, creek hopping along the way on this designated Scenic and Recreational River. You'll begin the trail with a jog over gravel roads and through gates, bringing you to an access point of a beach on an eddy. From there, despite both the private residences and ruins you'll sometimes pass, things get wilder. A shorter stretch can be made out to the halfway point and back for a good 12-mile day, but the ambitious can tackle the whole canyon and even arrange for a shuttle with the myriad providers who do just that for boaters and hikers.

From the lot, walk the trail to a crossing of Rilea Creek and a junction. Here the trail becomes a road to the left, passing through farm property and several gates. Just after the road climbs, the trail picks up on the right. The next 2.1 miles passes a 400-foot elevation viewpoint of the Rogue's Copper Canyon and

Painted Rock Creek, where you'll climb at the 1.5-mile mark to a dirt road, where the trail heads left, crossing Blue Jay Creek before bearing right. You'll arrive at painted Rock creek at the 3.1-mile mark, followed by Leo, Stonehouse, Spring, and Sundown Creeks. This is a good turnaround point, but if you're up for more, the next 4.8 miles reaches a high point of 750 feet at the Adams Prairie, with a spur trail leading into an exploration of its meadows. You'll reach Auberry Creek at the 8.7-mile mark, the campground on Dog Creek at the 9.1-mile mark, and Slide Creek at the 11-mile point. The trail ends at the trailhead on Road 3533 another 2.5 miles past that.

User Groups: Hikers and dogs only. No mountain bikes or horses allowed. No wheelchair facilities.

Permits: Permits are not required. Parking and access are free.

Maps: For a map of the Siskiyou National Forest, contact the Rogue River–Siskiyou National Forest headquarters, 3040 Biddle Road, Medford, OR, 97504, 541/618-2200. For a topographic map, ask the USGS for Agness.

Directions: From U.S. 101, at the south end of the Gold Beach Bridge, follow Jerrys Flat Road for 32 miles along the Rogue River; the road becomes Road 33. Just after a river crossing, turn left at a sign for Agness. Follow this one-lane paved road three miles to the Agness Store and turn right on Cougar Lane for 0.2 mile. Park in the Agness Community Library gravel lot. Walk straight on the gravel road, following trail signs and passing two gates to the trail's start on the right. To shuttle and do the entire length of this trail, leave a vehicle at the west trailhead. To get there, take Jerrys Flat Road from Gold Beach (the road becomes FS 33) about 9.8 miles to the Lobster Creek Bridge. Cross the bridge and take the first right on FS Road 3533, continuing 3.7 miles to FS Road 340. Follow signs about three miles to the trailhead.

Contact: Siskiyou National Forest, Gold Beach Ranger District, 29279 Ellensburg Avenue, Gold Beach, OR, 97444, 541/247-3600.

78 ILLINOIS RIVER
5.0-17.2 mi/3.0 hr-2 days 🏃5 ⛰10

northeast of Gold Beach in Siskiyou National Forest

A tributary of the Rogue River, the Illinois River is every bit as rugged as the famous waterway, the difference being that this National Recreation Trail never comes close to the river. Instead, this trail traverses into the Kalmiopsis Wilderness and even goes up and over Bald Mountain. The river itself holds a Wild and Scenic River designation, in no small part because of its substantial beauty—and good fishing. If the whole trail is not an option for the day, an easy hike to the Buzzards Roost is a good destination. But if you're in the mood and in tip-top shape, the strenuous hike to Silver Creek will test your endurance. When you've warmed up, then you may be ready to tackle the entire 27-mile length. This trail is located in the area charred by the 2002 Biscuit Fire burn; take caution and proceed knowingly. Along the way, look for recovering madrone, tanoak, myrtlewood, and black huckleberry.

The Illinois River Trail sets out from Oak Flat and climbs the canyon wall for 2.5 miles to Buzzards Roost, hung over 1,000 feet in the air above the river. This makes for a good day trip. Continuing 1.7 miles up the trail, you'll come to Indigo Creek and Indian Flat, with a left-hand spur trail leading into the meadows just before the creek. From there the trail descends slowly for 3.7 miles past the old Fantz Ranch, now USFS property, crossing numerous creeks before arriving at the canyon of Silver Creek.

User Groups: Hikers, dogs, and horses. No mountain bikes allowed. No wheelchair facilities.

Permits: Permits are not required. Parking and access are free.

Maps: For a map of the Siskiyou National Forest and the Kalmiopsis Wilderness, contact the Rogue River–Siskiyou National Forest headquarters, 3040 Biddle Road, Medford, OR, 97504, 541/618-2200. For a topographic map, ask the USGS for Agness.

Directions: From U.S. 101, at the south end of the Gold Beach Bridge, follow Jerrys Flat Road for 28 miles along the Rogue River to the bridge over the Illinois River. On the far side of the crossing, turn right on Oak Flat Road for three miles. The trailhead lot is on the left along a gravel road just beyond the end of the pavement.

Contact: Siskiyou National Forest, Gold Beach Ranger District, 29279 Ellensburg Avenue, Gold Beach, OR, 97444, 541/247-3600.

79 INDIAN MARY PARK
2.8 mi/1.5 hr   🏃1 ⛰7

west of Grants Pass on the Rogue River

This historic park has a long history in an area known for its wars between white settlers and Native Americans. In 1855, one Umpqua Joe warned the white settlers of an impending attack, which they thwarted. For this he was awarded a piece of land from where he operated a ferry. He died in 1886, and his daughter, Indian Mary, kept operating the ferry crossing. Once she left for Grants Pass, the land changed hands several times until 1958, when Josephine County bought it and made it into the park it is today. The sole trail in the park is named for Umpqua Joe and climbs to a viewpoint over the Rogue River.

The trail starts across the highway from the campground and day parking lot. The trail alternates between steep and easy, climbing 0.8 mile to a 0.2-mile viewpoint loop fork to the left. Returning to the main trail, climb 0.5 mile through black oaks to the official trail's end high above the river.

User Groups: Hikers and dogs. No wheelchair facilities.

Permits: Permits are not required. A $2-per-car day-use pass is required, or you can purchase a $25 annual pass.

HIKING

HIKING

Maps: For a topographic map, ask the USGS for Galice.

Directions: From I-5, take the Merlin exit 61 north of Grants Pass and follow signs 3.6 miles to Merlin on the Merlin-Galice Road, then go straight seven miles to the park entrance on the right.

Contact: Josephine County Parks, 125 Ringuette Street, Grants Pass, OR, 97527, 541/474-5285.

80 SHRADER OLD-GROWTH TRAIL

0.8 mi/0.5 hr   🏃1 ▲6

northeast of Gold Beach in Siskiyou National Forest

BEST (

This easy loop trail is the home of Laddie Gale Douglas fir, 220 feet high and 10 feet thick, named for a legendary University of Oregon basketball player who led the team to a national championship victory way back in 1939. Quite the commemoration. The wide and easy trail is perfect for families. This is a fine trail to take slowly, savoring the forest that a typical hiker may normally move through at a quick clip.

From the parking area, the loop is an easy stroll through not only stately Douglas fir and cedars, but deciduous tanoak. Just inside the forest, the trail splits for the loop. Go left and in 0.2 mile cross a stream on a footbridge. From here, follow the loop through the colossal trees another 0.6 mile, gradually ascending back to the start of the loop. Along the way you'll pass the Laddie Gale commemorative tree.

User Groups: Hikers and dogs only. No wheelchair facilities.

Permits: Permits are not required. Parking and access are free.

Maps: For a map of the Siskiyou National Forest, contact the Rogue River–Siskiyou National Forest headquarters, 3040 Biddle Road, Medford, OR, 97504, 541/618-2200. A brochure map is available at the trailhead. For a topographic map, ask the USGS for Brushy Bald Mountain.

Directions: From U.S. 101, at the south end of the Gold Beach Bridge, follow Jerrys Flat Road for 11.2 miles. Pass Lobster Creek Campground on the left and turn right at a sign for the Frances Schrader memorial Trail. Follow Road 3300-090 for 2.1 steep miles to a lot on the left.

Contact: Siskiyou National Forest, Gold Beach Ranger District, 29279 Ellensburg Avenue, Gold Beach, OR, 97444, 541/247-3600.

81 OTTER POINT

1.4 mi/0.5 hr   🏃1 ▲7

north of Gold Beach on the Pacific Ocean

This seldom-seen series of trails are off the beaten path a bit, though not far from nearby U.S. 101. Wind-sculpted sandstone formations and a long beach laid bare by waves are only a short distance from all the traffic—and are worth a visit. From the parking area at this State Recreation Area, it's a 0.4-mile round-trip to the headland of Otter Point, with its view out over a long southern beach, and a short scramble trail to a hidden beach on the north face. A second trail heads south from the lot, descending to a beach with plenty of room to run.

User Groups: Hikers and dogs. No wheelchair facilities.

Permits: Permits are not required. Parking and access are free.

Maps: For a topographic map, ask the USGS for Gold Beach.

Directions: From Gold Beach, drive north on U.S. 101 for three miles. Near milepost 325, take a right at a sign for "Old Coast Road" and drive west to a T-junction. Turn right for 0.6 mile, then left at a state park sign, driving to the end at a parking area.

Contact: Oregon Parks and Recreation Department, 1115 Commercial Street NE,

Salem, OR, 97301, 800/551-6949, www.or-egonstateparks.org.

82 BIG PINE INTERPRETIVE LOOP
2.5 mi/1.0 hr 👫1 △8

west of Grants Pass in Siskiyou National Forest

BEST (

Along a stretch of Myers Creek, a network of four looping trails goes through a forest centered around "Big Pine," a 250-foot-high, double-topped ponderosa pine tree with a six-foot diameter. It's anyone's guess how many people it would take to get their arms around it. This is a great hike for the family, especially if you're staying at the Big Pine Campground. With wheelchair-friendly paths and more great trails nearby, this makes for a good launch point into the area. A second trail extending from the loop further surveys the old-growth Douglas fir and ponderosa pine in the area.

To walk the Big Pine Interpretive Loop, cross the bridge over Myers Creek and bear right. You'll find Big Pine in the first 0.1 mile. Continue around the loop 0.3 mile to find a marginally maintained spur, the Taylor Camp Trail. This trail is steeper and brushier, but makes for an added exploration of up to a mile one-way, before it ends at an old logging road. Return as you came and continue counterclockwise on the Big Pine Trail to complete the loop.

User Groups: Hikers and dogs. The path is wheelchair accessible.

Permits: Permits are not required. A federal Northwest Forest Pass is required to park here; the cost is $5 a day or $30 for an annual pass. You can buy a day pass at the trailhead, at ranger stations, or through private vendors.

Maps: For a map of the Siskiyou National Forest, contact the Rogue River–Siskiyou National Forest headquarters, 3040 Biddle Road, Medford, OR, 97504, 541/618-2200. For a topographic map, ask the USGS for Chrome Ridge.

Directions: From I-5, take the Merlin exit 61 north of Grants Pass and follow signs 3.6 miles to Merlin on the Merlin-Galice Road, then go straight 8.5 miles toward Galice and turn left on Briggs Valley Road/FS 25 for 12.5 miles. Turn right at the Big Pine Campground entrance and keep right for the day-use parking area.

Contact: Siskiyou National Forest, Wild Rivers Ranger District, 2164 Spalding Avenue, Grants Pass, OR, 97526, 541/471-6500.

83 TAYLOR CREEK
10.1 mi one-way/1-2 days 👫3 △7

west of Grants Pass in Siskiyou National Forest

Taylor Creek's watershed in the Siskiyou Mountains offers many opportunities to explore in many directions. Briggs Creek, Minnow Creek, China Creek, Dutchy Creek, and two interpretive trails, including the Big Pine Loop (see *Big Pine Interpretive Loop,* previous listing) and the Burned Timber Nature Trail all extend from Taylor Creek's trail. It is possible to hike the creek in differing lengths, as the trail ducks in an out of the forest, meeting the road. Active claims are still to be found along the way, as this area has a mining legacy going way back.

From the lower trailhead, hike into the forest of red-barked madrone, live oak, and Douglas fir. Watch for miner's claim notices tacked to trees. Within the first 1.8 miles, the path crosses Taylor Creek on a 60-foot-high bridge, passes the Burned Timber Loop, and meets up with another bridge to the Tin Can Campground. After another 1.4 miles, the trail crosses Road 052 and continues another 0.6 mile to the next trailhead. The next 2.6 miles crosses the creek twice and arrives at Lone Tree Pass. The final 3.6 miles leaves the creek and heads into the woods, passing a 0.7-mile spur trail to the Big Pine Campground before reaching the final trailhead.

HIKING

User Groups: Hikers, dogs, horses, and mountain bikes. No wheelchair facilities.

Permits: Permits are not required. A federal Northwest Forest Pass is required to park here; the cost is $5 a day or $30 for an annual pass. You can buy a day pass at the trailhead, at ranger stations, or through private vendors.

Maps: For a map of the Siskiyou National Forest, contact the Rogue River–Siskiyou National Forest headquarters, 3040 Biddle Road, Medford, OR, 97504, 541/618-2200. For a topographic map, ask the USGS for Chrome Ridge and Galice.

Directions: From I-5, take the Merlin exit 61 north of Grants Pass and follow signs 3.6 miles to Merlin on the Merlin-Galice Road, then go straight 8.5 miles toward Galice and turn left on Briggs Valley Road/FS 25 for 3.1 miles to a pullout on the left marked "Taylor Creek Trailhead." Consider a shuttle at the Big Pine Campground, which connects to the Taylor Creek Trail. To find the campground from the town of Merlin, follow Galice Road 8.5 miles and go left at Road 25, continuing 12.5 miles to the campground on the right.

Contact: Siskiyou National Forest, Wild Rivers Ranger District, 2164 Spalding Avenue, Grants Pass, OR, 97526, 541/471-6500.

84 BRIGGS CREEK

9.5 mi/1 day

west of Grants Pass in Siskiyou National Forest

Briggs Creek has mining history to spare, and in this section of the Siskiyous, there are even some modern mining claims continuing today. Though this trail goes on much farther, there is a great option of visiting the abandoned Courier Mine Cabin, making for a great day. This trail is easiest in low water, as several fords are required. It's also popular for its abundance of swimming holes. In the meadow at Sam Brown Campground, once the site of an entire mining town, the only thing left is the grave of Sam Brown himself, one of the first African American men in southern Oregon, shot for allegedly conferencing with the miners' wives in a way the miners didn't appreciate.

The trail sets out, alternately following dirt roads and trail, from clear-cut to forests of fir, yew, and cedar, for 2.4 miles along the creek, passing the Elkhorn Mine, with its rusty machinery still left behind, and reaching the 30-foot-wide creek ford. The trail continues another 1.5 miles past tanoak, madrone, and sugar pine to the abandoned flume of the Courier Mine and finally to the one-room cabin. From here, the trail fords the creek again, continuing on to its end at Soldier Creek.

User Groups: Hikers, dogs, horses, and mountain bikes. No wheelchair facilities.

Permits: Permits are not required. A federal Northwest Forest Pass is required to park here; the cost is $5 a day or $30 for an annual pass. You can buy a day pass at the trailhead, at ranger stations, or through private vendors.

Maps: For a map of the Siskiyou National Forest, contact the Rogue River–Siskiyou National Forest headquarters, 3040 Biddle Road, Medford, OR, 97504, 541/618-2200. For a topographic map, ask the USGS for York Butte.

Directions: From I-5, take the Merlin exit 61 north of Grants Pass and follow signs 3.6 miles to Merlin on the Merlin-Galice Road, then go straight 8.5 miles toward Galice and turn left on Briggs Valley Road/FS 25 for 13.4 miles. One mile after the Big Pine Campground, turn right on FS Road 2512 for 0.3 mile, then turn left into the Sam Brown Campground, keeping left. Park in the large trailhead lot on the right.

Contact: Siskiyou National Forest, Wild Rivers Ranger District, 2164 Spalding Avenue, Grants Pass, OR, 97526, 541/471-6500.

85 ILLINOIS RIVER TRAIL TO BALD MOUNTAIN
20.6 mi/1–2 days

northwest of Cave Junction in Kalmiopsis Wilderness

Many hikers think of this trail as one of the best in southern Oregon. This entry into the Kalmiopsis Wilderness, overlooking the Wild and Scenic Illinois River, has plenty to brag about. Pounding rapids, sweet campsites, and an abundance of creeks, all crowned by 3,917-foot Bald Mountain, are enough to suit anyone's taste. Although the 2002 Biscuit Fire started with a lightning strike at Florence Creek near this trail, many of the towering trees survived. In other areas, pine are repopulating the area, slowly but surely, and scrub oak and tanoak have already made their comeback.

The Illinois River Trail begins at a 140-foot steel bridge over Briggs Creek and the site of an old homestead. The first 4.5 miles heads into the wilderness area and crosses several creeks beneath York Butte, with views to the river below. At a junction, a loop trail begins with the goal being Bald Mountain. Go left 0.8 mile on the Pine Flat Trail to get to Pine Flat, a great camping spot overlooking Boat Eater Rapids, a granite island and six-foot drop whose name speaks for itself. Continue 2.6 steep miles to a junction. If you're tired, go to the right on a spur trail for 1.3 miles to connect to and follow the Illinois River Trail to the right four miles back to the junction above Pine Flat. If not, endure another 1.8-mile climb on the Pine Flat Trail to a campsite by a spring, keeping left at a junction with the Illinois River Trail to ascend to a 0.2-mile loop around lofty Bald Mountain's summit. Then descend, following the Illinois River Trail down 5.6 miles to the junction above Pine Flat, going left on the Illinois River Trail to return to the trailhead.

User Groups: Hikers, dogs, and horses. No mountain bikes allowed. No wheelchair facilities.

Permits: Permits are not required. A federal Northwest Forest Pass is required to park here; the cost is $5 a day or $30 for an annual pass. You can buy a day pass at the trailhead, at ranger stations, or through private vendors.

Maps: For a map of the Siskiyou National Forest and the Kalmiopsis Wilderness, contact the Rogue River–Siskiyou National Forest headquarters, 3040 Biddle Road, Medford, OR, 97504, 541/618-2200. For a topographic map, ask the USGS for Agness, York Butte, and Silver Peak.

Directions: From Grants Pass, head south on U.S. 199 toward Crescent City for 20 miles to a flashing yellow light in Selma. Turn right on Illinois River Road 4103 for 18.6 miles to the end of a rough gravel road at the Briggs Creek Trailhead.

Contact: Siskiyou National Forest, Wild Rivers Ranger District, 2164 Spalding Avenue, Grants Pass, OR, 97526, 541/471-6500.

86 CAPE SEBASTIAN
3.8–5.8 mi/2.0–3.0 hr

south of Gold Beach in Cape Sebastian State Park

In 1603, the Spanish explorer Sebastian Vizcaino named this cape—not so much for himself as for Saint Sebastian. The views on a clear day extend 43 miles to the north to Humbug Mountain. To the south, a 50-mile view extends all the way to California. The cape itself hosts a dense Sitka spruce forest and overlooks Hunters Cove and Hunters Island, where cormorants hang out.

From the lot, the trail heads out over the cape for 1.4 miles, descending in the last portion to a striking lookout. The next 0.5-mile section follows the headland for more views before descending to the beach. For a longer hike, follow the beach towards the sea stacks for another mile to the Myers Creek pullout, a good turnaround point.

User Groups: Hikers and dogs. Paved trails are wheelchair accessible.

Permits: Permits are not required. Parking and access are free.

Maps: For a topographic map, ask the USGS for Cape Sebastian.

Directions: Drive south of Gold Beach seven miles on U.S. 101 and near milepost 335 turn at a "Cape Sebastian Viewpoint" sign, following this road 0.6 mile up the cape to a parking area.

Contact: Oregon Parks and Recreation Department, 1115 Commercial Street NE, Salem, OR, 97301, 800/551-6949, www.oregonstateparks.org.

87 SNOW CAMP LOOKOUT
7.0 mi/3.5 hr   👥2 ⛰8

northeast of Brookings in Kalmiopsis Wilderness

One of the losses of the Biscuit Fire was the original Snow Camp Lookout, a 15-by-15-foot lookout that had been restored prior to the fire. The good news is, it's been rebuilt yet again. From the new lookout, rentable for $30 a night, the ocean is visible on clear days—and in fact, this site offers a 360-degree view. The longer trail to the lookout is one of the oldest in the Siskiyou National Forest, dating at least as far back as 1911, and portions of it have been identified as an old Native American trail.

Snow Camp Trail passes through wildflower heaven in the spring and summer, including azalea, beargrass, iris, cat's ear lilies, death camas, and Indian paintbrush. The first 1.7 miles pass the ruins of an old shelter, a rocky knoll, and eventually meeting up with Windy Creek. Take the left-hand turn here, fording the deep and cold Windy Creek and continuing steeply another mile. It is not a difficult ford but is best done in summer. A left-hand junction heads to Panther Lake, but stick to the right another 0.7 mile, climbing Snow Camp Mountain. At the next junction,

go right again 0.6 mile on the Snow Camp Lookout Trail to the lookout road and head for the top.

User Groups: Hikers, dogs, and horses. No mountain bikes allowed. No wheelchair facilities.

Permits: Permits are not required. Parking and access are free.

Maps: For a map of the Siskiyou National Forest, contact the Rogue River–Siskiyou National Forest headquarters, 3040 Biddle Road, Medford, OR, 97504, 541/618-2200. For a topographic map, ask the USGS for Collier Butte.

Directions: From Brookings and the U.S. 101 bridge, take the North Bank Road east eight miles and continue straight on Road 1376 an additional eight miles to a junction after the South Fork Chetco Bridge. Turn left, following "Snow Camp Lookout" signs on Road 1376 another 13 miles to a trailhead on the left a few hundred yards after milepost 21.

Contact: Siskiyou National Forest, Chetco Ranger District, 539 Chetco Lane, Brookings, OR, 97415, 541/412-6000.

88 WINDY VALLEY
4.4 mi/2.5 hr   👥1 ⛰7

northeast of Brookings in Siskiyou National Forest

The Klamath Mountains rise above the ocean at the southernmost stretch of the Oregon coast, playing host to a wild diversity of trees and wildflowers. The Windy Valley Trail, unfortunately, is located along a stretch burned by the 2002 Biscuit Fire, one of the biggest in Oregon's history. Yet, for a learning experience, trails like this are a great way to see how a forest regenerates itself. One thing that colonizes this area is the Darlingtonia californica, the carnivorous pitcher plant also known as the cobra lily, which makes a meal of local bugs. This strange flower is native to this area and is rarely found anywhere else.

The Windy Valley Trail will pass through wildflower heaven in the spring and summer, including azalea, beargrass, iris, cat's ear lilies, death camas, and Indian paintbrush. The first 1.7 miles pass the ruins of an old shelter, a rocky knoll, and eventually meeting up with Windy Creek. Stay to the right for 0.5 mile to another crossing (there may still be a log there) and continuing into Windy Valley's meadows to the foundations of an old cabin beside a pool and small waterfall. Return as you came.

User Groups: Hikers, dogs, and horses. No mountain bikes allowed. No wheelchair facilities.

Permits: Permits are not required. Parking and access are free.

Maps: For a map of the Siskiyou National Forest, contact the Rogue River-Siskiyou National Forest headquarters, 3040 Biddle Road, Medford, OR, 97504, 541/618-2200. For a topographic map, ask the USGS for Collier Butte.

Directions: From Brookings and the U.S. 101 bridge, take the North Bank Road east 8 miles and continue straight on Road 1376 an additional 8 miles to a junction after the South Fork Chetco Bridge. Turn left, following "Snow Camp Lookout" signs on Road 1376 another 13 miles to a trailhead on the left a few hundred yards after milepost 21.

Contact: Siskiyou National Forest, Chetco Ranger District, 539 Chetco Lane, Brookings, OR, 97415, 541/412-6000.

89 MISLATNAH TRAIL TO MISLATNAH PEAK
9.6 mi/4.5 hr   🥾3 ⛰8

northeast of Brookings in Kalmiopsis Wilderness

There is only one route into the Big Craggies Botanical Area deep in the Kalmiopsis Wilderness, and this is it. The Big Craggies is a rocky, densely brushed area requiring cross-country travel. On top of that, this trail also

tops Mislatnah Peak, the site of a former lookout. Access to this trail is somewhat sketchy, as there is a slide on the Tincup Trail, which provides access to this trail about 0.9 mile from the trailhead. Also, you have to watch as you cross the prairies, as the trail has a way of vanishing and reappearing like magic. Check current conditions before you go.

From the parking area, start out on the Tincup Trail, descending 0.9 mile to Mislatnah Creek and the woodsy, grassy bench of Mislatnah Camp. Follow the trail upstream 0.1 mile to a horse crossing and ford the creek. Continue downstream for 0.3 mile and turn left on the Mislatnah Trail. In 0.6 mile, you'll pass a spring and enter the Upper Mislatnah Prairie in 0.2 mile beyond that. Here is where to really watch for the trail as it crosses the prairie 0.3 mile, entering the trees on the far side. The trail continues through a dry tanoak and madrone woodland for 1.4 miles to Jacks Camp, where signs point out a spring. Beyond the camp, the Kalmiopsis Wilderness begins, and the brush grows thicker along this steep ridge. Only 1.0 mile farther, the trail ascends to the 3,124-foot Mislatnah Peak, with views to the Big Craggies.

User Groups: Hikers, dogs, and horses. No mountain bikes allowed. No wheelchair facilities.

Permits: Permits are not required. Parking and access are free.

Maps: For a map of the Siskiyou National Forest and the Kalmiopsis Wilderness, contact the Rogue River–Siskiyou National Forest headquarters, 3040 Biddle Road, Medford, OR, 97504, 541/618-2200. For a topographic map, ask the USGS for Big Craggies.

Directions: From Brookings and the U.S. 101 bridge, take North Bank Road east eight miles and continue straight on Road 1376 an additional eight miles to a junction after the South Fork Chetco Bridge. Turn left, following Road 1376 another 10 miles to milepost 18, then fork right onto Road 360 for 1.5 miles, keeping right at Road 365 for the last 0.8 mile to the Tincup Trailhead.

HIKING

Contact: Siskiyou National Forest, Chetco Ranger District, 539 Chetco Lane, Brookings, OR, 97415, 541/412-6000.

90 TINCUP TRAIL TO BOULDER CREEK CAMP
7.2 mi/3.0 hr   🏃3 △7

northeast of Brookings in Kalmiopsis Wilderness

The Tincup Trail makes its way into the Kalmiopsis Wilderness following the Chetco River along an old gold prospectors' trail, heading across Bronson Prairie to the confluence of the Chetco and Boulder Creek, a good turnaround for a 7.2-mile day. Note that fords are necessary and those fords can only be done in late summer. Also, access to this trail is limited due to a slide on the Tincup Trail at Mislatnah Creek 0.9 mile from the trailhead, though there are other options to get to the trail. Check current conditions before you go.

From the parking area, start out on the Tincup Trail, descending 0.9 mile to Mislatnah Creek and the woodsy, grassy bench of Mislatnah Camp. Follow the trail upstream a mile to a horse crossing and ford the creek. Continue downstream for 0.3 mile to a junction with the Mislatnah Trail. Continue 2.3 miles upstream to Boulder Creek Camp, with access to water and campsites—meaning this a great place to cool your heels. Hardy hikers can continue on the nearly 20-mile trail to its end at Darling Creek.

User Groups: Hikers, dogs, and horses. No mountain bikes allowed. No wheelchair facilities.

Permits: Permits are not required. Parking and access are free.

Maps: For a map of the Siskiyou National Forest and the Kalmiopsis Wilderness, contact the Rogue River–Siskiyou National Forest headquarters, 3040 Biddle Road, Medford, OR, 97504, 541/618-2200. For a topographic map, ask the USGS for Big Craggies.

Directions: From Brookings and the U.S. 101 bridge, take North Bank Road east eight miles and continue straight on Road 1376 an additional eight miles to a junction after the South Fork Chetco Bridge. Turn left, following Road 1376 another 10 miles to milepost 18, then fork right onto Road 360 for 1.5 miles, keeping right at Road 365 for the last 0.8 mile to the Tincup Trailhead.

Contact: Siskiyou National Forest, Chetco Ranger District, 539 Chetco Lane, Brookings, OR, 97415, 541/412-6000.

91 ILLINOIS RIVER FALLS
1.2 mi/0.5 hr   🏃1 △6

northwest of Cave Junction in Siskiyou National Forest

Heavily damaged during the Biscuit Fire, the Fall Creek Trail was closed due to a burned-out bridge; check on the status of this trail with the U.S. Forest Service before attempting it. If you can get there, it's an easy hike across a bridge to the far side of the Illinois River. Go left 0.4 mile, then head cross country along the river about 300 yards to a view of the 10-foot Illinois River Falls. Watch out for poison oak, as it grows back viciously after fires.

User Groups: Hikers, dogs, and horses. No mountain bikes allowed. No wheelchair facilities.

Permits: Permits are not required. Parking and access are free.

Maps: For a map of the Siskiyou National Forest, contact the Rogue River–Siskiyou National Forest headquarters, 3040 Biddle Road, Medford, OR, 97504, 541/618-2200. For a topographic map, ask the USGS for Pearsoll Peak.

Directions: From Grants Pass, head south on U.S. 199 toward Crescent City for 20 miles to a flashing yellow light in Selma. Turn right on Illinois River Road 4103 for 11 miles. At an "End Maintenance" sign, turn left at a gravel pullout onto Road 087, a rough descent 0.5 mile to a bridge.

Contact: Siskiyou National Forest, Wild Rivers Ranger District, 2164 Spalding Avenue, Grants Pass, OR, 97526, 541/471-6500.

92 BABYFOOT LAKE
2.4-5.3 mi/1.0-2.5 hr

west of Cave Junction in Siskiyou National Forest

For a firsthand look at the devastation—and survival—of flora in a wildfire, head to Babyfoot Lake. The trail passes through a ghost wilderness of black snags that nevertheless harbor new blooms of beargrass and Oregon grape, feeding on sunlight from the opened canopy. The lake itself is an oasis, and the trail passes through the Babyfoot Lake Botanical Area: Western red cedar, incense cedar, and Port Orford cedar all survived here, as did Jeffrey pine and Brewer's weeping spruce. Tanoak trees along the way simply sprout new trees from their roots. The entire hike is a valuable lesson in fire ecology. The lake itself is a high mountain lake in a glacial cirque.

From the trailhead, enter the burned forest on the Babyfoot Lake Trail, going 0.3 mile to a junction. From there, head to the right, descending gently 0.9 mile to the Kalmiopsis Wilderness border and Babyfoot Lake. For an interesting loop, continue past Babyfoot to Trail 1124, an old road, in 0.5 mile. Go left, following this Kalmiopsis Rim Trail along 1.8 miles to a rock cairn and a burned sign marking the trail to the left. Follow the Ridge Trail for another view down to Babyfoot Lake, keeping right at the next two junctions for 1.8 miles back to the trailhead.

User Groups: Hikers and dogs. No horses or mountain bikes allowed. No wheelchair facilities.

Permits: Permits are not required. A federal Northwest Forest Pass is required to park here; the cost is $5 a day or $30 for an annual pass.

You can buy a day pass at the trailhead, at ranger stations, or through private vendors.

Maps: For a map of the Siskiyou National Forest and the Kalmiopsis Wilderness, contact the Rogue River–Siskiyou National Forest headquarters, 3040 Biddle Road, Medford, OR, 97504, 541/618-2200. For a topographic map, ask the USGS for Josephine Mountain.

Directions: Drive U.S. 199 south of Grants Pass 24 miles and turn west on Eight Dollar Road, following signs for Kalmiopsis Wilderness. The road becomes Road 4201 and crosses the Illinois River in three miles then continues on gravel for 12 more miles. At a fork, follow signs for Babyfoot lake and go left on Road 140 for 0.7 mile to a trailhead spur on the right.

Contact: Siskiyou National Forest, Wild Rivers Ranger District, 2164 Spalding Avenue, Grants Pass, OR, 97526, 541/471-6500.

93 VULCAN PEAK
2.6 mi/2.0 hr

east of Brookings in Kalmiopsis Wilderness

Atop Vulcan Peak lie the remains of an old fire watchtower, a few metal pieces, some bits of glass. The view is expansive across, ironically, the massive burn of the 2002 Biscuit Fire. Nonetheless, this is a straightforward climb with views extending down to Vulcan Lake (see *Vulcan Lake,* next listing) and the Chetco River drainage system.

From the trailhead, walk up an abandoned roadbed 0.2 mile to a junction with the Chetco Divide Trail. Fork left and climb 1.1 miles and nearly 1,000 feet to a view encompassing the Siskiyou Mountains, the Kalmiopsis Wilderness, and the Pacific Ocean.

User Groups: Hikers, dogs, and horses. No mountain bikes allowed. No wheelchair facilities.

Permits: A free wilderness permit is required and available at the trailhead. Parking and access are free.

HIKING

HIKING

Maps: For a map of the Siskiyou National Forest and the Kalmiopsis Wilderness, contact the Rogue River–Siskiyou National Forest headquarters, 3040 Biddle Road, Medford, OR, 97504, 541/618-2200. For a topographic map, ask the USGS for Chetco Peak.

Directions: From the U.S. 101 bridge in Brookings, head east on North Bank Road for eight miles, continuing straight on Road 1376 another eight miles. At a junction just beyond the South Fork Chetco Bridge, turn right on gravel Road 1909 for 13.4 miles, following signs for Kalmiopsis Wilderness. At a fork, go right into the Vulcan Peak Trailhead.

Contact: Siskiyou National Forest, Chetco Ranger District, 539 Chetco Lane, Brookings, OR, 97415, 541/412-6000.

94 VULCAN LAKE

3.7 mi/2.5 hr

east of Brookings in Kalmiopsis Wilderness

BEST (

Every good explorer can recount some beautiful mountain lake stumbled upon in the heat of the day, and how refreshing it was to sink down into some cold mountain water and feel all tensions slip away. Vulcan Lake is certainly one of these places, and as a destination it seems fitting: Its loop trail leads over some serious rocky country scarred by the 2002 Biscuit Fire but, all things considered, is recovering nicely. It makes for a hot hike and a cool finish. On the way, the trail passes the remains of the old Gardner Mine, the Sorvaag Bog, and two lovely lakes in the presence of Vulcan Peak. The lakes themselves lie in a prehistoric cirque, when this area was scoured down to bedrock by glaciers. Vulcan Lake is not only great for swimming on a hot day, it's also a great entry point for a backpacking exploration.

From the trailhead at road's end, head to the right on the Vulcan Lake Trail for 1.4 miles, climbing to a pass overlooking not one, but two lakes (a bit farther in the distance is Little

Vulcan Lake) before heading down to Vulcan Lake. Here you'll find a junction; go right to Vulcan Lake, straight to Little Vulcan, and to the left for a challenging loop. This left-hand trail leads 1.1 miles along a barely discernable path, so watch the cairns stacked here. You'll pass the bog and the mine—both good for exploration—before joining the Johnson Butte Trail. Go left 0.8 mile along this old roadbed to return to the trailhead.

User Groups: Hikers, dogs, and horses. No mountain bikes allowed. No wheelchair facilities.

Permits: A free wilderness permit is required and available at the trailhead. Parking and access are free.

Maps: For a map of the Siskiyou National Forest and the Kalmiopsis Wilderness, contact the Rogue River–Siskiyou National Forest headquarters, 3040 Biddle Road, Medford, OR, 97504, 541/618-2200. For a topographic map, ask the USGS for Chetco Peak and Tincup Peak.

Directions: From the U.S. 101 bridge in Brookings, head east on North Bank Road for eight miles, continuing straight on Road 1376 another eight miles. At a junction just beyond the South Fork Chetco Bridge, turn right on gravel Road 1909 for 13.4 miles, following signs for Kalmiopsis Wilderness. At a fork, go left 1.7 miles to road's end at the trailhead.

Contact: Siskiyou National Forest, Chetco Ranger District, 539 Chetco Lane, Brookings, OR, 97415, 541/412-6000.

95 JOHNSON BUTTE

12.6 mi/6.5 hr

northeast of Brookings in Kalmiopsis Wilderness

The Kalmiopsis Wilderness is so named for the bug-eating blooms of the *Kalmiopsis* carnivorous plant that grow in profusion along the Johnson Butte Trail. The best times to see the flowers are May and June, about when the snows melt in this remote section of the Klamath Mountains. The trail follows an old mining road, long abandoned. But the ridge it follows offers substantive views, especially in light of the 2002 Biscuit Fire, which did a number on this part of the world. Still, the trail passes accessible, lily-covered Salamander Lake along the way, as well as a rare azalea found in patches in this wilderness area.

From the trailhead, the Johnson Butte Trail is a single run at 6.3 miles one-way. It follows a ridge on an old road for 1.5 miles before turning to trail, then crosses the ridge 0.4 mile later. After four miles, the trail rounds Dry Butte and arrives at a spur trail to Salamander Lake. About 1.1 miles beyond this lake is a spur trail on the right that leads to a spring. From here, it's a 1.2-mile run to a junction with the Upper Chetco Trail in the shadow of Johnson Butte, at a flat good for camping—but there's no water. Return as you came.

User Groups: Hikers, dogs, and horses. No mountain bikes permitted. No wheelchair facilities.

Permits: A free wilderness permit is required and available at the trailhead. Parking and access are free.

Maps: For a map of the Siskiyou National Forest and the Kalmiopsis Wilderness, contact the Rogue River–Siskiyou National Forest headquarters, 3040 Biddle Road, Medford, OR, 97504, 541/618-2200. For a topographic map, ask the USGS for Chetco Peak and Tincup Peak.

Directions: From the U.S. 101 bridge in Brookings, head east on North Bank Road for eight miles, continuing straight on Road 1376 another eight miles. At a junction just beyond the South Fork Chetco Bridge, turn right on gravel Road 1909 for 13.4 miles, following signs for Kalmiopsis Wilderness. At a fork, go left 1.7 miles to road's end at the trailhead.

Contact: Siskiyou National Forest, Chetco Ranger District, 539 Chetco Lane, Brookings, OR, 97415, 541/412-6000.

96 BOARDMAN STATE PARK
12.6 mi one-way/1-2 days 👣5 ⛰10

north of Brookings on the Pacific Ocean

Samuel Boardman—a 21-year veteran of the Oregon State Parks, and in fact the first superintendent of that newly created system back in the early 1900s—left Oregon with the firm foundations of a supreme park system as his legacy. No wonder that what is now Boardman State Park is named for him. It's grandiose, epic, and as far as the Oregon coast goes, you can get just about every pleasure out of it you could imagine: 300-year-old Sitka spruce, rock arches and natural bridges, amazing vistas, cove beaches, timbered sea stacks, and old midden mounds left by Native Americans. What's more, this park is easily sampled in short stretches, as the trail itself—part of the Oregon Coast Trail—parallels U.S. 101, with a number of pullouts for easy access. To do the whole trail, or to backpack it, you'll want to have tide charts handy, as some stretches will require some beach portages. Be prepared for wonder at a discount, as all sections are free. But where to start?

The southernmost stretch begins at the Lone Ranch Picnic Area on a nice beach and heads north immediately onto Cape Ferrelo, named for a 1542 Spanish explorer, traversing its grassy and wildflower-strewn meadows 1.2 miles to a viewpoint parking area. The next 1.4 miles provides a side trail down to a beach on the north end of the cape and continues through Sitka spruce forests over House Rock Creek to a viewpoint of the same name. The trail continues over the rocky headlands 1.3 miles then dives down for a 1.2-mile beach crossing before heading up to the Whalehead Beach Picnic Area—the "whalehead" being a sea stack that spouts water out its head when the tide comes in just right. You'll need to follow the entry road up 0.3 mile to connect with the rest of the trail. Continue 1.4 mile for some stunning viewpoints, arriving at the Indian Sands, a series of strange wind-sculpted

HIKING

sandstone formations. Follow the headlands north 1.4 miles to U.S. 101, where the trail briefly joins the highway to cross the highest bridge in Oregon at 345 feet over the canyon of Thomas Creek. The next 1.3 miles follows the cliffs and drops down to China Beach, passable only at low tide. Cross the beach and head back to the highway for 0.6 mile. Then in 1.1 miles, pass over the beautiful Natural Bridges with a viewpoint. The final 1.4-mile stretch again follows the cliffs with views out to Spruce Island and Arch Rock. The trail ends at Arch Rock Picnic Area.

User Groups: Hikers and dogs. The Arch Rock and Cape Ferrelo Viewpoints are wheelchair accessible.

Permits: Permits are not required. Parking and access are free.

Maps: For a free park brochure, call Oregon Parks and Recreation, 800/551-6949, or download a free map at www.oregonstateparks. org. For a topographic map, ask the USGS for Brookings.

Directions: Drive north of Brookings on U.S. 101 about four miles. The southernmost start of the trail is at the Lone Ranch Picnic Area between mileposts 352 and 353. The northernmost start of the trail at Arch Rock Picnic Area is between mileposts 344 and 345.

Contact: Oregon Parks and Recreation Department, 1115 Commercial Street NE, Salem, OR, 97301, 800/551-6949, www.oregonstateparks.org.

97 REDWOOD NATURE TRAIL
2.6 mi/1.0 hr   🥾1 🏔7

east of Brookings in Siskiyou National Forest

BEST (

Though California gets all the fame for its redwood trees, Oregon has its own share. They extend, in fact, about this far north into the state, and an easy tour in Loeb State Park visits the *Sequoia sempervirens* on land donated to the state by a group called Save the Myrtlewoods. That's not all they saved:

The park is also a haven for red alder, tanoak, evergreen huckleberries, and salmonberries. The Riverview Trail follows the Chetco River for some grand views of the rocky-bottomed river, as well.

From the picnic area, head out 0.7 mile along the Riverview Trail on the Chetco River, home to river otters and fish-hunting osprey. The trail ends at the North Bank Road, so cross the road to the Redwood Nature Trail parking area and follow this trail along Elk Creek. Head to the left for the 1.2-mile loop uphill into the stately redwood grove. Return along the Riverview Trail.

User Groups: Hikers and dogs. No wheelchair facilities.

Permits: Permits are not required. Parking and access are free.

Maps: A trail guide is available at the trailhead. For a topographic map, ask the USGS for Mount Emily.

Directions: From the U.S. 101 bridge in Brookings, head east on North Bank Road for 7.3 miles and turn right into Loeb State Park and drive to the trailhead parking area.

Contact: Oregon Parks and Recreation Department, 1115 Commercial Street NE, Salem, OR, 97301, 800/551-6949, www.oregonstateparks.org.

98 WHEELER RIDGE
1.6 mi/1.0 hr   🥾1 🏔7

east of Brookings in Wheeler Creek Research Natural Area

On September 9, 1942, a Japanese submarine surfaced off the coast of southern Oregon, and a small aircraft was launched by catapult. The pilot, Nobuo Fujita, carrying his family's 400-year-old samurai sword, dropped two incendiary bombs. The plan was to start massive forest fires. The plan failed, as the fires on Wheeler Ridge were quickly put out, and another bomb dropped on Grassy Knob (see *Grassy Knob* listing in this chapter) never went off—and indeed was never found. The pilot got away scot-free. Later, though, the pilot returned, first in 1962 to present his family's samurai sword to the city of Brookings, and then in 1992 as an act of reconciliation when he hiked this ridge and planted a redwood tree.

To find the bomb site, hike from the trailhead 0.8 mile into the Wheeler Creek Research Natural Area. This easy path weaves through big Douglas fir, tanoak, pine, and huge redwoods. The trail ends at an interpretive sign and the redwood seedling planted as a gesture of peace.

User Groups: Hikers and dogs. No wheelchair facilities.

Permits: Permits are not required. Parking and access are free.

Maps: For a map of the Siskiyou National Forest, contact the Rogue River–Siskiyou National Forest headquarters, 3040 Biddle Road, Medford, OR, 97504, 541/618-2200. For a topographic map, ask the USGS for Fourth of July Creek.

Directions: From the south end of the U.S. 101 bridge in Brookings, drive inland on South Bank Road five miles, then turn right on gravel Mount Emily Road, following "Bombsite Trail" signs 13 miles to the trailhead sign. Park along the road.

Contact: Siskiyou National Forest, Chetco Ranger District, 539 Chetco Lane, Brookings, OR, 97415, 541/412-6000.

HIKING

Index

www.moon.com

DESTINATIONS | ACTIVITIES | BLOGS | MAPS | BOOKS

MOON.COM is ready to help plan your next trip! Filled with fresh trip ideas and strategies, author interviews, informative travel blogs, a detailed map library, and descriptions of all the Moon guidebooks, Moon.com is all you need to get out and explore the world—or even places in your own backyard. While at Moon.com, sign up for our monthly e-newsletter for updates on new releases, travel tips, and expert advice from our on-the-go Moon authors. As always, when you travel with Moon, expect an experience that is uncommon and truly unique.

MOON IS ON FACEBOOK—BECOME A FAN!
JOIN THE MOON PHOTO GROUP ON FLICKR

MOON OUTDOORS

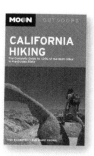

"Well written, thoroughly researched, and packed full of useful information and advice. These guides really do get you into the outdoors."

—GORP.COM

ALSO AVAILABLE AS FOGHORN OUTDOORS ACTIVITY GUIDES:

MOON OREGON COAST CAMPING & HIKING

Avalon Travel
a member of the Perseus Books Group
1700 Fourth Street
Berkeley, CA 94710, USA
www.moon.com

Editors: Elizabeth Hollis Hansen, Sabrina Young
Series Manager: Sabrina Young
Senior Research Editor: Kathie Morgan
Research Editor: Glenn Mayeda
Copy Editor: Valerie Sellers Blanton
Graphics Coordinators: Elizabeth Jang,
    Domini Dragoone
Production Coordinators: Elizabeth Jang,
    Domini Dragoone
Cover Designer: Kathryn Osgood
Interior Designer: Darren Alessi
Map Editor: Mike Morgenfeld
Cartographers: Michelle Trame, Brice Ticen,
    Kat Bennett
Illustrations: Bob Race

ISBN-13: 978-1-59880-573-4

Text © 2010 by Tom Stienstra and Sean Patrick Hill.
Maps © 2010 by Avalon Travel.
All rights reserved.

Front cover photo: Coast trail, north of Brookings, Oregon © Weldon Schloneger/ Dreamstime.com
Title page photo: driftwood on Oregon coast © Ingrid Perlstrom / 123rf.com

Printed in the United States of America

ABOUT THE AUTHORS

© JOHN BEATH

Tom Stienstra

For 30 years, Tom Stienstra's full-time job has been to capture and communicate the outdoor experience. Tom writes a weekly outdoors column that is distributed across America. He has won more than 100 national and regional writing awards, and has twice been named National Outdoors Writer of the Year. His television show, *The Great Outdoors*, is broadcast weekly on CBS/CW. His first edition of *Pacific Northwest Camping* was acclaimed by the Portland Oregonian.

Tom takes part in all facets of the outdoors, and as a pilot and airplane owner, can cover great distances quickly in the pursuit of adventure. He lives with his wife Stephani at their ranch in the "State of Jefferson," near the Oregon border.

You can contact Tom directly via his website at www.tom stienstra.com. His guidebooks include:

Moon Oregon Camping
Moon Washington Camping
Moon Pacific Northwest Camping
Moon West Coast RV Camping
Moon California Camping
Moon California Hiking (with Ann Marie Brown)
Moon California Fishing
Moon California Recreational Lakes & Rivers
California Wildlife
Moon Northern California Cabins & Cottages
Tom Stienstra's Bay Area Recreation

© ANDY BUDOR

Sean Patrick Hill

Sean Patrick Hill is a freelance writer, poet, and teacher who has spent many weekends and summers exploring the best of Oregon's mountains, deserts, and coastlines. Born and raised in upstate New York, Hill moved to Oregon after graduating from the University of Buffalo. He lived in Eugene, Bend, and then Portland, graduating with a masters in writing from Portland State University. For two summers he worked with the Oregon Youth Conservation Corps, leading teenage crews into the Cascade Mountains to do every-thing from maintaining trails to building bridges to counting frogs. Later, as an AmeriCorps volunteer, he organized tree plantings in local parks, clean-ups of riverside environments, and field trips into the wilderness for high school students.

Hill has written outdoor travel articles for *The Oregonian*, *The Source Weekly*, *Columbia Gorge Magazine*, and *Oregon Coast*. His poetry appears widely in online and print journals, and his first book of poems, *The Imagined Fields*, will be published this year.

Made in the USA
San Bernardino, CA
16 June 2015